D1260343

Flicker

Flicker
Your Brain on Movies

Jeffrey M. Zacks

OXFORD
UNIVERSITY PRESS

OXFORD
UNIVERSITY PRESS

Oxford University Press is a department of the University of
Oxford. It furthers the University's objective of excellence in research,
scholarship, and education by publishing worldwide.

Oxford   New York
Auckland   Cape Town   Dar es Salaam   Hong Kong   Karachi
Kuala Lumpur   Madrid   Melbourne   Mexico City   Nairobi
New Delhi   Shanghai   Taipei   Toronto

With offices in
Argentina   Austria   Brazil   Chile   Czech Republic   France   Greece
Guatemala   Hungary   Italy   Japan   Poland   Portugal   Singapore
South Korea   Switzerland   Thailand   Turkey   Ukraine   Vietnam

Oxford is a registered trademark of Oxford University Press
in the UK and certain other countries.

Published in the United States of America by
Oxford University Press
198 Madison Avenue, New York, NY 10016

Library of Congress Cataloging-in-Publication Data
Zacks, Jeffrey M.
Flicker : your brain on movies/Jeffrey M. Zacks.
    pages cm
Includes bibliographical references and index.
ISBN 978–0–19–998287–5
1. Motion picture audiences—Psychology.   2. Motion pictures—Psychological aspects.
3. Emotions.   4. Cognition.   I. Title.
PN1995.9.A8Z33 2014
791.4301'9—dc23
2014013120

9 8 7 6 5 4 3 2 1
Printed in the United States of America
on acid-free paper

CONTENTS ■

PROLOGUE ■
A Trailer

> Whenever I hear people dismiss movies as "fantasy" and
> make a hard distinction between film and life, I think to
> myself that it's just a way of avoiding the power of
> cinema. Of course it's not life—it's the invocation of life,
> it's in an ongoing dialogue with life.
> —Martin Scorsese, 2013 Jefferson Lecture at the
> National Academy of the Humanities

I love movies. And it seems that most everyone else does
too. Over the past century, the projection of moving pictures has grown from a carnival curiosity to a popular
entertainment to an art form to a global industry. In 2009,
1.4 billion movie tickets were sold—in just the United States
and Canada! Why do people pony up time and money to
sit in a dark room and look at a flickering wall? And how
does it work? How can a sequence of images, none of which
ever moves a micron, be transformed into a leaping lion or
a plummeting parachutist? Why do we flinch at a mere

picture of a jet careening toward the mere idea of a control tower? Why do we cry at the misfortunes of people conjured from wisps of light, whose most painful suffering ends with the final credits? Is living vicariously through the movies good for you or bad? Does watching on-screen carnage desensitize you to real-world violence?

As a scientist who studies the mind and the brain, I'm prone to obsessing about these sorts of questions while I'm waiting for the previews to start. For the past 12 years or so, my laboratory has been showing people movies and trying to figure out what is going on in their heads. I didn't get into this to try to figure out how movies work, but to understand how we perceive, comprehend, and remember in the real world. Along the way I realized that filmmakers know a tremendous amount about perception, cognition, and emotion—though they may not be able to put what they know into words. You can't make a movie like *Avatar* or *The Science of Sleep* without having a lot of insight into perception, and you can't write *Memento* or *The Usual Suspects* without a great feel for how people think about events.

At the same time, I realized that my field of science might be able to help explain some of how this works and what we experience as members of an audience in the theater. That field is called *cognitive neuroscience*; it is the study of the mind and the brain and how they relate. In my research, I started to explore how our experience at the movies co-opts mechanisms we evolved for understanding the real world. I also started reading a small but fascinating literature by scientists interested in film and film theorists who care about science. I became convinced that if you are interested in what goes on in your head when you watch a movie, there is a science base that is very informative.

I also started teaching a seminar called "The Cognitive Neuroscience of Film." For 2½ hours a week one semester of each year, I had the privilege of discussing and debating the topics of this book with a gifted group of advanced undergraduate and graduate students at Washington University in St. Louis. This book owes an enormous amount to their keen eyes and ears and their curiosity. They found a bunch of fantastic examples to illustrate things we talked about; I've tried to give shout-outs in the footnotes, but let me also say "Thanks, guys!" right here. Thanks also to a wonderful, sensitive group of friends and colleagues who read beta versions of pieces of the manuscript: Steve Abbott, Todd Braver, Bruce Christensen, James Cutting, Fred Kleinberg, Dan Levin, Mark Plattner, Khena Swallow, Barbara Tversky, and Jim Zacks. Thanks to Joan Bossert at Oxford University Press, who guided me through the editorial process from start to finish. For sitting through interviews, providing information, and clueing me in to various stages of the book-writing process, many thanks to Sian Beilock, Bruce Bridgeman, Bob Buderi, Brad Bushman, Andrew Butler, Chris Ferguson, Peter Guber, Dan Levitin, Pamela Speh, Wendy Strothman, and Andrew B. Watson. The biggest piece of the book's writing took place during a sabbatical at Clare Hall, Cambridge University; thanks to Clare Hall and to Washington University for making that possible, and to Trevor Robbins and the Department of Experimental Psychology of Cambridge University for their generous hospitality and intellectual support. Over the years, my research has been supported by the James S. McDonnell Foundation, the National Science Foundation, the National Institutes of Health, and the Defense Advanced Projects Agency, for which I am deeply appreciative. Finally, many thanks to my family for sitting through second and third viewings of some of the movies I discuss, and for putting up with my too-frequent sequestration in the study.

Every movie has a trailer, so here's a trailer for the rest of the book. It's a tale in two acts. Part I, "From Up on a Screen to Inside Your Head," is about what it's like to experience a movie. It tries to answer the questions that people ask me when they hear I work on movies and the brain. How it is that movies, which are patently fake and obviously flat, evoke responses in us that are as "juicy" as the experiences we have in real life? In Chapter 1, "Your Brain Wasn't Built for Movies," I propose a couple of principles that evolved to govern our actions and emotional responses in real life, which are commandeered by movie-watching. In the next two chapters, "The Movie in Your Head" and "Tearjerkers and Sitcoms," I show how those principles help explain what makes stories so gripping, whether they are written on a page or flickered on a screen, and I consider why movies have such a surprising power to make us laugh and cry. If experiences at the movies are so close to experiences in real life, where do we draw the line? That's the question of Chapter 4, "Living Vicariously." And if movies are such powerful experiences, does consuming bad movies make us bad people? That's the question of Chapter 5, "The Dark Side."

Part II, "The Tricks That Make Movies Work," is about all the things that happen outside our awareness to produce the rich illusions we experience when watching films. It tries to answer the questions that nobody asks me, but when I bring these questions up, people thump their forehead and say, "Wow! I had no idea it was that cool." Chapter 6, "Action!" asks, how is it that movies move at all? Chapter 7, "Cut!" asks, why we don't get hopelessly confused when two totally different shots are edited together. Chapter 8, "Bottlenecks, Spotlights, and Chunks," asks how our very limited brains cope with the vast amount of sensory information that a feature film blasts at us. Chapter 9, "Sleight of Hand," is for movie geeks and those who find movie geeks annoying. It looks at continuity errors—like when Harry Potter is sitting on the left side of the table in one shot and on the right side in the next—and why they are so easy to create and surprisingly difficult to notice.[1]

The last chapter, "Virtual Futures," asks what the movies will be like in twenty years. Will our entertainment be jacked directly into our brains? Will video games and movies fuse? I'll consider how the architecture of the brain will shape the future of entertainment.

So if this book were a movie, what kind of movie would it be? A documentary, of course. Everything I'm going to tell you is true as far as I know it, and based on the best psychological and neuroscientific data I can find. But don't let that freak you out. My heroes in the documentary film world are storytellers—Errol Morris, Werner Herzog, and Michael Moore. And it turns out that movies and the brain have some great stories. So grab some popcorn and take a seat.

PART I

From Up on a Screen to Inside Your Head

1 ■

Your Brain Wasn't Built for Movies

Rocky II. It's round 15 of the rematch between Rocky Balboa and Apollo Creed. The two fighters are beating each other into hamburger. As the final round builds, the camera pulls in close to the fighters. Creed delivers a series of haymakers with his right, and Balboa answers with punishing alternating body blows. These are the punches that in a few moments will bring *both* fighters to the mat. Most of the shots are over-the-shoulder views from the perspective of the boxer receiving the blows. So as you sit in the audience, for about 20 seconds fists are popping out of the screen toward your face almost continuously. It is exhausting to watch, and almost impossible not to flinch.

Alice in Wonderland. When Alice slays the Jabberwock in Tim Burton's film version, the head tumbles down directly toward you. Try not to duck just a little. I saw this movie with my 7-year-old son, who likes to sit up front. Jonah wiggled around in his chair as if he were really there, craning to see through the crowds in the castle grounds and flinching at the looming Jabberwock. As the camera swooped and dove and the action heated up, eventually the sense of movement became too strong—he turned to me and said, "Dad, I think I'm gonna barf." I had him close his eyes for a little bit and he was fine.

Sitting in a theater, it is not at all uncommon to experience bodily responses—to feel as if you are preparing to move, perhaps even squirming a little in your seat. You may feel as though you are ready to jump into the action at a moment's notice, yet you are sitting perfectly still and nothing is touching you. What is going on? Your eyes and ears are telling you that something exciting is happening in front of you and your brain is preparing you to react. Of course, you *know* it's just a movie. But large parts of your brain don't process that distinction. This makes sense because our brains evolved long before movies were invented, and our perceptual systems are honed to deal with the problems posed by the real world. Our brains didn't evolve to watch movies: Movies evolved to take advantage of the brains we have. Our tendency to want to respond physically to them highlights this.

William James described the tendency of visual images to evoke motor actions more than a hundred years ago, using the term *ideomotor actions*: "Wherever movement follows *unhesitatingly and immediately* the notion of it in the mind, we have ideo-motor action." The term had originally been coined to describe involuntary actions during hypnosis and séances, but James pointed out that seeing something and responding automatically with an appropriate movement is one of most common ways movements are caused, "the normal process stripped of disguise."[1] These days, we distinguish between two different ways in which an action can be associated with an event in the world. We can describe these as two different rules that people are built to follow. I will call these the *mirror rule* and the *success rule*.

The mirror rule says "Do what you see." Everyday life is replete with examples of the mirror rule, though we often don't notice them. Imagine that you and I are sitting across from each other at a desk. If I cross my arms or legs, you are much more likely to cross yours. Same thing if I tug my ear or scratch my neck. As the conversation progresses, you will start adapting your accent and the pace at which you talk so that it is more like mine. At the same time, I am imitating your physical and verbal mannerisms in exactly the same way. Neither of us is likely to notice it, but the phenomenon is easy to identify in a lab. In a number of experiments over the years, psychologists have crossed their arms, scratched their ears, and varied the pacing of their speech and then measured the effects on their conversational partners. Once you start looking for them, the effects are dramatic and actually pretty funny. They also show convincingly that we mimic whether we intend to or not, often without noticing. For example, in one study an experimenter told a story about attending a crowded Christmas party, at which she had to duck to avoid bumping into someone. As she told the story, she ducked to demonstrate. A videotape of the audience showed that just as she ducked to the right, they ducked to the left, performing a mirror image of her action. In another experiment, researchers paired participants with an experimenter who either rubbed her face or shook her foot throughout the interaction. Sure enough, people who were paired with a face-rubber rubbed their own faces more often, and people paired with a foot-shaker shook their own feet. Afterward, neither group was aware that they had been performing the behavior.[2]

There is an even more powerful way to see the mirror rule in action: Ask people to move their bodies in ways that either mirror or mismatch what someone else is doing. Suppose I ask you to perform this simple task: Stick out your hand and rest it, palm down, on the table. When a number "1" appears on the screen, raise your index finger a few inches as quickly as possible. When a "2" appears, raise your middle finger. This is an easy discrimination task, and people can do it in a few tenths of a second. Now, suppose I were to stand across from you and do the same discrimination but with the opposite movements: middle finger for 1, index finger for 2. Both of us would perform much more slowly, and if we were really trying to go fast, we would probably start making mistakes.[3] When I do a task like this, it feels as if something outside me is making my finger want to go down just as I am trying to lift it up. It feels like it takes concentration to resist. An experiment from the University of British Columbia shows that this feeling is on target: If someone makes a startling noise while I'm watching you raise your left finger, it breaks my concentration and makes it quite likely that the finger I shouldn't be lifting will twitch.[4]

You can experience this feeling at the movies, too. In Stanley Kubrick's *Dr. Strangelove*, the title character (one of several played by Peter Sellers) has an involuntary habit of snapping Nazi salutes when he gets excited. You can almost feel your own arm going up. Watch *The Natural*, and it's hard not to feel yourself swinging a virtual bat along with Robert Redford. These are times when the effects of the mirror rule really stand out. I'm suggesting that this is driving your movie experience all the time, only you don't notice it.

If you go to an action movie with a lot of kids, you can literally *see* the mirror rule operating. For example, during a martial arts scene, you will see a good portion of the audience waving their arms and legs along with the characters. At my house, my kids fully jump out of their chairs and leap around the living room.

More subtle, but even more ineluctable, is the mimicking of facial expression. Watch audience members' faces sometime when you go to the movies. If a character on screen is grinning, people will tend to smile. If a character is angry, viewers' brows will knit. If someone starts crying, mouths will turn down and you may even see tears. What is particularly striking is that this seems to work even when you don't particularly like or identify with the character. Facial imitation is particularly powerful—and particularly difficult to override. In Chapter 2 we will come back to this, because it is part of why movies can have such a powerful emotional impact.

But for now let me mention one action that is especially subject to the mirror rule: laughing. In one study conducted at the University of Indiana in the 1960s, researchers asked people to listen to jokes either alone or in groups. The group audiences laughed more. Interestingly, they didn't rate the jokes as any funnier; perhaps they laughed more not because they thought the jokes were any funnier, but as a direct result of seeing or hearing their fellow audience members yukking it up. The entertainment industry is definitely wise to this, whether or not producers can cite the relevant experimental studies. Sitcoms have been filmed in front of live audiences for 5 decades because producers know that audiences at home laugh more when they hear a live audience laughing. In fact, when a live audience does not laugh sufficiently, canned laughter will often be added to the soundtrack. And it works: People laugh more when a laugh track is added.[5]

Why are we built to follow the mirror rule? We are an intensely social species, often dependent on other humans for our survival, and mirroring probably provides several benefits for fitting our own behavior in with that of others. Imitation is an efficient way to coordinate behavior: If you and I need to pull a rope or row a boat together, you can just say "Do what I do," rather than trying to explain exactly how to execute and time my movements so that they will match yours. This sort of coordination is present across a wide phylogenetic swath. For example, if one of a flock of shorebirds takes off, others will tend to imitate it. They do this so that if one bird detects an approaching predator, the whole flock can quickly evacuate. Imitation is also an efficient way to learn new skills. An automatic pathway from what you see to what you do can shortcut a lot of trial and error. If you have ever studied a musical instrument or dance, you know that imitation is a powerful means of instruction.

All of the preceding examples are examples of the simple, immediate control of behavior. But in some species, ours included, the mirror rule has been leveraged to enable smarter behavior. The trick is that once a motor representation of an action is activated, you can use that representation to recognize the action, and you can use your motor experiences to make predictions about what is going to happen next. For example, suppose a man on the screen is shown grasping a doorknob. As you watch this, it activates a motor representation for doorknob grasping in your brain. Throughout your life, when you have grasped a doorknob, you have usually opened the door, and often walked through it. So, when you activate your grasping representation, this causes your opening and walking representations to activate as well. If the character then walks out the door, you have a head start on processing this sequence because your motor representation of walking is pre-activated. None of this is likely to be conscious or deliberate—it happens quickly, outside of awareness. Nonetheless, it is an important form of understanding.

Furthermore, this sort of priming may allow you access to the mental state of the character. Most of the time when you executed this sequence of movements, it was accompanied by the sense of "I am intending to walk through this door." So observing the grasping can activate the motor sequence, which in turn can activate the intention. This chain of association can provide a mechanism for "mind reading"—for working out what characters are thinking or intending based on what they are doing. I want to emphasize that this mechanism is a bit smarter than simply imitating the behavior, but is still pretty simple—simple enough to operate fast, automatically, and outside of awareness. There is good evidence that we rely on this mechanism all the time.[6]

In short, our behavior often follows the mirror rule, such that when we see an action performed we have a tendency to perform the same action ourselves. If the circumstances are not appropriate—say, sitting in a movie theater—we may suppress the overt execution of the action. Sometimes we'll achieve only partial success at this. The mirror rule helps us get ready to perform appropriate actions quickly, to learn sequences of actions, and to represent the mental states of other people based on their behavior. You've probably heard the phrase "monkey see, monkey do" used in a pejorative way to describe shallow imitation without understanding. The mirror rule is exactly "monkey see, monkey do." But the next time you use this phrase, think about a few things: First, it's not just monkeys. The mirror rule is prominent in species from birds to prairie gophers to us. Second, the mirror rule is a pretty valuable trick, so don't look on it too condescendingly. Third, although the mirror rule does indeed function without our understanding—that's what makes it so valuable—it can provide a basis for our understanding.

Now to the second rule: the success rule. The success rule says, "Do what has worked." It is obvious why we would be built to follow the success rule—doing what works is better than the alternative. You can feel the success rule working powerfully in situations where you need to react fast. When a traffic light turns red and your foot presses the brake seemingly before you could think of it, that's the success rue. If you play a lot of solitaire or chess, you may notice that when you encounter a common configuration you can make the next move almost as if without thinking. That's the success rule. The success rule is a pervasive factor in everyday action, and a significant component of how we learn new skills. It underpins a lot of "practice makes perfect."

Psychologists talk about the success rule in terms of stimuli, which are the things the world presents to us, and responses, which are the actions we take. Its formal name is "operant conditioning." The success rule says that if you experience a stimulus, make a particular response to it, and things work out, then next time you experience that stimulus you should be more prone to making the same response. Suppose I'm standing in a batting cage and baseballs are flying at me. I take a swing and miss low. Another swing, another miss. Then, on the third swing, I make contact. I probably cannot articulate what it was about that third swing that worked. (I may even just have gotten lucky.) But chances are my next swing will repeat a little bit of what was different about the swing that made contact. As I practice more and more, the bits that are associated with successfully hitting the ball will tend to predominate, and the bits associated with missing will die out. For most skills, particularly those we learn deliberately like batting or chess, the success rule is not the only thing operating. We may read books or get coaching from an expert, and we may consciously try to alter what we are doing. But the success rule is always working away hand in hand with these deliberate strategies to refine our performance.[7]

The success rule shows up not just in simple motor skills, but also in more subtle, complex social interactions. Suppose you stop at the same coffee shop on the way to work each morning, and it has two lines at the counter, staffed by two regular servers. Now, suppose both provide perfectly reliable service, but one of the servers always smiles when tallying up your order, whereas the other is stone-faced. Over time we would probably see you selecting the line of the smiling server more and more often. You might not be at all aware of it, but for most of us being smiled at is rewarding and the success rule says that we will adjust our behavior to make it happen more often.

The success rule builds up habits that drive our behavior. When we go to the movies we cannot just turn these habits off. If we have experienced a stimulus repeatedly and by the success rule learned a response, we will tend to produce that response when the stimulus shows up on the screen. So, the success rule explains why you might duck a little when the Jabberwock's head falls in *Alice in Wonderland*. You have a lifetime of experience with falling objects approaching our heads. A lot of them you ducked and it worked out OK. Some you failed to duck and the consequences probably weren't good. So, when it looks like something is falling toward your head, you have been trained by your previous experiences to duck.

Toward the beginning of *The Truman Show* there is a shot in which Truman waves at the neighbors from his porch. Jim Carrey's wave is filmed from the viewpoint of the neighbor, so it is as if Carrey is waving at you, the viewer. You may feel a tendency to wave back. That's the success rule operating in the social domain. Ignoring someone who waves at you is rude and produces bad outcomes; waving back is friendly and produces good outcomes. Over a lifetime, this builds up a tendency to wave back when someone waves at you. This tendency follows you into the theater.

So is there a mirror rule brain center? A success rule brain center? It turns out the answer is no. So how does the brain implement the mirror rule and the success rule? To explain that, I need to tell you a bit about how the brain is organized.

The perceptual parts of our brain take up a lot of the brain's real estate, and they are composed of a huge number of nerve cells, or neurons. Perceptual brain areas are organized according to three principles. First, many of them are neural *maps* of our visual world. A neural map is a representation in the brain built so that when two locations are nearby in the world, they will activate groups of neurons that are nearby in your brain. This is just like how in a road map, when two locations are nearby in the world, they will correspond with nearby spots on the road map. If you consider the map as a whole, it forms a picture of the world. How well defined are these brain maps? They vary: Some have higher resolution and some have lower resolution, and most are spatially distorted—squished. But some—particularly in the visual system—are clear enough that that they can be read off like blurry photographs.[8]

A second principle of brain organization is that visual areas *specialize*, dividing up the labor of visual processing, with different visual areas focusing on different visual features. Some areas are very sensitive to relative brightness, others to color, and still others to line orientation or shape.

A third principle governing the visual brain is that areas are arranged *hierarchically* in successive levels. "Early" levels receive signals from the eyes after passing through only a few neurons; "later" levels are more neurons away from the retina. Importantly, each level does not just feed forward to the next level, but also feeds back to the previous level. This feedback is critical for the sophisticated processing our visual systems do.

These three principles have been studied most fully in the visual system, though we also know a fair bit about hearing and touch sensation. In vision, the earliest processing area is called primary visual cortex, or V1. V1 is located in the back of the brain, and it is where visual information first arrives when it is transmitted from the eye. Neurons in V1 are sensitive to simple contrasts of brightness, to location, and to changes over time. As we move up the hierarchy, we move forward in the brain and the features to which areas are sensitive get more complex. One area specializes in color, and damage to this area can make you color-blind. Another area specializes in motion; we'll spend a bit of time on this one in Chapter 6. One set of high-level areas in the visual system is located on the bottom surface of the back of your brain. These areas receive input from upstream areas that are sensitive to visual features like color and shape, and integrate these features to play a major role in identifying and categorizing objects. These feature-sensitive visual areas feed into areas that are right in front of them, which contain cells that respond to very specific categories of objects or people—sometimes essentially to specific individuals. These cells are the closest thing we have to "grandmother cells"—cells that respond to your grandmother and only your grandmother.

As we go up each of the perceptual hierarchies, interactions *across* these hierarchies also increase. The highest levels in the perceptual processing hierarchies integrate information from multiple senses. Cells in these areas respond to specific kinds of objects not just when they are seen, but also when the same type of object is heard or touched.[9] In fact, we can think of the whole perceptual system as one big hierarchy, starting from sense-specific maps that represent low-level sensory features and working up to cross-modal maps representing abstract features of our environment.

The motor system is also organized hierarchically, but the motor hierarchy can be thought of as the reverse of the perceptual hierarchy. Whereas the earliest levels in the visual hierarchy are closest to the eye, the *latest* levels in the motor hierarchy are closest to the hand. The last stage before most voluntary motor commands leave the brain is primary motor cortex. Primary motor cortex occupies a strip from along the middle of your brain, running from the crown of your head down to just in front of your ears. It controls simple movements of your body, and it is organized as a map of your body with the feet represented on top and the hands toward the bottom. Higher levels in the motor system control more complex movements.[10]

The perceptual hierarchy and the motor hierarchy are both changing and adapting all the time. Specifically, the connections between neurons are adjusting to increase or decrease the effect that one neuron has on others. Neuroscientists call this *plasticity*. Plasticity is critical for adapting behavior to a changing environment; it is our brain adjusting itself, tuning itself up over time to work better. Plasticity is responsible for much of the operation of the mirror rule and the success rule. Let's start by looking more closely at the mirror rule.

In *The Karate Kid* (the original, from 1984), Mr. Miyagi gives Daniel the task of waxing a car. He shows him the proper technique—"wax on" (a circular motion), "wax off" (a circle in the other direction). Daniel executes probably a thousand repetitions of this action before he is done. On each repetition, he is performing a motor action and experiencing the perceptual consequences of that action. This gives plasticity a chance to adjust connections between his neurons to strengthen the association between what the movement feels like and what it looks like (and sounds like and feels like). It is no surprise that when Daniel needs to produce the same movement for karate, now without the waxing cloth, he is smooth and proficient.

Most of the actions you mirror are not subject to this kind of intense practice, but it helps us to see what is going on. In everyday life you have vast amounts of experience acting and experiencing the perceptual consequences of those actions. Plasticity leverages that experience to tune up the connections between your perceptual system and your motor system so that you can imitate a vast repertoire of movements. Importantly, you can stitch these bits together in novel ways, like assembling a new sentence from your preexisting vocabulary. Often we find ourselves imitating new combinations of actions that we may not have experienced before. This generativity is just what makes the mirror rule so useful.

Likewise, plasticity underpins the success rule by adjusting connections between neurons. In *The Red Violin*, the orphan prodigy Kaspar Weiss is instructed to practice a piece over and over, slowly increasing the tempo, until he can play the piece perfectly. This sort of practice modifies the neural connections throughout Kaspar's motor cortex, strengthening connections that work together and weakening connections that interfere with the performance. Over time, this huge number of small adjustments can have significant effects on the function—and even the physical layout—of our brains. One especially neat thing about violin playing is that it is asymmetric—the left arm executes fine movements with the hand on the fingerboard, while the right hand performs large movements with the upper arm. Does this produce hand-specific changes in the brain? Yes. A group of researchers in Germany found that touching the left hands of violinists leads to larger brain responses than does touching the left hands of non-violinists. It turns out that the hand area in primary motor cortex usually sits on a distinctive knob-shaped fold in the brain's surface. In violinists, this knob is more pronounced—so much so that trained neuroanatomists can see the difference just by looking at an MRI scan![11]

The mirror rule and the success rule operate mostly because our brains constantly adjust themselves as we sense and act. However, some of our behaviors are so important that evolution has built them into our hardware. This is particularly important for behaviors that must be up and running early in development, before we have had a lot of experience with the world. For example, there is evidence that mirroring the social behaviors of other humans is inborn. In one famous study, Andrew Meltzoff got permission to visit the maternity ward of Swedish

Hospital in Seattle to make faces at newborn babies. Half of the time he stuck out his tongue; the other times he opened his mouth in an "O." Each time, he then recorded how often the newborns stuck out *their* tongues or opened their mouths. The babies were by no means perfect mimics, but more than half of the babies spent substantially more time performing the gesture that matched Meltzoff's gesture, and did so for both gestures. This is way too high a rate to happen by chance.[12]

Some instances of the success rule follow this same pattern. One example is the ducking response we talked about earlier. Studies using baby humans and other species have studied a particular visual pattern called *looming*, in which a shape becomes larger and increases its rate of expansion. This is what happens when an object is coming toward you and is going to hit you. When you see this, you will instinctively pull your head back. Newborn infants do the same thing.[13]

So, you can see that there is no "mirror rule system" and no "success rule system" in the brain. Instead, these rules are general principles of how the brain adapts to the environment. They are implemented in disparate brain systems, many of which are organized according to the three principles I described: maps, distributed representations, and hierarchical organization. Most perceptual, motor, and cognitive brain functions accord with these principles and with the mirror rule and the success rule. In short, the two rules are properties of the system as a whole, not of just one brain area. But just as there are special cases in which evolution has built in instances of the rules, there are bits of special-purpose hardware that are implemented in certain instances. One of particular note is the *mirror neuron*.

Mirror neurons were discovered in 1996 by Giacomo Rizzolatti and his colleagues at the University of Parma, who made electrical recordings of cells in the brains of monkeys while they performed goal-directed actions like reaching for a peanut. The researchers were recording from one of the higher-level areas in the motor hierarchy. Cells in this area were very selective for particular goal-directed actions: One cell might respond when the monkey picked up a peanut with its right hand by pinching the nut between its first and second fingers, but not when the monkey used its whole fist to grasp the nut or pinched its fingers without the nut being there. The experimenters trained the monkeys to perform particular actions by example. One day during training they noticed something amazing: Some of the cells that fired for particular actions fired not just when the monkey performed the action, but also when the monkey saw the experimenter demonstrating! They had found a piece of the neural representation of action that wasn't just perceptual, or just motor, but both.[14]

Mirror neurons are a fascinating phenomenon. The fact that single cells are selective for specific goal-directed actions whether they are perceived or performed is important, and it didn't have to be that way. It could have turned out that action representations were broadly distributed across many neurons, so that no particular neuron would be so selective for a particular action. It could have turned out that the cells that responded to both perception and action cared only about the movement pattern and not about the goal. The particular constellation of features possessed by mirror neurons is pretty nifty, and has captured the imagination of scientists and laypeople alike.

At the same time, we should keep in mind that mirror neurons provide only a small piece of the puzzle. We already knew that the brain had the ability to map quickly and accurately from perceived movements to performed movements. This had to be the case because we can imitate others' movements in real time. Moreover, we knew that the mapping was in part automatic because the experiments showed that other people's movements affect our own whether we are trying to imitate them or not. Mirror neurons have been offered as an explanation of everything from culture to autism.[15] My own feeling is that this is a bit premature. Often it is tempting to think that because we have found *where* in the brain a phenomenon happens we understand *how* it happens. That is sort of like pointing to the combustion chamber in a gasoline-powered car and saying that this piece explains how the car moves. For now, we need to learn a lot more about how the system of which mirror neurons are a part works.

The mirror rule and the success rule describe how what we see can determine what we do. But if we are constantly acting so as to mirror others' actions and to perform the actions, how do we ever do what we *want* to do? If we are sitting in a movie theater, why are we not waving our arms whenever the onscreen characters do, smiling or grimacing in response to their expressions, or reaching for the steering wheel whenever we see an obstacle in a car chase?

The first answer is that we *do* imitate on-screen actions, a little bit. But for the most part we are able to keep a lid on the automatic connections between our perceptual systems and our motor systems. More broadly, we are able to modulate the connections depending on the task at hand. When we play a tennis match our brain is configured to move according to a particular set of rules that relate the look of the ball to the movements of our feet and arms. These rules were honed by learning according to the success rule. When we watch a tennis match on TV, those connections are turned down; a different set of rules controls our movements. This switching of rules depends in part on the *prefrontal cortex*, the front-most part of the brain. The prefrontal cortex is thought to maintain representations of which task we are trying to do, which turn some rules up and other rules down.

The prefrontal cortex is just about the slowest part of the brain to develop as we grow up. It is not fully mature until the late teens. Thus, it makes sense that if we look around a movie theater, it is the kids that we see ducking, grimacing, and squirming the most in response to the action on the screen. They are less able to turn down the automatic influences of the mirror rule and the success rule.

More dramatically, we can see neurological cases in which the ability to suppress the mirror rule and the success rule is impaired. When the mirror rule runs amok, this is called *echopraxia*. Here is a description from a pair of British psychiatrists, writing in the 1960s, of one catatonic patient, A.S. (he is referred to by his initials; this is the norm when neuropsychological patients consent to have their cases described in the scientific literature, and is done to protect their privacy):

> A.S. was sitting rigidly immobile on the right side of a second patient J.W., looking at a point on the floor. The latter patient, J.W., then moved back in his chair and took up a slouching posture with his left hand on his chin, his left elbow leaning on the arm of the chair and his right leg crossed over his left. He also had put his right hand in his trouser pocket and his whole body was tilted towards the left. A.S. looked up at this patient as the latter was moving and then moved from his original position into one identical with that of J.W., including the body tilt.... The number of such automatic repetitions of visually perceived actions performed by this patient amounted to between 30 and 40 in any session of one hour in the group situation.

A.S. seemed aware of what he was doing, at least in part. When he started copying others' actions, he would often cover or close his eyes—but as soon as he opened them again he recommenced his involuntary mimicry. The psychiatrists go on to describe a second patient, E.H., who imitated not only other people there in the room but also people on television. When asked whether he was enjoying the program, he replied, "Yes, but I don't know which is myself."[16]

Patients who lose the ability to suppress the success rule exhibit *utilization behavior*: When confronted with an object, they have a hard time not using it for its typical purpose. For example, the English psychologist Tim Shallice and his colleagues asked a patient to complete some paper-and-pencil tests in the presence of extraneous objects. For example, the patient's tray might have a pencil and ruler on it, which would be helpful for doing the task, but also a plastic toy gun and a candle. The patient frequently handled the extraneous objects, for instance picking up the candle, finding some matches, and lighting it. It was as if the object called out to have its appropriate action performed, despite the task at hand. (Perhaps this call of objects explained why the patient smoked 40 cigarettes a day!)[17] As far as I know, no one has examined whether patients with utilization behavior perform actions in response to objects on a TV or movie screen. It may be that if the initial action of grasping for the object does not meet with success, the action dies out, and so little overt utilization behavior would be seen in front of a screen. But the existence of this phenomenon shows us that when we see objects, motor plans for acting on those objects might immediately start bubbling under the surface.

Echopraxia and utilization behavior have been associated with lesions in the brain's frontal lobes. The idea is that our perceptual and motor systems are constantly building representations of actions that might be appropriate to the current situation. These representations live mostly in the parietal lobes. The prefrontal cortex acts as a kind of editor, exerting control over which of these potential actions are executed. When the prefrontal cortex is damaged, it cannot edit effectively and some of the prepared actions that should be suppressed are carried out.[18]

As evolution shaped the rule-tuning mechanism, why did it not do a more thorough job? Why do echoes of the mirror rule and the success rule leak out even when we are trying to hold still in a movie theater? Why is our control system so vulnerable that it doesn't quite work in kids and can be impaired by neurological injury? I do not think this is just a design flaw. I think it is part of a trade-off: By not quite shutting down the rules that are the "wrong" ones right now, your brain is helping to ready you for the time when those are the right rules. I think the ability to run rules in an "offline" mode and appropriately inhibit their actions is an important component of what makes us smart. In Chapter 4, I will develop the implications of this idea.

But before we get there, I want to point out just how peculiar movies are in their dependence on inhibiting the output of the mirror rule and the success rule. Does any other animal spend its time sitting around watching a screen that it cannot control? For most animals most of the time, when they see something in the environment that is associated with an action, they go ahead and execute the action. Movies are strange because they present perceptual experiences that can be vivid and realistic evokers of behavior, but they are necessarily passive. You can't change what is happening on the screen—for now.

It may turn out that we are in the early stages of a revolution in entertainment, in which movies will be transmuted into interactive experiences. I am frankly not quite sure whether this is going to happen. There are practical reasons that movies may remain passive. For one thing, the experience of watching something on a large screen would be prohibitively expensive if everyone needed to have their own screen. There also are social factors that may keep mainstream movies from becoming too interactive. Movies give us a shared social experience, both when we watch as a group and when we get together to talk about them later. If movies become interactive, then even if you and I go to the same movie we will not have gone to the same movie. Gamers certainly talk with each other about the games they play, but would that conversation replace the sort of conversation people have about movies?

If movies do mutate into a fully interactive form of entertainment, we will be able to look back and conclude that by 2010, when I started writing this book, it had already begun. Video games have been popular since the 1970s, and the visual richness of games continues to approach that of commercial cinema. Interaction techniques, which have taken their cue from *virtual reality*, have become more sophisticated and prevalent since the 1980s. Some now include head-mounted displays that show pictures stereoscopically with a wide field of view; motion-tracking hardware and software that can record your body's position in real time; and force-feedback actuators that can vibrate or push back on your body.

In the last few years, technologies for integrating realistic bodily action into movies and games have gone mainstream. The two most popular as I write this are the Nintendo Wii and the Microsoft Xbox Kinect. The Wii works by having the gamer hold a wand that can sense direction and acceleration. The Kinect works by using cameras and an infrared depth sensor to track movement without the user wearing or carrying anything. Using these systems, game designers can create situations in which it is totally appropriate to interact with the objects on the screen—to pick up the treasure or hit the approaching tennis ball.

These technologies are one of several ways that the line between movies and games is blurring. This is a topic I'll return to at some length in the very last chapter of the book. If we do wind up with living in a world of interactive movies, then the mirror rule and the success rule will be free to shake off the shackles of inhibition.

The movie of the future may *expect* you to duck the boulder shaken loose by the landslide or swat the fly buzzing in front of your nose. If so, I have one prediction: that when we start acting out at the movies we will do it all of a piece or not at all. The whole body comes along for the ride. For example, when I watch people play Wii games, it seems to me they don't just move the wand, but move their whole bodies in a way that approximates how they would move if they were really playing tennis or bowling or playing soccer. Now, suppose that sometime in the future we bring something like Kinect technology to the movie theaters, so that a big group of us can sit in our seats in the theater but also interact with the action on the screen. In this situation, we would probably need to restrict the motion sensing to our upper bodies; if people were up out of their seats someone could get hurt! But even if you know that this is how the system works, I'll bet when the soccer ball on the screen rolls toward your feet you'll kick at it. Here's why: The prefrontal cortex system that controls how our potential actions get executed probably does not have fine-grained enough control to do otherwise. It can tell you to hold on to an action or let it out, but probably can't do a great job modulating which parts of the action get executed. This has an interesting implication: A little bit of interactivity may go a long way. If the system has to respond to only a little part of what we do with our body to get us to move the whole thing, it may turn out that we don't need whole-body tracking to have a deeply involving experience, as long as the screen responds to part of what we do.

2 ∎

The Movie in Your Head

Harry watched the dragon nearest to them teeter
dangerously on its back legs; its jaws were stretched
wide in a suddenly silent howl; its nostrils were
suddenly devoid of flame, though still smoking—
then, very slowly, it fell—several tons of sinewy,
scaly black dragon hit the ground with a thud that
Harry could have sworn had made the trees behind
him quake.

    —J. K. Rowling, *Harry Potter and the Goblet of Fire*

The movie sucked me in from the very beginning.
I jumped at some parts of the movie and almost cried at
the ending. . . . While the movie was not exactly like the
book, I am not in the least bit disappointed. . . . When
Harry is fighting for his life against a deadly dragon you
feel scared for him. When Hermione yells at Ron you feel
mad at Ron as well. When Ron feels dumb for doing
something idiotic you feel embarrassed for him. This is

what made the original Star Wars trilogy characters great, and the same formula goes into the Harry Potter films. That's what makes them classics.

—groovygirl112006 and FMACDONALD, commenting
   on Mike Newell's *Goblet of Fire* film adaptation

J. K. Rowling's description of the Hungarian Horntail dragon is oozing with perceptual detail—the smell of smoke, the color and texture of its skin, the sound and feel of its fall.[1] As groovygirl112006 tells us, there is something in common between our response to such a description and our response to seeing the same events depicted on a screen. No doubt movies are a deeply visual phenomenon, but of course that is not the whole picture. When people talk about movies, they may slip in a word or two about the special effects or the soundtrack, but mostly they talk about the *story*—the characters, the actions, the causes and effects. When filmmakers adapt a book, they are usually trying to translate the story to the screen.

What does it mean to understand a story? What is it about what goes on in our heads that is the same whether we read a story on a page or watch it on a screen? When you get "lost in a book," what is going on? In this chapter I am going to propose an account that answers these questions and explains how words on a page can tap into the perceptual and motor patterns that we have built up by means of the mirror rule and the success rule. The explanation is speculative in places, but if it is correct, it will not just help us understand how movies work but also may have some broader implications.

The basic idea is this: To understand a story, we construct *models* of the story's events. An event model is a representation in your head that corresponds systematically to the situation in the story. It is not a perfect copy—it simplifies a lot and distorts some things, but it is accurate enough that you can use it to run simulations that can tell you about parts of the situation you may have missed and to infer what might happen soon.[2]

As you were reading the passage from *Harry Potter* on the opening page of this chapter, you constructed an event model that represented Harry, the dragon, the smoke, and the trees. If you had come to this passage in the larger setting of the book, your model also would have represented Harry's broom, the field of spectators watching him fight the dragon in a tournament, and his competitors facing their own dragons. It might have included information that was not explicitly mentioned in the text, but was filled in, such as the smell of the smoke, the color of Harry's robes, and Harry's thrill and happiness at overcoming this obstacle.

If you watched Mike Newell's movie version of *The Goblet of Fire*, you would likewise build up a model of the scene. The model would not be exactly the same, but it would have a lot of the same elements: Harry, the dragon, and so forth. An event model is a representation of what the situation is about, not of how you learned about the situation. It ought to be more or less the same whether you witnessed the situation yourself, watched it in a movie, or read about it in a newspaper or a novel.

OK, there are *some* differences. One reason that a book and a movie adaptation give rise to different event models is that filmmakers change elements of the situation when they adapt a story for the screen. These are the things that fans of *Harry Potter* or the *Lord of the Rings* books fixate on when they debate the merits of a book-based movie. But this is not really a difference between models based on movie watching and models based on reading. The same thing would hold if you compared two different written versions of a folk tale or two different movie adaptations of a book.

Subtler differences arise because moving pictures and written language tend to convey different sorts of information. Movies almost always give you information about the color, shape, and size of the people and objects they depict. In a book, it is the author's choice whether to describe those features or not. When the dragon appears in the *Harry Potter* movie, you get information about its color, shape, and size "for free," whereas in the book, J. K. Rowling had to decide which aspects of the creature to describe.

On the other hand, books almost always tell you about objects' and people's names and categories, whereas movies don't have to. In language, it is almost impossible to mention an object, person, or animal without categorizing it. People are usually referred to by name or else by categories such as their gender and age group and by categorical descriptions of their hair color, height, and so forth. Animals are referred to by their species or by a name if the animal is a pet. Here is the beginning of Annie Proulx's *The Shipping News*:

> Here is an account of a few years in the life of Quoyle,
> born in Brooklyn and raised in a shuffle of dreary upstate
> towns. Hive-spangled, gut roaring with gas and cramp,
> he survived childhood; at the state university, hand
> clapped over his chin, he camouflaged torment with
> smiles and silence. Stumbled through his twenties and
> into his thirties learning to separate his feelings from his
> life, counting on nothing. He ate prodigiously, liked a
> ham knuckle, buttered spuds. His jobs: distributor of
> vending machine candy, all-night clerk in a convenience
> store, a third-rate newspaperman. At thirty-six, bereft,
> brimming with grief and thwarted love, Quoyle steered
> away to Newfoundland, the rock that had generated his
> ancestors, a place he had never been nor thought to go.[3]

In a few short lines, you get a lot of information about Quoyle's experiences and torments, but nothing about what he looks like or sounds like.

So, when you watch a movie, some parts of your model are more fleshed out and others are left sketchy; when you read a book, different parts of your model will be filled in. These differences are not absolutes: Occasionally a movie presents a person or animal without giving color information, but showing only a shadow or silhouette. And if a book author wants to keep a character's age or gender ambiguous, it is possible to do so by using descriptive phrases that explicitly refrain from committing to these categories. "A figure appeared in the door; it was impossible to say whether it was a man or woman, old or young." But such descriptions are unusual and they call attention to themselves.

So there are definitely differences, but event models from movies and from books are more alike than different. Why? Because the neural architecture we possess for model building did not evolve to help us understand movies *or* novels: It evolved to help us deal with the real world. When you go to a grocery store or have lunch with a friend, you have to keep track of multiple people, objects, places, and how they relate to one another. A lot of the information you need just to walk the aisles of the grocery store or carry on a conversation with your lunch partner is not physically present in front of you. Some of it may be missing from the information you have available: Part of a store shelf may be hidden by a display case, part of what your friend said may have been drowned out by the sound of a door opening and closing. Other parts of the situation *were* present but are no longer there—the shelves on the aisle you just left or what your friend said a minute ago. In order to behave effectively, you need to keep track of all of this. So we, along with a number of other species, have evolved a memory system that can take input from lots of sources—vision, hearing, touch, and so forth—and integrate it with our general knowledge to maintain a representation of the situation we are part of. As human language evolved, we added another input line to the mechanisms for event model construction. But the basic architecture is designed to take a diverse set of inputs and construct a coherent representation of a situation.

The notion of a model can be a slippery one, so let me elaborate.[4] One way to pin down what event models are is to say what they are *not*. First, an event model is not a description in anything like language. Language is amazing in part because the relations between elements of language need not correspond in any way to the things that language is about. The word *sun* has nothing round, hot, or yellow about it. This means that the similarity between two sentences does not tell us much about the similarity between the situations they describe. Consider this sentence:

The fire truck arrived after the warehouse burned down.

Here is another sentence that is very similar but describes a very different situation:

The fire truck arrived before the warehouse burned down.

This next sentence is much less similar, but describes the same situation as the first:

The warehouse burned down before the fire truck arrived.

In an event model, unlike in language, the representation is systematically related to the thing being represented. Remember in Chapter 1 when I described *maps* in the brain? In the visual system, locations in space that are near each other are mapped to places in the brain that are near each other. Maps in the visual cortex process the information your eyes provide about your world. Another set of maps processes information about your body from your skin and muscles. These maps sit on either side of your central sulcus, a large fold that runs from just in front of your ears up to the top of your head. The cortex just behind the sulcus, your primary somatosensory cortex (*somatosensory* means "body sense"), contains a map of the body, with the head on the bottom, the hands just above the ears, and the feet on the top. Across the sulcus, on the front side, is your primary motor cortex. It contains another map, aligned with the somatosensory map, which plays a major role in controlling your body's movements.

For both the visual maps and the somatosensory and motor maps, the brain uses spatial location in the head to represent spatial location in the world: It is the spatial arrangement of neurons that implements the map, and what is mapped is the spatial arrangement of visual features, somatosensory features, or muscular actions. But maps do not have to use space to do the representing, and they do not have to be representations *of* space. The part of your brain that is primarily responsible for hearing is the auditory cortex. The auditory cortex sits on the side of your brain near your ears. It contains a set of maps that use space to represent sounds' pitch. Low-pitched sounds activate the part nearest the surface of the brain. As the pitch becomes higher, activation moves back a bit and into folds in the brain's surface.[5] Even though the dimension being represented is not spatial, there is a systematic and smooth relationship between the representation and the situation it represents.[6]

Because event models are layered on top of maps, they inherit this property of having a smooth relationship between the situation being represented and the representation in your head. The neural hardware that implements event models includes parts of the perceptual system that are laid out as maps. Another reason that models map smoothly on to situations is that they are also layered on top of the mirror rule and the success rule, principles we examined in Chapter 1. The mirror rule says that when you see someone wave his or her arm, you activate a motor representation of arm waving. Once that mechanism is in place, you can use it to represent waving in your event model. The success rule says that when a movie shows a ball rolling toward you, you will ready an appropriate response—a jump, kick, or dodge. Once this response is in place, you can use it to represent parts of the situation that are not explicit in a movie or text—to build inferences into your model that line up with the structure of the world about which you are inferring.

Event models are not just *pictures* in the head. Pictures do not have components, but models do. Think of the difference between a photograph of Robert Downey Jr. as *Iron Man* and an Iron Man action figure. The action figure has components that can move relative to one another. The figure changes when you move the arms and legs, whereas in a picture, you are stuck with the one configuration. (If you cut out the arms and legs from the picture to move them around, you have created a model, albeit a crummy one.) Components are critical for running simulations. A good model has parts that correspond to the real situation in relevant ways, so that by manipulating the parts you can produce a result that corresponds to what would happen in the world.

Our models are by no means always perfect. Flawed event models provide one of the bottomless wells for slapstick. For example, in Jacques Tati's *Mon Oncle*, Tati plays a Luddite Parisian visiting his sister's newfangled house in the suburbs. None of the knobs and buttons in the kitchen does what he expects. Eventually he figures out how to open the cupboard and pulls out a water jug. He is surprised to see that it is made of some kind of rubber such that it bounces when dropped on the floor. Intrigued, he pulls a water glass from the cupboard and drops it—and then sheepishly tries to brush the broken glass under the oven.

Models of other people are even more prone to error. Much of the conflict in movie plots—and in real life—happens because someone has an incorrect model of someone else they care about.

An event model is not a perfect copy of the situation it represents. Models are abstractions. They leave out lots of information and distort some of the remainder. Abstraction is necessary because even a simple situation has way too much information to represent in the mind; if our brains tried to capture it all, they would quickly run out of storage capacity. But even if we could store it all, we wouldn't want to. Abstraction is what allows us to fill in missing information and make useful inferences. A perfect copy is no more or less useful than the thing it represents.

I think this was put best by the comedian Richard Wright (you have to imagine him saying this very slowly and drily): "I have a map of the United States...Actual size. It says, 'Scale: 1 mile = 1 mile.' I spent last summer folding it. I also have a full-size map of the world. I hardly ever unroll it. People ask me where I live, and I say, 'E6.'" Models are useful precisely because they boil a situation down to a point at which our cognitive capacities can deal with it.

The combination of mapping, separating into components, and abstracting is a powerful one. It allows you to build mental models that can allow you to discover new things, sometimes counterintuitive ones. It is said that this is how Newton arrived at his account of how gravity produces orbits. As the story has it, Newton imagined firing a powerful cannon from a mountaintop. He knew that objects accelerate toward the earth at a constant rate. And he knew that the earth was round. So, he mentally simulated firing the shot with larger and larger charges. As the charges became big enough, the shot would travel far enough that it would have farther to fall because of the earth's curve. If the charge were just big enough, the shot would just keep falling around the earth—an orbit.

How do we construct event models? Everyday life is complicated, and most of the time no single sense can give us a full picture of the situation around us. So we have to combine information from vision, hearing, touch, and smell. And even the combination still may leave our model incomplete in important ways, so we fill in from our memories. If you sit down to breakfast in your kitchen at home, your model probably includes information about the adjacent rooms even if you haven't been in them yet this morning. Finally, we often receive help from others to fill out our models using language. If you can't see what's in a box, you might ask your friend sitting across the table. In short, to navigate complex situations with incomplete information, we have had to evolve a highly opportunistic set of mechanisms for model building.

You can see all this in play in *The Matrix*, when Neo, Morpheus, and the rest go to visit the Oracle. After their interview, they discover they have been betrayed, and a game of cat-and-mouse with the agents ensues. Neo and the gang are navigating a complex apartment building that they have never visited before. They look and listen intently. At the same time, Tank is sitting back on their ship, looking at a structural diagram of the building and talking to them on the phone. The team has to quickly combine what they see, hear, and remember with what Tank tells them so that they can act fast—turning just before they are discovered or head-butting through a bathroom wall to uncover a hidden way out.

We think that information from all these sources is integrated into a common model. This means that whether you experience it live, watch it on a screen, or read about it, you wind up with a model that includes information about how things look and feel and sound, where objects and people are located, and how you might act. In other words, when you understand a story, you are simulating the events in the story—whether you see them on a screen or read about them on a page.

The idea that event models underlie understanding is a pretty strong claim. Not every cognitive psychologist or neuroscientist buys it. It makes some counterintuitive predictions: The hard-core version of the model-building account says that when we understand a story just by reading it, we fire off the same neural systems that we use to build models of the real world. So, if you read about a blue sky, does this activate the parts of your visual cortex that represent color? If you watch runners on a beach in *Chariots of Fire*, do the parts of your brain that move your legs start firing away? If so, why does this not interfere with your processing of the real world—why don't you start hallucinating and acting out?

In the last few years, a number of laboratories around the world have been asking these questions.[7] In my laboratory, we have mostly used functional MRI (fMRI), which is a good choice for this work because it allows us to record from the whole brain at once, tracking changes in the brain down to scales of a few millimeters and a few seconds. It is also noninvasive: It doesn't require us to implant electrodes and doesn't require the participants to do anything. They simply lie on their backs in a big tube with an angled mirror in front of their faces through which they can watch a movie. And fMRI is safe—though not nearly as comfortable as a theater—so our participants can remain in our experiments for as long as they have the patience to do so. In these experiments viewers watched Albert Lamorisse's *The Red Balloon*, a 1956 French film that follows a young boy as he frees and befriends a balloon that appears to have a strong will of its own.[8] The film had a bunch of attractive features for us: It is shot and edited in a straightforward naturalistic style, it has almost no dialogue, and it does not use flashbacks or large temporal gaps.

Before we scanned anyone, we analyzed the movie very carefully to try to identify those points at which new information would be incorporated into the participant's event model. *The Red Balloon* tells the story of a little boy who, on his way to school in Paris, finds a big red balloon that appears, magically, to be a sentient creature. The balloon follows him and they have adventures. (I won't give away the ending.) The film tells a poignant little story with efficient editing and almost no language. A raft of data, mostly from studies of reading, suggested that people incorporate new information into their models when the information changes. This makes sense. In *The Red Balloon*, when the boy enters the school you might update spatial aspects of your event model. When he unties the balloon you might activate motor features related to grasping and manipulating. We went through the movie and found all the spatial changes, such as when the camera pans through a door into a new room or the film cuts from an outside shot to an interior view. We also recorded all the changes in the objects characters interacted with—reaching for a broom or grabbing a door handle. And we recorded several social features that might be important, such as changes in characters. Finally, we coded for cuts because the large visual discontinuities at cuts produce big visual responses. (More on that in Chapter 7.)

We were interested in brain responses in two particular areas. The first location, found in the bottom of the temporal lobe, is called the *parahippocampal place area*, and is known to be important for representing space in humans.[9] In fMRI experiments, this area is activated more by looking at pictures of buildings and rooms than by any other visual stimulus. Patients with lesions in this area have trouble learning or remembering their way around. We looked to see which areas of the brain became more active when the movie action in *The Red Balloon* shifted from one location to another. Sure enough, there was a large increase in a small part of the temporal lobes, right where the parahippocampal place area should be. We think this is the trace of your brain updating your model of the space in which the action is taking place.

Next, we investigated which brain areas were particularly active when characters in the film picked up new objects. We were especially interested in the somatosensory and motor maps of the body. For example, when you see a character reach for an object, if you incorporate information about the act of reaching and what it feels like, we would expect to see activity in one or both of these maps. More important, we should see it in the area corresponding to the hand. The somatosensory cortex is organized contralaterally, which means that the right hand is represented in the left hemisphere and vice versa. Our participants were all right-handed, so we'd expect to see activity in the left motor cortex. That is what we observed.[10]

Data like these, from my lab and from others, started to convince me that a relatively hard-core version of the model-building theory might be correct. But I do worry about an alternative possibility: What if these responses just reflect a hardwired connection between our visual systems and the systems that represent spatial location or motor action? Humans are intensely visual creatures, and it's not crazy to think that we might have some simple hardware rigged to translate patches of light in our visual fields into representations of spatial location or actions. That would be a lot less powerful and flexible than the event models I've described.

Luckily, we already had a dataset available to test these two alternatives. If the effects we saw were due to a simple translation from visual patterns to locations or actions, then the effects we observed ought to look very different when our participants were getting their information about the situation by some means other than watching it. On the other hand, if people are really building event models, we would expect to see similar responses to new spaces and new objects when people read about them. The data were part of Nicole Speer's PhD thesis in my lab. Nicole wanted to know how people construct models of events from texts. To study this, she asked people to read approximately 40 minutes' worth of stories in the MRI scanner. If watching movies in the scanner seems weird, reading is even weirder. We had readers lay on their backs looking at the mirror in front of their face, while a computer projected one word at a time in the middle of their visual field. The words went by at a rate of about four per second—pretty brisk, but with a little practice not hard to follow. We presented the stories this way for two reasons. First, during normal reading people have to move their eyes all over the place, and this generates a lot of brain responses that we were not interested in. Second, by presenting the words one at a time we knew exactly when each reader was processing each word. Like we did with the movies, we gave people breaks every 10 minutes or so, during which we asked them questions about what they had just read.

The stories described the activities of a young boy over the course during a single day in a town in Kansas in the 1940s. How these stories came about is a story in and of itself. Roger Barker was chair of the Department of Psychology at the University of Kansas in the 1940s. He was trained in the traditions of experimental psychology, with a PhD from Stanford. In those days the field was focused tightly on basic measurements of perception and learning. Perception experiments were a huge challenge—imagine trying to present controlled visual stimuli without computers—so psychologists became experts at working with complex mechanical and electrical timers, shutters, and projectors. Somewhere along the way, Barker became convinced that there was something missing.

Psychology was learning a lot about the fine structure of behavior in the lab, but it knew precious little about when, where, and with whom various behaviors occurred out in the wild. He decided that the world needed a new "ecological psychology," which would answer these questions. Someone at the university must have agreed, because Barker obtained funding to establish a field research station at a town in Kansas (Oskaloosa) that was referred to in publications as "Midwest." Barker and his team set about characterizing how the people of Midwest behaved: what they did, where they did it, and with whom. One of their techniques was to collect what they dubbed "specimen records," detailed descriptions of the activities of a person over the course of a day. One of these specimen records described a day in the life of Raymond Birch (not his real name). A team of 12 observers working in rotating shifts of 3 wrote down everything Raymond did, from the moment he awoke until the moment he went to bed in the evening. Published as a book called, appropriately enough, *One Boy's Day* in 1951, it runs to 540 pages. Here is an excerpt:

> Susan Hebb (a second grader) went by on her bike and said to Raymond, "Hello," in a pleasant tone. Raymond walked toward the corner of the school, carrying his jacket. Susan fell in step behind him. They had some whispered conversation, and giggled in a breathless way. They were not boisterous, but each breath came out in the form of a giggle or a happy sigh. Wheeling around, Raymond walked over to Susan's bike, which was parked near the front door, and pushed his jacket into Susan's basket. Susan said, "Hey, you," and laughed. She said this in a demanding, warning, but very good-natured tone of voice. Both giggled quietly as before. Raymond ran up the terrace of the lot next door to the school. Susan chased him. They ran in and out of the bushes. Raymond ran quickly down the terrace. He stood still, taunting

Susan, but not saying anything. He looked quite cocky with his legs spread apart and his arms akimbo, just defying Susan to catch him. Susan ran quickly down after him. Raymond then raced up the terrace and the chase continued. Susan followed and they went in and out of the bushes. Raymond raced down the terrace again. Susan called good-naturedly, "Oh, what's the use, what's the use." Raymond ran up the terrace with Susan after him. He slowed down as he came back down the terrace. A big grin spread on Raymond's face. He suddenly took off again, running up the terrace. He was followed by Susan, but she ran right past him to meet Betty Reeves, who had come up the road. He picked a leaf off a bush, put it in his mouth, and nibbled on it. Suddenly Susan ran after him. Raymond giggled and went chasing off in the direction of a tree that stood across the walk from the bushes. Susan, giggling, pursued him.[11]

I think of *One Boy's Day* as like James Joyce's *Ulysses*, except that it's all true—and if you read it straight through it's really boring. It may not make great literature, but the daily entries and other evidence generated by Barker's team are a treasure trove for psychology and sociology. The theoretical work that accompanied these data-gathering missions was creative and insightful. It contributed to the founding of a new subfield of psychology. But somehow Barker's vision never caught hold within the larger field. Today, his work is only modestly cited in the scientific literature, and *One Boy's Day* is barely ever mentioned. Buried treasure.

But back to model building. Ten-minute chunks of *One Boy's Day* were ideally suited for our experimental purposes because they really do describe a set of true events, and they describe them in a workmanlike, unadorned fashion, allowing us to focus on the situations. And although the piece as a whole is pretty dull, the short excerpts are perfectly pleasant reading. We coded the *One Boy's Day* excerpts just as we coded *The Red Balloon*, recording changes in spatial location, objects, and the rest. For example, in the foregoing excerpt, "Raymond walked very briskly onto the school grounds" and "Raymond ran up the terrace of the lot next door to the school" are both changes in space. Changes in objects include "pushed his jacket into Susan's basket" and "he picked a leaf off a bush."

With this coding in hand, we looked at the fMRI data to see what was happening in our participants' brains as they read about changes in space and objects. Sure enough, when the text described Raymond entering the school grounds or running up the next-door terrace, we saw activity in what looked to be the parahippocampal place area. The location of the effect was so similar to what we had seen for movies that it was striking. And when the text described Raymond pushing his jacket into Susan's bike basket, we saw activity in the hand area of the somatosensory cortex. In fact, the result in this case was stronger for the texts than it had been for the movies; this time we saw activity in the motor cortex as well. Just as with the movies, the response at object changes was almost exclusively in the left hemisphere. Again, this makes perfect sense, because all our participants were right-handed and the motor cortex is organized contralaterally.

A few months later, as we were finishing up the data analysis and writing up our findings for publication, my daughter Delia came home from preschool to find a package on our doorstep. Inside the package was a book from her grandparents. Excited, she ripped open the brown wrapper to find a bright pink dust jacket with a cute illustration of little girls in tutus and tights. Delia had just started taking ballet lessons, and her grandparents had sent her a story set in a ballet class. Bouncing with expectation, she grabbed the book, asked me to read to her, and opened it. Then she paused. She turned a couple pages, and her face fell. "What's wrong?" I asked. The pages were covered with words; no pictures. I gave her a squeeze and, without thinking about it, told her, "It's okay, don't worry. Sometimes there are pictures on the page, and sometimes you make the pictures in your head." Models are not pictures, of course, but I think I must have been under the influence of these results.

These sorts of data support the idea that when you read a book, you construct a model of the situation described in the book that is in important ways similar to the model you would build if you watched a movie of the same situation. Professional storytellers know this intuitively. Here's the animator John Kahrs: "Whenever I read something, I'm picturing it in my head like a movie. If the worlds are fully realized in the text, you can have those wonderful visuals. I think everybody has a little bit of the director in them, envisioning these stories."[12] The similarity of the movie results and the book results lends support to the idea that our event models are abstractions. Translating a set of letters on a page or screen into a representation of the space of the terrace steps or the feel of pushing a jacket requires abstraction, much more than translating pictures, because the letters are so different from the form of the information being represented.

However, one thing these data do not say a lot about is the role of the brain's maps in model building. If the hard-core version of the model-building story is true, we should be able to see that reading or watching a movie produces responses not just in the right general area of the brain, but the specific portions of that area that correspond to the situation in the movie or story. For example, if you see Pelé kick a soccer ball with his left foot in John Huston's *Victory*, you should activate the part of your right motor cortex that represents your left leg. In fact, there *is* pretty good evidence on this point. In one of the first fMRI studies, Giovanni Buccino and his colleagues at the University of Parma had viewers watch short film clips in which a person did things like biting an apple, grabbing a cup, and kicking a ball. Notice that these actions are performed with the mouth, the hand, and the feet, respectively. The fMRI activity associated with each of these actions lined up nicely with the map in the motor cortex and in the somatosensory cortex next door. Again, there is evidence that watching movies works in a similar fashion to reading words. Olaf Hauk and his colleagues at the Cognition and Brain Sciences Unit of the Medical Research Council in Cambridge, England, asked people to read words describing actions that are always performed with a particular body part: "lick" (mouth), "pick" (hand), and "kick" (foot). Again, the data tracked the motor and somatosensory maps.[13]

The experiments mentioned thus far have used short, isolated movie clips and words. So one important question that still remains unanswered is, do these effects hold up with movies and stories that are more realistic or more like the movies and stories we consume for enjoyment?

Also, just how far do these simulations go—how much of the neural apparatus for representing perceptual and motor reality do they use? Remember that the sensory and motor parts of the brain are organized hierarchically. Do simulations from reading affect the whole system or just the higher level areas? Most of the neuroimaging evidence finds effects in higher level areas but not in the lower levels. For example, in the Hauk et al. studies, the somatotopic activity evoked by reading verbs was found in regions a little more frontal than the primary motor cortex. In studies of deliberate mental imagery, there is some evidence for simulation responses in primary areas, but the evidence is still sparse. There must be *some* differences between simulation and perception, or else we would confuse the two. Going forward, the name of the game for research in this area will be to determine the exact differences in the mechanisms for reading a story, watching a movie, and performing an action in real life.[14]

How is information about a situation integrated from different sources into one event model? Think about Neo's mission in *The Matrix*. If a model of the situation really sits at the center of his understanding, then in order to react so quickly he must be putting together the sights and sounds with the words coming over his earpiece in real time, constantly updating the map-like parts of his event model. This leads to a pretty provocative suggestion: If reading leads to model building, and model building depends on the same maps as perception and action, then what we are reading about should directly influence our perceptions and actions. Does this really happen?

Two of the people who have pushed theories of event models the hardest over the last few years have been asking just this question. They each came to this question from very different directions. Rolf Zwaan started his career to study literature. But as a PhD student in the Netherlands in the late 1980s, he became interested in describing literature quantitatively, using computer models and statistics. Over time he became increasingly interested with how features of stories affected the ways readers processed them. He now directs the brain and cognition group at Erasmus University Rotterdam. Art Glenberg studied experimental psychology, writing his dissertation on memory for lists of words. Gradually he became convinced that memory did not evolve for memorizing word lists, and focused more and more on the kinds of representations that memory builds. By the 1990s, both Zwaan and Glenberg believed that when we read stories, we construct models of the sort I have been describing, models that represent perceptual and motor information in its native format. Each of them, together with their colleagues, set out to explore the nature of these models.

In 2002, Zwaan, Rob Stanfield, and Rich Yaxley set out to test the idea that model building from reading affects perception. They asked people to alternate between a reading task and a perceptual task. First, they read a sentence, such as "The park ranger saw the eagle in the sky." Then, they pushed a button, bringing up a picture like one of the ones in Figure 2.1. They were asked to name the object as quickly as possible, and the computer recorded the exact moment at which they began to speak. People can do this pretty fast; the average speaking time was about 2/3 of a second. But just how fast depends on the relationship between the sentence and the picture—and in a very specific way. Suppose you read the sentence and build a model of the situation. It should contain a representation of the ranger and a representation of the eagle, and in the model the eagle should have its wings outstretched to fly. If your perceptual maps support this representation, and these are the same maps you use to perceive the picture, then this ought to help with the perceptual task. Sure enough, people were faster to say "eagle" in response to the picture on the left than to the picture on the right. This was not just something funny about these particular pictures. When Zwaan's group changed the sentence to "The park ranger saw the eagle in the nest," people named the second picture fastest. One worry is that if the pictures always show something mentioned by the sentence, then the people in the experiment might change their strategy to take advantage of this, over-emphasizing their tendency to build models. To discourage this, the experimenters included a bunch of trials with pictures like the third one in Figure 2.1—pictures unrelated to the sentences.

They proposed that when people read the sentences, they build a model of the situation with the ranger and the eagle. If the eagle is in the sky, the map-like part of the model represents the spread-wing shape. If the eagle is in the nest, it represents the closed-wing shape. Then, when

FIGURE 2.1 People read "The ranger saw the eagle in the nest" or "The ranger saw the eagle in the sky," and then were asked to verify whether one of these pictures matched a word in the sentence. For both sentences, the correct response to the left and middle pictures was "yes." Responses were faster when the eagle's pose matched the visual description in the sentence, though this was not relevant to the task.

visual information comes in from the eyes that is consistent with the model, people have a head start on processing it and can respond faster. If the information is inconsistent, it slows them down.

At just about the same time that Zwaan and his students were conducting their experiments, Art Glenberg and Mike Kaschak were setting up an experiment to test the idea that model building from reading affects our actions. They asked people to read sentences and decide as quickly as possible whether the sentences made sense. Here are a few examples:

1. Joe sang the cards to you.
2. Courtney handed you the notebook.
3. You handed Courtney the notebook.

The first one is nonsense. The second two make sense, and describe actions that involve moving toward you ("Courtney handed you the notebook") or away from you ("You handed Courtney the notebook"). Glenberg and Kaschak asked their readers to respond by pushing or pulling a lever. For half of the readers, they were to push for sensible sentences and pull for nonsense sentences; the other half did the opposite.

The nonsense sentences were not of interest; they were needed just to make the readers think about the sentence. Number 2 and number 3 are where the action is. If readers built event models that used motor maps to represent the actions in the situation, they ought to construct two different models: After reading 2, the reader's model should include a motor representation of receiving the notebook, with the arms coming toward the body. For these sentences, people were faster in the "pull" condition than in the "push" condition. After reading sentence 3, the reader's model should include a motor representation of giving the notebook, with the arms going away from the body. In this condition, people were faster in the "push" condition than in the "pull" condition. Glenberg and Kaschak concluded that their readers were building models that included map-like motor representations of the situation, and that these interacted with the representations required to *actually* move.

Let me emphasize one point about both of these studies: In each case, you can do the task without using a map-like representation. In the eagle experiment, you are never asked about the shape of the wings. In fact, you are never asked about the sentence at all; you are asked simply to name the picture.[15] In the lever experiment, you are never asked about the direction of transfer; you simply have to decide whether the sentence is nonsense or not. There is no reason that thinking about shape or the direction of movement would give you information to help you complete the task. The fact that you see these effects under such conditions makes me think that this is likely to be a normal part of how we read.

For aficionados of speeded response time tasks such as myself, results like these get the blood pumping. But perhaps not everybody becomes so excited. What do a few tens of milliseconds to name a picture or pull a lever really matter in the real world? Hopefully you can see that the real importance of such results is what they tell us about what is going on inside our heads. But it also helps to connect the dots, to show how the processes of model building play out in real life.

If skilled readers such as yourself construct event models while they read, does giving people a leg up on model construction make them better readers? Art Glenberg and his colleagues have been asking exactly this question. Their approach combines book reading with toy playing—which sounds pretty good to the kids they are working with. Here's how it works: To help teach an elementary school class a story about a kid named Ben feeding the animals on the farm, a teacher sits the kids down with a toy farm set with pieces representing Ben, the animals, the barn, and the feed. The students are instructed that each time they see a drawing of a green stoplight, they should act out the sentence with the toy. Each student then reads the story, with help if necessary. When the students encounter a stoplight, they act out that sentence with the toy. In this way, they are updating a *physical* model of the situation as they read. After they finish, the teacher chats with them for a couple minutes, asking them to recall as much of the story as they could. When Glenberg and his colleagues tested this technique experimentally, they found that acting out the sentences almost doubled memory for them.

So far so good, but what if the kid wants to read about something other than Ben's farm or doesn't happen to have a Playskool toy set handy? The important thing about skilled reading is being able to build a *mental* model, not a physical one. This is what Glenberg's group was trying to teach—and at first it didn't work. When they brought the kids back a few weeks later and had them read without any toys, the children did no better than a control group who hadn't had the model-building training. So the researchers went back to the drawing board and added an additional training phase. This time, after the kids read with the physical models, they did more reading during which the teacher instructed them directly to construct a model in their heads. This time it stuck—weeks later, the kids with the training were able to read a new story, with no toys, and retain more than a control group of children who did not get the training.

Testing a child's memory is a great way to find out how much they have understood, but reproduction is not why you build a model when you watch or read. Models are for thinking. For inferring the pieces you missed. For antici-pating what will happen. Most important, your ability to form models did not develop so that you could watch mov-ies or read stories. It developed so that you could *act*. Remembering what happened in the past is sometimes helpful for planning actions, but much more important is inferring what will happen in the future. The key is the simulation facility that models provide. Say you are cook-ing dinner and have a pot of pasta on the stove. As you are chopping vegetables or setting the table, your model of the situation allows you to simulate that the noodles are get-ting softer, and that simulated change can prompt you to check the stove and take them off.

Part of what is astonishing about stories, whether in written language or in pictures, is that they are a means by which a storyteller can build a series of event models in someone else's head. This can be hugely helpful, and it's been proposed as the rationale for why we evolved the capacity to tell and understand stories. This point was brought home vividly for me in a conversation with Peter Guber. Guber ought to know. He's a very successful movie executive, having run Sony Pictures and founded Mandalay Entertainment. Here's what he said when I asked him why we have stories:

> Around 100,000 or 150,000 years ago, when our species started having oral language, we sat around the campfire and we passed down the rules, values, and beliefs of the tribe, which held it together. That was how we taught the young people to hunt, how to be safe, what not to do. It was all through stories. We sat in front of the campfire with the flickering images: the first movie theatre. And people were carried away with it, were mesmerized. That oral narrative had bound inside of it, like a Trojan horse, the rules and beliefs of the tribe which allowed the tribe to be congruent, coherent, together. This allowed the tribe to work together, to outsmart their prey, become successful, and climb up the food chain. So that's been baked into our DNA.[16]

I have focused on the physical properties of event models, for a good reason. They are the easiest to study because we know a lot about the perceptual and motor maps that play key roles in implementing them. But your models do not stop with the physical. If the situation has people in it, your event model probably represents a host of social features: Who is in charge? Who are friends and enemies? It often will represent the emotions and goals of the characters. Some stories appeal because they require you to build up this social information from sparse, incomplete information.

The novelist Henry James was a master of this, and his books have been perpetually adapted into movies for exactly this reason. Consider this scene from *Washington*

Square, when the protagonist Catherine Sloper meets the man she will fall in love with, Morris Townsend:

> He looked straight into Catherine's eyes. She answered nothing; she only listened, and looked at him; and he, as if he expected no particular reply, went on to say many other things in the same comfortable and natural manner. Catherine, though she felt tongue-tied, was conscious of no embarrassment; it seemed proper that he should talk, and that she should simply look at him. What made it natural was that he was so handsome, or rather, as she phrased it to herself, so beautiful. The music had been silent for a while, but it suddenly began again; and then he asked her, with a deeper, intenser smile, if she would do him the honour of dancing with him. Even to this inquiry she gave no audible assent; she simply let him put his arm round her waist.[17]

James's description is like light filtered through leaves in a forest: Some of the physical scene is illuminated directly, and some of the interior of the characters' thoughts are described like cast shadows. While reading, you have to assemble these pieces to construct a situation. For those of us who take pleasure in James's novels, this process of construction is what it is all about. The 1997 movie of *Washington Square*, directed by Agnieszka Holland, also requires the viewer to construct from a patchwork of cues, but the mix is different. In the book, James can authoritatively describe the characters' inner states using an omniscient narrator. A movie adaptation could use voice-over to do the same thing, but that would come across as ham-handed. Instead, Jennifer Jason Leigh as Catherine provides physical cues to Catherine's state of mind. She raises her fan to cover her face. Her mouth hangs open, revealing clenched teeth. Carol Doyle's screenplay adds some dialogue among the other characters to call attention to Catherine's muteness. The film scene conveys just as vividly the nature of Catherine's captivation, but using completely different means. So, it may be that whether you tend to prefer the book or the movie depends in part on whether you prefer to build your models from categorical descriptions of abstract and internal features, or from depictions of people's appearances and actions.

One genre that puts the work of model building at the center of the experience is the detective story. An event has occurred—a murder, usually, or perhaps a heist. The action of the story reveals bits and pieces of what happened through dialogue, the discovery of evidence, and sometimes flashbacks. You are to use these pieces to construct a model of the situation of the crime. The pieces are designed to provide only partial information, to conflict, and to mislead. The detective protagonist is usually a proxy for your own problem-solving process. One of the tricks of this technique, I think, is that your proxy can be preternaturally gifted. Sherlock Holmes and Hercule Poirot are miles ahead of their compatriots. By reading along as they solve the mystery, we are placed in their shoes and flattered to think that we are just as smart. As the genre has developed, it has picked up riffs and variations. In Stieg Larsson's novel *The Girl with the Dragon Tattoo* and the movie adaptations, the problem solver is split into two people: Mikhail Blomquist the reporter, and Lisbeth Salander the investigator. In Alan Parker's *Angel Heart,* the problem solver and the problem are folded into one person.

In the hard-boiled detective stories of Raymond Chandler, you may identify with Philip Marlowe not so much for his brains as for his guts and his ability to take a punch. Most of the movie adaptations of Chandler de-emphasize the problem-solving part of model building in favor of the characters' emotions and the ethical themes of honor and betrayal—think of Humphrey

Bogart in *The Big Sleep*. But one of them puts the building of a model of the crime's situation front and center. In adapting *Lady in the Lake*, Robert Montgomery shot virtually the whole movie from the first-person perspective of Marlowe. When he picks up a gun to look at it, you see the gun rise into the frame of the camera. When he gets hit in the face, the fist looms into the camera. The main story is framed by opening and closing shots that are filmed conventionally with Montgomery facing the camera. In the opening, he says,

> Right now, you're reading your newspapers and hearing over your radios about a murder. They're calling it the case of the lady in the lake. It's a good title. It fits. What you've read and what you've heard is one thing. The real thing is something else. There's only one guy who knows that. I know it.... You'll see it just as I saw it. You'll meet the people; you'll see the clues. And maybe you'll solve it quick, and maybe you won't. You think you will, eh? OK, you're smart. But let me give you a tip: You've gotta watch them. You've gotta watch them all the time. Because things happen when you least expect them.[18]

The trailer for *Lady in the Lake* promoted it as a major landmark in filmmaking. Does filming a whole movie in point-of-view shots work? For me...not so much. Certainly it has not been widely imitated. I think this has to do with how our attention works—a topic we'll dig deeper into in Chapter 8. The director working solely with point-of-view shots is forced to severely limit what is available to our eyes, to take over with the camera much of the filtering that our attentional system would do in a film shot more conventionally with shots of wide and medium angle. But at the same time the camera can't jump around as much as our eyes do in real life, so the point-of-view shot winds up constraining our view severely and poorly. But I would say there is no question that if you like detective stories for the game of getting a jump on the detective, then this is a film for you.

Is the movie version of *Lady in the Lake* as good as the book? When it comes to adaptations, this is the recurring question. Sometimes the debate can become fierce. When Peter Jackson adapted the *Lord of the Rings* books, he was responding to the concerns of die-hard Tolkien fans long before the first film was even released. In this book, I mostly want to duck the question of what is a good movie and what is not. I don't think that science should generally be in the business of making esthetic pronouncements. But as a psychologist and a brain scientist I am intensely interested in what *works* for people, and adaptations present a notable case.

Most of the time, the cognoscenti conclude that the adaptation is but a pale reflection.[19] Is there a general answer about whether an adaptation is as good as the original? One easy way to answer would be to say, "It's a matter of opinion; everyone comes to their own conclusion." There is something right about that, I think, because novels and movies afford very different routes to event model construction. Language categorizes—a color has to be described as red or orange or explicitly as a combination of the two. A shape has to be a circle or an ellipse or at least a blob. A writer can stretch: a color might be "red-orange," and to describe the shape of a puddle, Nabokov in *Pale Fire* called it "spatulate." Neologisms and hyper-precise descriptions can extend the expressive limits of description, but at a cost of length and effort. A film can simply show the puddle. This means that novels directly present more categorical information about the situation, while leaving more perceptual information to simulation. As a reader, you have to work to construct the sights and sounds as they are described. There are more degrees of freedom in the appearance of things. Movies do the opposite: You are given the sights and sounds, and have to work to sort them into categories and causes. The screenwriter Christopher Keane gives six practical rules for writers adapting novels for the screen:[20]

1. If you're adapting a novel to the screen, forget about what the characters think.
2. In movies, what you see is what you get.
3. If you have no storyline, you have no story.
4. Compress time.
5. Reduce the number of characters.
6. Watch out for too many subplots.

See what I mean? "What you see is what you get" means that the viewer is going to have very different material from which to build an event model than the reader.

Another way of putting it comes from the novelist and screenwriter William Goldman. He's written original screenplays (*Butch Cassidy and the Sundance Kid, Chaplin*), adapted other authors' novels (*Misery, The Chamber, The Stepford Wives*), and adapted his own books (*Marathon Man, Heat, The Princess Bride*), so he knows whereof he speaks:

> When people say, "Is it like the book?" the answer is, "There has never in the history of the world been a movie that's really been like the book." Everybody says how faithful *Gone With the Wind* was. Well, *Gone With the Wind* was a three-and-a-half-hour movie, which means you are talking about maybe a two-hundred-page screenplay of a nine-hundred-page novel in which the novel has, say, five hundred words per page; and the screenplay has maybe forty, maybe sixty, depending on what's on the screen, maybe one hundred and fifty words per page. But you're taking a little, teeny slice; you're just extracting little, teeny *essences* of scenes. All you can ever do in an adaptation is [be] faithful in spirit."[21]

You may prefer one kind of model building to the other, or you may prefer one sometimes and the other at other times. If you find pleasure in imagining perceptual details based on categorical descriptions, you're going to prefer reading. If you revel in beautiful images, you'll probably prefer watching. Or you may find that one way of building models is more rewarding for some kinds of situations, and the other way is more satisfying for other kinds of stories.

But often our friends and the movie critics mostly agree about whether an adaption was successful. These cases overcome our individual variations and achieve a consensus response, be it good or bad. A few adaptations from the last few years that have gone over well include *L.A. Confidential*, the *Bourne* movies, *Fight Club*, *The Diving Bell and the Butterfly*, and *There Will Be Blood*. What is it that makes some adaptations broadly successful? My hunch is that in most of these consensus cases, the movie takes advantage of the unique tools of film for building event models. Often, successful adaptations are action movies, in which the mirror rule and the success rule have ample room to take viewers for a thrill ride. Other times, they allow the filmmaker to create visual images for situations where description falls short (think of *Out of Africa* or *Blade Runner*).

The bottom line is that both books and movies are tools for helping you build models of situations. If the situation is interesting to you and the tool allows you to build a vivid event model, I think you will tend to enjoy the experience. But, as we have seen, words and moving pictures are quite different sorts of tools. Think of a situation as being like a piece of furniture. One piece might be a chair. If you have glue, a set of fine chisels and woodworking knives, and you know what you are doing, you will tend to build one sort of chair. If you have a lathe, sander, and power saw, you will tend to build a different sort of chair. The basics of what it is to be a chair will be preserved, but the results will be quite different. If the chair holds weight and is pleasing to the eye, it will be a success either way. When a filmmaker takes a story and adapts it, it is like taking a piece of furniture made with one set of tools and using it as the basis for a new piece made with a different set of tools. If it works, the new piece probably will not look quite like the original; it will be an *adaptation.*

3 ■

Tearjerkers and Sitcoms

In 1976, Armistead Maupin started writing a fiction column called "Tales of the City" for the *San Francisco Chronicle*. The columns grew to a series of six novels published over 12 years. After a break, Maupin returned in 2007 with a novel that checked in on his central character, Michael Tolliver, and those close to him. In this scene from *Michael Tolliver Lives*,[1] Michael is packing to visit his mother, who is dying. His boyfriend, Ben, is concerned about him:

> Ben left the suitcase and pressed against my back, wrapping his arms around me.
>
> "Are you okay?"
>
> "Yeah, sweetie, I'm fine. Why do you keep asking that?"
>
> His cheek was against my shoulder blade. "Because you're not crying."
>
> Ben knew better than anyone that I can cry at the drop of a hat. I had cried the night before when we were

watching Victor/Victoria on Logo, the new queer channel.

. . .

"I'm not gonna cry about Mama," I said.
Ben tightened his grip on me.
"Does that sound awful?"
"No."
"I'm not sure she wants to go...but...that's not the point. It's just not in me anymore."
"Some things are just too big, I guess."
"Or too late," I said.

Do you cry at the movies? This passage rings all kinds of bells for me because I can remember big events in my life when I expected, even *wanted*, to cry but it didn't come out, and at the same time I can remember clenching my face and turning away to hold off tears in movies that weren't even all that great. What is going on here?

One thing that is striking about emotional responses to movies is their rapidity. A good piece of slapstick can quickly induce laughter and euphoria, and a good crying scene can just as quickly have you weeping. A second striking feature of movie emotions is their strength. A good melodrama can really make you sad—sometimes, apparently, sadder than you would feel if you encountered the same situation in real life. Finally, a feature of movie emotion that I find especially perplexing is that it is in some sense so inappropriate. What's the point in getting angry at a fictional villain? You can't do anything to thwart his nefarious aims. First of all, the situation is fictional (assuming we're talking about a fiction film). Second, nothing you do in your seat can change the outcome. In this chapter, I am going to develop an explanation of why movies can make us feel emotions that are fast, strong, and independent of our ability to take action. I'll say up front that this story is by no means complete;

this is an area where there is lots of great science yet to come.

For the first part of the explanation, I'm going to appeal the mirror rule again. Just as when you see someone wave you have a tendency to wave back, when you see someone smile you will find yourself smiling as well. See someone frown and your lips will tend to droop. These responses have the same properties as the mirror movements I described in the last chapter: They happen automatically—you don't have to be trying to mimic. They happen fast. And they are hard to suppress—if you try to frown just as someone else starts smiling it is quite difficult.

This was recognized early on in the history of film. In 1916, Hugo Münsterberg wrote a book called *The Photoplay: A Psychological Study.* Münsterberg had taken over the psychological laboratory established by William James at Harvard. He leveraged that position to become a major public intellectual in the early 20th century in America, writing books on eyewitness testimony, worker performance, and psychotherapy. *The Photoplay* is considered by some to be the first real book of film criticism, and it is astonishing for the depth of its insight into how perception at the movies works. Münsterberg proposed the mirror rule (though he didn't call it that, of course) as one of two basic means by which movies produce emotion:

> Our imitation of the emotions which we see expressed
> brings vividness and affective tone into our grasping of
> the [movie's] action. We sympathize with the sufferer and
> that means that the pain which he expresses becomes our
> own pain. We share the joy of the happy lover and the
> grief of the despondent mourner, we feel the indignation
> of the betrayed wife and the fear of the man in danger.
> The visual perception of the various forms of expression
> of these emotions fuses in our mind with the conscious
> awareness of the emotion expressed; we feel as if we

were directly seeing and observing the emotion itself. Moreover the idea awakens in us the appropriate reactions. The horror which we see makes us really shrink, the happiness which we witness makes us relax, the pain which we observe brings contractions in our muscles; and all the resulting sensations from muscles, joints, tendons, from skin and viscera, from blood circulation and breathing, give the color of living experience to the emotional reflection in our mind.[2]

Münsterberg didn't have a way to test this proposal very carefully, but these days we can measure the effects of facial mirroring accurately in real time. One laboratory demonstration shows just how robust facial mimicry is. Researchers asked people to watch a series of pictures showing people with neutral expressions. Each was presented for a nice slow interval, 5 seconds. Unbeknown to the participants, just before each of the slow faces was shown, *another* face was presented very briefly, between 25 and 35 milliseconds. This quick face was presented so briefly that none of the participants was even aware it was there; it was completely masked by the slow face that immediately followed. The quick face sometimes displayed a neutral expression just like the slow face, but sometimes it was smiling or frowning. The researchers measured contraction of the viewers' facial muscles using a technique called electromyography. When viewers were shown quick faces that were smiling, their muscles took on more of a smiling expression. When they were shown pictures of a quick face that was angry, they took on more of an angry expression. They were imitating the expressions of faces they couldn't even detect![3]

Getting a clean measure of facial mimicry during movies is tricky, because the facial expression is embedded in a larger situation. If someone in the audience smiles, is it because the actor smiled or because of the joke she told?

That said, there is evidence that viewers' expressions match those of the actors. In one study, researchers made movies of people describing a happy or sad experience. As you would expect, the happy movie included more smiling and the sad movie more sad expressions. The researchers then showed both movies to viewers, while videotaping the viewers. Sure enough, the viewers smiled more during the movie with more smiling and displayed more sad expressions during the movies with more of those. This could have happened because of the actors' expressions, but we can't rule out that it happened because of what the actors were talking about. In any case, it does happen.[4]

So, part of why we smile and grimace at the movies might be mirroring. Just as we mimic the postures and movements of people we see, we also copy their facial expressions—monkey see, monkey do. But the mirror rule doesn't explain all of the postures and expressions we adopt when watching a movie. In *Big Night*, when a waiter brings out a delicious-looking dish, you probably smile even though the diner's back is to you, hiding his face. In *Rain Man*, you probably smile when the cards come up blackjack whether or not you can see any of the characters. What explains these sorts of smiles? The answer comes from an unlikely source—someone immensely famous, but whom few of us associate with emotion: Charles Darwin.

Darwin first became famous for his observations of plant and animal structure made aboard the exploring vessel *The Beagle* and published in 1839 when he was 29 years old. Twenty years later, those observations—and volumes more—coalesced into the theory of natural selection laid out in *Origin of Species*. But at the same time that he was observing the physical structure of the natural world, he was filling notebook after notebook with observations of animal and human expressive behavior. In 1872, he would publish his observations together with an integrative theory as *The Expression of Emotions in Man and Animals*. It sold well at the time, but for a hundred years it had little impact on thinking in psychology, biology, or anthropology. This has turned around in the last few years, in part as a result of a scholarly new edition edited in 1998 by the psychologist Paul Ekman,[5] and perhaps in part as a result of attention around the bicentenary of Darwin's birth. Even in the dark period when the book was ignored, scientists all were quick to praise his careful and sympathetic descriptions of behavior. But in light of current psychology and neuroscience, it is impressive to see how much of Darwin's account rings true.

Darwin started by asking what functions emotions serve in humans *and in other species*. Based on observing how emotional expressions work, mostly in animals other than humans, and inferring what their function was for the organism, Darwin proposed a theory of emotional expression in terms of three principles. The first principle turns out to be the success rule; the other two are derived from it.

Darwin called his first principle "the principle of serviceable associated habits." This is just the success rule. It says that if particular action has tended to work in response to a particular situation or cue in the past, then that situation or cue will tend to evoke the action. For Darwin, the success rule applied both to a particular person's learning of habits within a lifetime and to a species' acquisition of a habit by natural selection. For example, Darwin wrote about the curling up of the lip on one side, as in a sneer or snarl. This is an expression many of us form when we feel negative and aggressive toward someone else. Darwin argues that we produce this expression because it prepares us to bite with our canine teeth. When you snarl at someone, you probably are not going to actually bite them—but your ancestors might well have.[6]

Darwin's second principle is "the principle of antithesis." This one states that if the success rule makes an association between a cue and an expressive response, the opposite of that cue will tend to evoke the opposite of the response. Darwin suggested that a dog's submissive posture may have arisen as the antithesis of a threat posture. In threat, the head and tail are elevated, hairs bristle, and the ears prick forward. Submission is the opposite: head and tail down, hairs slack, ears pinned back. The antithesis may have originated as simply the relaxation of the muscles involved in the threat posture, but it now also serves an important communicative purpose: *not* threat.[7] In humans, Darwin proposed that the expression of astonishment or surprise is the result of antithesis:

> Now, a man in an ordinary frame of mind, doing nothing and thinking of nothing in particular, usually keeps his two arms suspended laxly by his sides, with his hands somewhat flexed, and the fingers near together. Therefore, to raise the arms suddenly, either the whole arms or the fore-arms, to open the palms flat, and to separate the fingers,—or, again, to straighten the arms, extending them backwards with separated fingers,—are movements in complete antithesis to those preserved under an indifferent frame of mind, and they are, in consequence, unconsciously assumed by an astonished man.[8]

Darwin's third principle is "the principle of direct action of the nervous system." With this, Darwin was essentially saying, "We are just built this way." Some emotional responses come about just because that is the way our nervous system is wired. But it turns out that the principle of direct action amounts to two applications of the success rule: a direct one and an indirect one. In the direct path, some emotional expressions are burned into the nervous system by natural selection because they are adaptive responses to particular situations. But Darwin also wants to account for responses that appear to be automatic, do not require learning, and cannot be traced to any adaptive response to a situation in our evolutionary history. Many of these are what Stephen Jay Gould called "spandrels"—side effects of adaptive associations that themselves have no adaptive value. For example, Darwin proposes that tears during crying are such a side effect. A baby's screaming contracts the muscles around the eye and puts pressure on the eye's surface. These trigger the tear ducts' reflexive contraction, which evolved to keep the eye lubricated. Examples like this are indirect applications of the success rule: The success rule produces an adaptive relationship between a situation and a useful response (screaming), and what we think of as an emotional expression (producing tears) comes along for the ride.

Let's pull all this together: The mirror rule states that when we see an actor laugh or frown onscreen, we tend to mimic that response. The success rule (Darwin's "principle of serviceable associated habits") states that we evolved to respond to environmental cues by readying our bodies to respond appropriately. Together, they can exert a powerful influence on how we move our faces and bodies while watching movies. In *Marathon Man*, when Dustin Hoffman is being chased by thugs and his face shows terror, and the mirror rule predicts that faces in the audience will also show terror. When the audience members see shots of him running and the chasers chasing, the success rule predicts that audience members' bodies will prepare to flee or fight. They'll hunch forward, their pulse will go up, and their pupils will dilate. When the actors' expressions fit with the situation the characters are in—which is most of the time in mainstream film—this two-pronged influence is sufficient to push the audience into the facial and bodily pose associated with a powerful emotion.

But there is still an important piece missing here. Mirroring a facial pose is one thing, but that's not emotion. Think about Michael Tolliver watching *Victor/Victoria*. Maupin is not just describing what is happening on Michael's face, but also what he feels inside—his experience of grief and sadness. What I find most surprising about the experience of emotion in the movies is not the grimacing and smiling, but the subjective *experience* of the emotion. What is it that produces *that*?

There are at least two mechanisms that could do the trick. One corresponds to an intuitive theory of emotions that most of us have lurking around, whether we think about it much or not. It goes something like this: First, something happens in the world. Say you find 100 bucks on the street or you learn that your best friend cancelled her holiday visit. You evaluate the impact of that event for you: 100 bucks—good; cancelled visit—bad. Your appraisal depends on your representation of the current situation and your goals. If you see something that indicates that, in the current situation, your goal is likely to be fulfilled, you feel good. If what you see indicates that your goal is likely to fail, you feel bad.[9] That appraisal causes an internal emotional response. It is this internal response that produces a particular facial expression. According to the appraisal account, facial mirroring may produce emotional *behavior* but not the *experience* of emotion. The experience results from your evaluation of whether the situation is good for you or bad for you.

This appraisal story fits common sense pretty well. There is a lot of evidence that appraisal is important for determining our emotional responses.[10] Also, it can account not just for why seeing a smile often makes you happy, but also for why seeing a hated villain's gloating leer might make you angry. In the latter case, your appraisal machine may have information that you are starting to form a smile, but when that information is combined with the other information about the scene, the net appraisal is negative—and your incipient mirror smile dissipates.

But I don't think the appraisal route is even close to the whole story. One limitation of the appraisal account is that it makes the fact that we experience strong emotions at the movies surprising. Nothing that happens on the screen can affect you, so you shouldn't evaluate it as good or bad. A movie might make you feel good if you appreciate the quality of the acting or special effects, or it might make you feel bad if you feel you got ripped off and wasted 2 hours on a dud, but an actor's smile or tears should be neither here nor there. In other words, the appraisal account fails to account for the main fact of emotional experience at the movies—that it happens at all. How can we patch the appraisal account to deal with this? In my view, the best solution is to propose that when we feel good for a protagonist's success—or a villain's defeat—we are appraising movie events in an "as if" mode. "As if" appraisals may have evolved to enable us to learn by observing other people's actions. This is another instance of movies hijacking an ability that evolved for dealing with real life. To some degree, we can tune the "as if" appraisal mode up or down: When we concentrate on the fact that *this is a movie*, we can exert top-down control on the appraisal mechanism, shortcutting these responses. But most of the time when we go to the theater, we deliberately allow ourselves to soak up the situation on the screen, develop rich and vivid appraisals, and thereby let ourselves get carried away. However, even when I think these appraisals are operating on their highest setting, "as if" appraisals don't seem to be convincing or powerful enough to account for the strength of the emotions we experience at the movies.

There's another problem with relying entirely on appraisal. Appraisals can be generated pretty fast, but they do take some time to compute. That doesn't seem to jibe with the immediacy and the power of emotional response that films can produce. Psychologists and neuroscientists have pointed out that for some aspects of emotion—particularly the initial evaluation of something as good or bad—it would be adaptive to hardwire stimuli to emotional responses. In particular, for many situations it might be a good idea to build a direct pathway from expressions of emotion to the experience of emotion.

This is a kind of wild idea; it turns common sense on its head. But it's an idea with a first-rate pedigree; it was at the center of the theory of emotion proposed in one of the classic texts in psychology, William James's 1881 *Principles of Psychology*. James emphatically presented his view as a radical one:

> Our natural way of thinking about these coarser emotions is that the mental perception of some fact excites the mental affection called the emotion, and that this latter state of mind gives rise to the bodily expression. My theory, on the contrary, is that *the bodily changes follow directly the perception of the exciting fact, and that our feeling of the same changes as they occur IS the emotion* [emphasis original]. Common-sense says, we lose our fortune, are sorry and weep; we meet a bear, are frightened and run; we are insulted by a rival, are angry and strike. The hypothesis here to be defended says that this order of sequence is incorrect, that the one mental state is not immediately induced by the other, that the bodily manifestations must first be interposed between, and that the more rational statement is that we feel sorry because we cry, angry because we strike, afraid because we tremble, and not that we cry, strike, or tremble, because we are sorry, angry, or fearful, as the case may be. Without the bodily states following on the perception, the latter would be purely cognitive in form, pale, colorless, destitute of emotional warmth. We might then

see the bear, and judge it best to run, receive the insult and deem it right to strike, but we should not actually *feel* afraid or angry.[11]

James was saying that the bodily experience of an emotion causes the subjective mental state. He thought there was no bright line between what goes on in the body and what goes on in the brain, and that when it came to emotions the body took the lead. This means that putting your body into the configuration associated with an emotion is not just *like* adopting part of the emotional state, it *is* part of the emotional state. Further, James argued that emotions are integrated systems, so when one part of the emotion is activated it spreads to the full package. In other words, if you adopt the physical forms and behaviors associated with an emotional state, the subjective experience will come along too.

Does this really happen, and, if so, does it happen in movie acting and movie watching? James quoted a number of contemporary stage actors who suggested that it does, though they differed in how necessary they thought it was:

> "I often turn pale," writes Miss Isabel Bateman, "in scenes of terror or great excitement. I have been told this many times, and I can feel myself getting very cold and shivering and pale in thrilling situations." "When I am playing rage or terror," writes Mr. Lionel Brough, "I believe I do turn pale. My mouth gets dry, my tongue cleaves to my palate. In Bob Acres, for instance (in the last act), I have to continually moisten my mouth, or I shall become inarticulate. I have to 'swallow the lump,' as I call it."[12]

The aspect of body configuration that is probably most important for movies is facial expression. James would say that smiling makes you happy and frowning makes you angry. Is it true? For decades, psychologists were skeptical, in part because it is hard to do the right experiment. If you tell someone to frown and then ask them how they feel, they'll probably figure out that there's a "right" answer. How could you get someone to frown or smile without realizing that's what they were doing with their face?

In 1988, a group of psychologists in Germany came up with a really clever way to do just that. Check out Figure 3.1, which illustrates the task. The researchers told participants that they were interested in how well people could perform cognitive tasks when they had to respond with body parts other than the ones they were accustomed to using. In one version, they asked people to respond by pushing together two golf tees stuck on their forehead—this makes a frown. In another task, they were asked to squeeze a pen between their teeth—this makes a smile. Each task was paired with a slightly tweaked version that didn't produce an emotion-related pose. When people looked at negative pictures, squeezing their forehead into a frown made them judge the pictures to be sadder. When they watched funny cartoons, clamping down on the pen to make a smile made the cartoons seem funnier. And all the while, they didn't notice that the tasks were making them pose like they were frowning or smiling—they just thought of it as moving their forehead or their mouth.[13]

Posing your face into a frown or smile doesn't just affect your subjective experience; it also affects your brain's response. A group of researchers in London asked people to imitate facial expressions and used fMRI scanning to measure their brains' responses. Some of the expressions were emotional—anger, sadness, and happiness. Others were eating behaviors—chewing and licking. You would expect that all of these behaviors would activate the somatosensory and motor cortices, and they do. But the emotional behaviors selectively activated other brain regions, some in a fashion that was specific to the

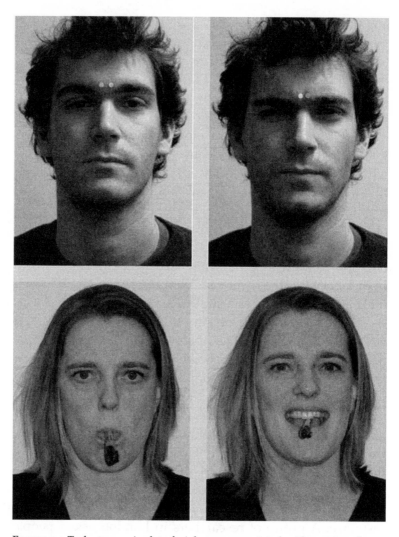

FIGURE 3.1 Tasks to manipulate facial poses associated with emotion. In the top two pictures, a man demonstrates the task in which people are asked to try to push the dots apart or bring them together. Bringing the dots together creates a frown. In the bottom two pictures, a woman demonstrates the task in which people are asked to hold a pen in their lips or teeth. Holding the pen in their teeth creates a smile.

From Niedenthal, P. M. (2007). Embodying Emotion. *Science*, 316, 1002–1005.

emotional expression being imitated. (More on the specific areas in a little bit.) Together with the picture judgment results, these data support James's notion that emotions are integrated systems that involve both the body and the brain, and specifically that activating the parts of an emotion system in the body can affect the parts in the brain.[14]

So let's talk about how the emotional brain responds to movies—particularly how a picture on a screen can evoke a strong emotional brain response. It's tempting to think that there are a bunch of little emotion centers in the brain, each corresponding to a different emotion. Stimulate the pain center and buckle in agony. Stimulate the joy center and smile gleefully. Stimulate the sadness center and cry pitiably. But that's not how it works. There are components we can localize, but they don't correspond one-to-one to emotions such as pain, joy, and sadness.

Emotions have parts and aspects. First is how the emotion *feels*. Fear is often described as negative and active, sadness as negative but quieter, satisfaction as still quiet but now positive. Second, there is what the emotion is *about*. You might be afraid of a person in a dark alley or of a precarious rock overhead. You could be satisfied about something you did or about something someone else did for you. Another important component of emotion is the *actions* that are associated with each one. Fear is associated with pulling back, and is part of an evolved response to remove yourself from danger. Lust is associated with, well,... The feelings, contents, and action associations of an emotion prepare you to take action in the situation that induced the emotion.

Given these multiple parts and aspects, it is not surprising that the experience of emotion is associated with a broad network of brain regions. The core feeling of emotion is thought to depend most on a set of regions in the ventral (lower) front part of the brain. Evolutionarily, some of these regions are tied especially strongly to areas involved in the sense of smell and the processing of body feelings. One worth singling out is the insula, a part of the lower frontal lobes that is deeply buried in a fold. Sniffing offensive odors strongly activates this area—and so does watching someone else sniff. Experiencing emotion also activates areas just above these in the medial part of the frontal lobes, areas that are also activated when people are asked to think about others' mental states. The association of these two sets of regions may have something to do with the similarity between you sniffing and seeing film of someone else sniffing.[15]

Another ventral frontal region that is worth singling out is the cortex in the middle of the brain in the lower front, the ventromedial prefrontal cortex. This region is in a perfect position to coordinate emotional responses to meaningful stimuli. It projects to a lot of regions in the midbrain that influence functions like breathing, heart rate, and sweating. At the same time, it has many connections to cortical regions that we think of as having a very "cognitive" function. The ventromedial prefrontal cortex itself is activated during many cognitive tasks. Its particular role in emotion may be in translating a cognitive representation of a situation into an emotional one. For example, suppose your friend proposes to take you for a hike. "It's a gorgeous trail, but it does hug a pretty huge cliff and it can get windy. You aren't afraid of heights, are you?" You probably don't need your ventromedial prefrontal cortex to feel anxiety when you are actually on the cliff, but you may need it to experience anxiety when your friend describes the route ahead of time and warns you what is coming.[16]

The ventral frontal cortex is also tightly connected to regions in the temporal lobes that are necessary for learning associations between neutral stimuli and emotionally significant consequences. The most important and best studied of these is the amygdala. Rats with lesions to the amygdala are unable to learn that a sound or a light warns them when a shock is coming. In humans, the situation is a little more complicated: People with amygdala lesions report that they can learn that after a visual cue a shock is coming, but they do not display the appropriate physiological anticipation. Such cases show us that although normally how we feel and what are thinking about are tightly coupled, they are not the same thing.[17]

Activation in these circuits produces specific effects out in the body. Fear is associated with increased heart rate and sweating, disgust with queasiness, anger with flushing, and so on. These reactions are part of programs that ready you to act. Bodily reactions also feed back to play an important role in the experience of emotion. The exact role of body sensations in emotional experience is controversial. Remember my explanation of William James's views? I focused mostly on the face, but he thought that bodily experiences were much more important to the experience of emotion. More recently, this view has been advocated most strongly by Antonio Damasio in his somatic marker hypothesis. However, other researchers have raised objections that the mapping from bodily sensations to emotional feelings is too inconsistent and too unreliable to be effective. A racing heart could mean you are afraid or angry, or that you just worked out or ate a hot pepper. I don't really have a dog in this fight. If the facial feedback story turns out to be wrong I'd have to change some of my thinking, but whether bodily sensations cause subjective emotion isn't so important. What is important is that they are reliably associated with the experience of emotion, and everyone agrees on that.[18]

Functional MRI studies show that circuits in the emotional brain can be activated by watching emotional expressions on the screen. In the London imitation study I described a little while ago, many of the regions we have discussed were activated when people watched emotional expressions. Some were activated only by specific emotions, and in some regions the amount of activation was related to how much the viewers imitated the emotion. These data help us fill in the pathway from the visual perception of emotion to the subjective experience of emotion, indicating that the brain systems involved behave in the right way.

So, here's how we get from watching an actor expressing emotion to feeling emotion in our seats. First, associations between visual facial expression and motor facial expression cause us to imitate; these result from the success rule, the mirror rule, or both. From here, there are two pathways, both of which can produce an emotion from the action of forming a facial expression. The appraisal path takes the expression you formed, and also the actor's expression and information about the situation at hand, and computes an emotional response. At the same time, the Jamesian pathway directly activates the emotion program that is congruent with our facial expression. As these two pathways play out, we settle into an integrated emotion program including emotion-specific brain circuits, the subjective experience of the emotion, and the priming of actions that are appropriate to the action.

Thinking about these two systems leads to a new hypothesis about one of the weird emotional things that can happen at the movies. Have you ever had the uncanny and uncomfortable feeling of watching a despicable character (say, Michael Douglas in *Wall Street*) expressing joy, finding yourself feeling great, and then suddenly catching yourself? My proposal—and I know of no data to back this up—is that this results from a race between a faster Jamesian pathway and a slower appraisal pathway. First, Douglas's smile gets you smiling. Quickly, the Jamesian pathway leads you to feel joy. Meanwhile, the appraisal pathway has started working out that the fact that he is happy is bad news for characters you care about. Once it catches up, you have a conflict between the two pathways, and when you notice it you think, "Why was I just feeling happy that something good happened to this creep?"

I want to be clear that I am *not* saying that facial mimicry is the only way we respond emotionally to the movies. When we watch *The Wizard of Oz*, we are sad in part because Dorothy can't go home when she wants to, and then happy when she does get to go home. That's due to the "as if" appraisal mechanism I described. But what surprises me about the experience is that it feels sudden and strong and involuntary. I think that this comes about because Judy Garland had a very expressive face, and when she smiles or cries on the screen our faces—and our emotions—follow along. I think the involuntary imitation of visually perceived expressions is probably the explanation for *that* piece.

I have focused on the visually evoked pathway because it makes the experience of movie watching distinctive. But let me say a just a few words about the more inferential path to feeling an emotion. This route depends on a particular form of reasoning that has come to be called *mind reading*—reasoning about other people's mental states. If I know that Dorothy would like to go home and I learn that she cannot, I can infer that she feels sad. I may do this by taking a first-person perspective on this situation—putting myself in Dorothy's shoes and thinking about how *I* would feel in that situation. Why do this kind of simulation? Because it allows me to use the same machinery to reason about the psychological consequences of events for myself and for others, and that makes it possible to do both more accurately and more efficiently. This kind of mind reading is strongly associated with the ventromedial prefrontal cortex, among other areas. This makes sense: I can use the same neural machinery I use to translate facts into emotions for myself to simulate the emotions those facts are producing for Dorothy.[19]

Alfred Hitchcock was a big believer in this sort of mind reading. In fact, he sometimes talked as if the actor's face was a distraction: "When a film has been properly staged, it isn't necessary to rely on the player's virtuosity or personality for tension and dramatic effects. In my opinion, the chief requisite for an actor is the ability to do nothing well, which is by no means as easy as it sounds." This comment came from a conversation with François Truffaut, just after describing a scene from *Sabotage*. In this scene, Mrs. Verloc (played by Sylvia Sidney) has just discovered that her husband is a saboteur who has just helped execute a bombing:

> We had a problem there. You see, to maintain the public's sympathy for Sylvia Sidney, her husband's death had to be accidental. And to bring this off, it was absolutely essential that the audience identify itself with Sylvia Sidney. Here, we weren't trying to frighten anyone; we had to make the viewer feel like killing a man, and that's a good deal tougher. This is the way I handled it. When Sylvia Sidney brings the vegetable platter to the table, the knife acts as a magnet; it's almost as if her hand, against her will, is compelled to grab it. The camera frames her hand, then her eyes, moving back and forth between the two until suddenly her look makes it clear that she's become aware of the potential meaning of that knife. At that moment the camera moves back to Verloc, absently chewing his food as on any other day. Then we pan back to the hand and the knife. The wrong way to go about this scene would have been to have the heroine convey her inner feelings to the audience by her facial expression. I'm against that. In real life, people's faces don't convey what they think or feel.[20]

Clearly, Hitchcock meant to get his audience to feel Sylvia Sidney's feelings by convincing them to simulate the situation she was in, not by mimicking the expression on her face.

Whether we experience an emotion directly, via facial imitation, or indirectly via simulation, what we see produces a kind of emotional contagion in which the audience is infected by the apparent emotional state of the actors. When this happens in real life, we call it *empathy*. Empathy is a crucial glue for social interactions. For example, suppose I am out with my 6-year-old daughter and her ice cream cone falls on the ground. She starts crying. I can see her crying, and I also can simulate how losing my ice cream would make me feel. Both of these routes make *me* feel sad and disappointed—but I have more tools to repair the situation than she does. I can give her my cone or buy her a new one, and I can comfort her. By experiencing her emotion empathetically, I am configured to take appropriate action. This is all very adaptive: It helps us solve problems, and it increases our trust that our friends and family will act to take care of us.

But empathy at the movies can play out in funny ways. For one thing, I can't do anything to help Dorothy get back to Kansas, so my disposition to act is left hanging. Worse yet, I can have empathic responses to despicable characters who are expressing reprehensible emotions. Here's François Truffaut talking with Alfred Hitchcock about Hitchcock's *Psycho*:

> One intriguing aspect is the way the picture makes the viewer constantly switch loyalties. At the beginning he hopes that Janet Leigh won't be caught. The murder is very shocking, but as soon as Perkins wipes away the traces of the killing, we begin to side with him, to hope that he won't be found out.... The viewer's emotions are not exactly wholesome.... When Perkins is looking at the car sinking in the pond, even though he's burying a body, when the car stops sinking for a moment, the public is

thinking, "I hope it goes all the way down!" It's a natural instinct.[21]

How does this play out over an extended film? A mood is like an emotion, but it's extended over a longer time and is not "about" something in particular in the way an emotion is. If you listen to people talk about their experience at movies, they certainly talk a lot about mood—what mood they were in when they went, what mood the movie put them in, how they picked a particular film because of the mood that they were in. Here are a few descriptions of one of the all-time heavy hitters for mood, *Terms of Endearment*, from IMDB:[22]

> Few movies can make you laugh and cry OVER and OVER again, but this one does it for me. Even when I catch a scene on cable, I find myself drawn in emotionally and grabbing for my box of tissues.

> TERMS OF ENDEARMENT is an undeniably gripping and emotional film experience that will have you rolling on the floor during one scene and weeping uncontrollably during the next.

Even viewers who dislike the movie (there are many) comment on how it develops a mood:

> This isn't exactly a film that I would recommend to everyone though, because... it does have a slow beginning and people with short attention spans are likely to think that this is the worst film ever, but I assure you that it's not. I got involved with each character, I really started to feel the pain and emotion of each character. It's a really heartbreaking film that caused me to get a lump in the back of my throat.

The film theorist Greg Smith offers a neat thesis: Movies are machines to put you in a particular mood. Smith argues that films are structured to create and maintain particular moods, and that this is part of what the filmmakers are composing as they assemble the movie. They do this in part by administering jolts of emotional experience. For example, he cites *Raiders of the Lost Ark*, in which each skeleton falling out of the wall or rope giving out serves to sustain the mood of suspense.[23]

Pulling all this together, movies can manipulate us because they hijack evolved mechanisms for responding to events in the real world. I have described a set of pathways by which visual perception of emotion can produce the experience of emotion. One pathway starts with the mirror rule—we tend to behave in a way that mirrors what we see. The other starts with the success rule—we tend to behave in a way that would be appropriate to acting in situations we have previously experienced that are similar to the one we are currently seeing. From either starting place, we arrive at a final common pathway in which we activate coordinated emotion programs that rely on distributed brain networks. These systems were built to ready us to act, but they fire off just the same even if we are planning on sitting tight in our seats until the movie ends.[24]

Now, let's return to Armistead Maupin's observation about *Victor/Victoria*. It's not just that the emotional response feels "just like being there." It's that the response seems inappropriately strong—in real life, we don't cry often over people we just met an hour ago. What is going on? I'm not sure, but here is an analogy that I think may be helpful. You may have heard of a set of famous experiments conducted by Niko Tinbergen with herring gulls. Herring gulls, like many bird species, feed nestling chicks by regurgitating food into their mouths. When the young birds see Mom or Dad coming, they start begging for food, by pecking at the red tip of the parent's beak. Tinbergen found that he could present a fake model of an adult gull's head and the chicks would go ahead and beg. Okay, so baby gulls aren't that smart. But then Tinbergen built an exaggerated fake gull consisting of a red knitting needle with three white bands painted around it. The nestlings begged *more* to the simplified fake head than to the realistic one. This came to be called a *supernormal stimulus*. Across a number of species and behaviors, exaggerated stimuli can be more effective at inducing a behavior than faithful reproductions of the normal stimulus.[25]

Thinking about supernormal stimuli led me to look differently at movies. My hunch is that emotional movies embed a great deal of supernormal stimuli—exaggerations of features of emotional expression, dialogue, physical action, setting, color, sound, and so on. Actors, directors, and editors have worked these out over the history of film by trial and error. You could think of these stimuli as being like processed foods with amped up sugar and salt: products that exaggerate dimensions of naturally occurring variation, producing an irresistible response.[26] A provocative corollary of this idea is that over-the-top movies could dull our emotional competence like junk food dulls our culinary competence. This suggestion has been pursued most vigorously in looking at the effects of viewing violent movies, a topic we'll return to in Chapter 5.

I do not have a theory of what one can exaggerate to better induce laughter—but I'll bet a good comedian does. I don't know how to make an audience cry on demand—but I'll bet a soap opera director could tell me how. I don't know how to terrify a theater full of people—but I'll bet a film editor who works on horror movies could tell me. There are stacks of books that relate this lore, just not in the terms of psychology and neuroscience. I would not be surprised if in the next few years researchers and filmmakers get together to do some of this translation and start testing out the theories in experiments. The result could be a whole new generation of techniques for making us laugh, making us cry, and scaring us witless.

4 ■
How Movies Make Memories

If movies and novels trigger experiences that are much like real events, are our memories of stories any different from our memories of our lives? One potential difference is that stories operate on very different timescales than real life. For starters, movies and novels generally unfold a lot faster. You can see this in action in the Hollywood epic. Richard Attenborough's *Gandhi* is long for Hollywood standards, 3 hours 11 minutes. But it sweeps across 55 years of Gandhi's life, so it covers about a year every 3 minutes. Along the way it describes the development of a new political and social philosophy and the founding of two nations. Clocking in at a relatively svelte 139 minutes, Arthur Penn's *Little Big Man* tells the story of Jack Crabb's 121-year life, tearing along at almost a year a minute! Along the way you get the battle of Little Big Horn and the death of Wild Bill Hickock.

There are exceptions, of course; story time can follow real time or even slow it down. Joyce's *Ulysses* describes one waking day of Leopold Bloom, and probably takes about 12 hours or so of reading time. And Nicholson Baker's *Mezzanine* expands a single escalator ride to 135 pages. In movies, *My Dinner With Andre* unfolds essentially in real time, consisting mostly of a single dinner conversation. And the recent TV series *24* made the match of screen time to story time its central device.

Novels and movies can do more than speed up (or occasionally slow down) time. They also can reorder events. The most common way to do this is in flashbacks. In some cases, a flashback is used to frame a story. Orson Welles's *Citizen Kane* is a canonical example. The film opens at the end of Kane's life, showing his death at his estate, Xanadu, and simulated newsreel footage summarizing his life. Then it cuts back to his childhood. The movie takes you back through his life so that movie time rejoins screen time at the end.

Another thing flashbacks can do is provide the audience with information at a critical juncture. In Tim Burton's 1989 *Batman*, Jack Nicholson as the Joker asks Michael Keaton as Batman, "Have you ever danced with the devil in the pale moonlight?" This prompts a flashback in which Keaton remembers the night, as a child, when his parents were shot by the petty criminal Jack Napier in a holdup. Napier drops the same line, allowing Batman—and the audience—to realize that the Joker is the man who killed Batman's parents.

Filmmakers have experimented with more dramatic disruptions of temporal ordering. In *Memento*, Christopher Nolan's protagonist, Leonard (played by Guy Pearce), suffers from anterograde amnesia—he is unable to form new long-term memories. For Leonard, each event is an island that disappears into the mist as soon as he leaves it. He has no way to relate the current moment to a larger timeline other than a set of tricks he has developed: taking pictures, writing notes, tattooing important information on his body. To convey this experience of being marooned in time—and also to build suspense—Nolan presents the events of the story out of order with few cues about the actual order in which they took place. Does this work? A pair of psychologists actually ran an experiment in which they re-edited *Memento* so that it ran in the "right" temporal order. Viewers were better able to figure out what was going on. This isn't too shocking—one point of telling the story this way is to create a puzzle to solve. But it does raise an interesting question: By the end of the movie, does the director want us to "get it" as well as possible? That is one goal. In general audiences probably prefer to be able to follow the story, and the techniques of mainstream cinema are optimized to make that as straightforward as possible. However, in *Memento* the goal of straightforward narration is subordinated to other conflicting esthetic goals. In the experiment, audiences' preferences lined up with the filmmakers' choices: They preferred the original version, despite having a fuzzier view of what they had just seen, suggesting that working on the puzzle and experiencing the suspense was more valuable to them than learning all the facts.[1]

Movies (and novels) can go further than *telling* the events of a story out of order. Sometimes within a story itself time passes in a funny way. In David Fincher's *The Curious Case of Benjamin Button*, time passes quickly—about a year per 1-1/2 minutes on-screen—but also sort of backward: Benjamin is born as an old man and becomes younger and younger as time goes by. Christopher Nolan's *Inception* layers multiple time frames running at different speeds. It takes off from the idea that events seem to pass quickly in dreams, and combines it with the notion of dreams within dreams, imagining multiple linked worlds with time running at different speeds.

Stories that tell events backward or link multiple timescales are tough to relate to real lives and our memories thereof. But for conventional narratives it makes a lot of sense to ask how our memories for stories line up with our memories of our lives. One of the basic and beautiful features of autobiographical memory is that it has a characteristic chronological *shape*—we have many memories from some parts of our lives but few from others. One way to map out the shape uses a method originally developed by Francis Galton in 1879. You can try it on yourself—that's how he originally did it.

Here's what you do. (*Important:* Don't look ahead while you try this, or it won't work.) First you will need a collection of random words. Twenty is a good number. There are random word generators on the web; google "random word generator." Or if that's not convenient, I have provided a list at the end of the chapter.

Find a blank sheet of paper and copy out your list, one word per line, on the left side of the sheet. Now, for each word on the list, think of an event in your life that is related to the word. For example, for the word *tobacco*, I thought of a time in high school when I decided I liked the smell of pipe tobacco. I had never smoked a pipe, but I bought a bag and kept it in a bowl in my room like potpourri. For each memory, write down a few words next to the cue that generated it, so you can remember it for later. Do this for all 20 words, and then turn the page.

Now, next to each memory description, write down, to the best of your ability, how old you were when the event occurred. Tally up the ages in 5- or 10-year increments. There! You have just plotted the shape of your memory for your life.

If you are older than 25 or so, chances are you will find that a lot of the memories you retrieved came from your teens and 20s. Most people do. This characteristic shape is called the *reminiscence bump*. If it happens that yours didn't pop up, don't sweat it. It may be that we just did not have you list enough memories to get a reliable sample, or it may be that you are one of those people whose memory has a unique shape. This happens, for example, if something big happens to you in your 40s or 50s.

But most of us will have a bump corresponding to late adolescence. This holds even as people look back from their 70s and 80s. We remember relatively little from the first few years of our lives, and a modest amount from our adult lives, but a lot from late adolescence. (Most of us also remember a lot about recent events, because we have had less time to forget them.) The reminiscence bump is tied up with all sorts of interesting things about who we are. If you ask people what sort of music they like, which books influenced them the most, which places they most enjoyed visiting, it turns out that late adolescence gets a disproportionate vote. The reminiscence bump does not just apply to personal events but also to the public events we live through. Ask people about the World Series or the Academy Awards, and they will tend to remember more about the ones that occurred during the bump.[2]

What causes the bump? One possibility is that it reflects the time course of how we mature during development. One version of the maturation story is biological—the reminiscence bump results from how the brain matures. Brain development is frantic during early childhood, and the frontal lobes are still sorting themselves out through the mid-teens. The bump pops up at just the time all systems are coming fully online. This period of peak performance is relatively brief. Just about the time the frontal lobes come up to speed the brain is starting to slowly shrink, a process that continues as we age. The total number of neurons slowly decreases, and the connections between neurons become slowly less efficacious. Does the bump occur because late adolescence is when our brains are most efficient at making memories?

Another version of the maturation story is psychological and social. It says that the bump happens because late adolescence is when we are figuring out who we are. The famous clinical psychologist Erik Erikson framed psychological development as a series of challenges, each of which is specific to a particular life stage. He proposed that the great psychological challenge of late adolescence is to form one's stable identity. Perhaps the reason we make lots of memories then is that we need to do so in order to work out who we are.

These are both reasonable possibilities—but they are both probably wrong. The evidence comes from a study conducted at Notre Dame by David Copeland, Gabriel Radvansky, and Kerri Goodwin. Here is how it worked. Copeland, Radvansky, and Goodwin got hold of an electronic version of the text of a novel, *The Stone Diaries*, by Carol Shields. *The Stone Diaries* was published in 1993 and won the Pulitzer Prize for fiction in 1995. It tells the story of Daisy Goodwill Flett from her birth in 1905 to her death in the early 1990s. Its 10 chapters run to 400 pages, so each chapter covers a little more than 8 years and each year spans a little less than 5 pages. Thirty-eight college students came into the lab to read *The Stone Diaries* on a computer. The computer presented one sentence at a time; they pressed a button to move on to the next sentence. (One thing I love about this study is how the participants were compensated: At the end of the study each got a paperback copy of the book. No course credit, no cash—a book. This tells me that immersing one's self in the story was its own reward.) Each time they came into the lab they could read as many chapters as they wanted; they were just asked not to stop in the middle of a chapter. When they were done, they were asked to write a summary of the book, and the experimenters asked them a bunch of specific questions about the story. Both measures showed a reminiscence bump for Chapter 3—late adolescence. They also showed a bump for Chapter 6. In this chapter, Daisy undergoes a major life change, going from housewife out into the working world. Life changes such as this produce reminiscence bumps in real life too.[3]

This study used a novel, but I'll bet it would work just the same with a movie like *Little Big Man*. The brains of the study's participants did not mature or age appreciably over the course of the study, so changes in brain function can't explain these results. Neither can changes in life stage challenges, because their life stage didn't change over the few weeks of reading the novel. So what produced the bump? One possibility is that the bump is due to relationships between the events themselves. One thing that helps memories to take hold is *distinctiveness*. Say you show me a hundred pictures of orchid species and teach me the name of each one. Then bring me back a week later, give me a species name and two of the pictures, and ask me which one it is. I would be hopeless—you might as well flip a coin. But suppose instead you had showed me a hundred different species spread all across the taxa—fish, trees, insects, slime molds...I would probably do a lot better because each picture would be more distinct. Adolescence is probably a time when a lot of distinctive events occur. That could explain why we experience bumps in our own lives, and in the lives of fictional characters.

Another possibility is that when you think about a life you use a *script*, just like the outline for a book or the script for a movie. A script specifies the cast, the setting, and the scenes, among other things. Scripts in this sense are cultural artifacts that we all share, which govern how we think about things. They emerge over time as members of a community talk about their lives and the lives of others. When two people get to know each other, they explain themselves to each other and the way they tell their stories is guided by the script. When an author writes a biography or an obituary, or when a filmmaker makes a movie, he or she is guided by the same script. This is helpful, because the script can help you fill in missing information, make inferences, and reinstate information you may have forgotten. For example, suppose you see a scene in which a young woman arrives at college and moves into her dorm, and then in the next scene she is working in an office. You can infer based on your script that she completed college and graduated, so the filmmaker doesn't need to show you all that happened in between. If something happened that violates the script—suppose she dropped out of school— the filmmaker would probably need to show that.

There is good evidence that the basic script for a life in most cultures has a particularly big cluster of scenes corresponding to late adolescence. According to the life script explanation, the bump occurs because people use their script to help them retrieve memories, and the script has a built-in bump. (What this story does not explain is how the script came to have a bump in it. In one sense it just pushes the explanation back from autobiographical memory to cultural knowledge.)[4]

The distinctiveness explanation and the cultural life script explanation share an important implication. They both say that memories of our lives and memories of stories have the same shape because they are formed by the same mechanisms. It's not the case that you have one bucket into which you drop all the real-life events, another for movie events, and a third for events in novels.

Remember, there is one model-building mechanism in there that grabs information from lots of different sources. The same machinery can combine what you see with what someone tells you to build a model of an event. That machinery is perfectly happy to operate on stuff from your life, from a movie, or from a book. I think that is a big part of the appeal of narrative films and books—they appeal to our model-building propensities.

If the same mechanisms are at work constructing event models from real life and from fiction, why do we not get confused about which is which? Most of the time, the movie or book is so different from our real-life experience that this is sufficient to do the trick. Neill Blomkamp's *District 9*, a surprise hit from 2009, is set in South Africa in the near future, and describes the society's response to the crash landing of a spaceship. When *District 9* came out, I had never been to South Africa, never seen a spaceship, and never met an extraterrestrial. (I'm now one for three.) So I was not likely to confuse events from my life with events from the film. Likewise, I am not likely to mistake my life for that of *Ben Hur* or *Henry the Fifth* (any of the movie versions); I have never worn a toga or a doublet, led an army, or driven a chariot.

Some people, however, do struggle to separate what they saw on screen or read about from what really happened. Take the case of the art dealer who developed an aneurysm that cut off blood flow to part of his left frontal lobe. In the acute phase of the injury he told wild stories, called *confabulations*, that mixed facts from his life with material from friends' lives, books, newspapers, movies, and sources that nobody could identify. He was convinced that all of this was true:

> When asked about his job, he stated that his
> responsibilities included negotiating with foreign

governments to buy their national treasures. He cited the governments of Egypt, France, Greece, and Cyprus as his negotiating partners. He insisted that one of his therapists and several of his friends were not real persons, but imposters.... He claimed that a certain building near the hospital was being used for sinister purposes. He later admitted that his interpretation of the building was due to a spy movie seen some 40 years ago, which flashed back whenever he looked at the building. This memory was highly vivid and real.[5]

Clearly, for this patient, the story of his life and the story of the film had fused.

Even those of us without brain disease can have trouble sorting our own memories from a movie, if the movie is close enough to our life. Ronald Reagan, the 40th president of the United States, served in the military in World War II. In that capacity he was involved with editing movie footage taken in the Nazi death camps at the end of the war. Later, it was reported that as president he confused that footage with his own personal experience, though he had never left the country during the war.[6] In another instance, President Reagan described a heroic bit of piloting he remembered having heard about during the war. When reporters tried to verify it, they could not find a corresponding real incident but did find an old movie that seemed to match the story.[7]

Most of us are not lucky (unlucky?) enough to have movies made about our lives. But we *do* watch movies about public events we took part in, or historical events we learned about from other sources. When we can't separate facts we learn from the real world from fictions we learn from the movies, we may find ourselves victims of distortion and propaganda.

Let's start with distortions that are probably not meant to deceive, but come about because a filmmaker is trying to tell a good story. David O. Russell's *Three Kings* is set during the first Gulf War. It depicts an adventure of three American soldiers in the chaotic late phase of the war, and paints a vivid picture of conflicting and corrupt political motivations for the conflict. Kathryn Bigelow's *The Hurt Locker* portrays a bomb disposal team during the second Gulf War. It emphasizes the great personal costs of the war, and suggests that it is ultimately futile. Both films give rich, vivid impressions of a place most viewers would have learned about from newspaper stories and news broadcasts but not visited directly. They convey a lot of information about the settings and situations they depict, and both directors have emphasized in interviews how important it was for them to "get it right." But these are ultimately works of fiction. When we watch them, do we incorporate their portrayals into our models of the historical events?

The situation can become even trickier when a movie presents itself as history but plays fast and loose with the facts. If I am trying to learn real history, does an inaccurate "true story" movie help or hurt? A group of psychologists led by Andrew Butler recently studied exactly this situation. They asked people to read accurate historical essays and also to watch clips from Hollywood movies about the same topics that contained inaccuracies. The historical periods spanned from the early 17th century with *Elizabeth*, about Queen Elizabeth I, up to World War II with *U-571*, about deciphering the Nazis' Enigma code. Each clip contained information that was inconsistent with history as far as we know, and inconsistent with the essays. Some of them were real howlers: The movie *Glory* depicts new recruits for the 54th Massachusetts infantry as former slaves, but in fact most of the regiment had been born free in the North. The film *U-571* depicts U.S. sailors sneaking on to the German submarine *U-571* in order to steal an encoding/decoding machine called the "Enigma." In the ensuing conflict, the machine is eventually sunk. There was a real *U-571*, and the

Enigma was central to German military secrecy. The real story of how a couple of Enigma machines were captured and the code was cracked is fascinating—but it has nothing to do with the events portrayed in the film. The British cracked the Enigma, and the *U-571* was sunk by Australians. (This "Americanisation" of history caused quite a stir in the United Kingdom when the movie was released. And the history of history flicks repeated itself when *Argo* came out in 2012, featuring a storyline that downplayed the role of Canadian diplomats in the rescue of six Americans trapped in postrevolutionary Iran.)

A surprising number of these distortions stuck with viewers when their memory was tested shortly thereafter. Even though they had read the "right" answer in the essay, viewers were willing to accept about 40% of the distortions as true. It didn't matter much whether they watched the movie before or after reading the essay. In a follow-up experiment, students were specifically given the task of detecting the historical inaccuracies. This didn't help a bit. These studies probably underestimate how influential bad information in historical movies can be, because most of the time when you watch a history flick you do not read an accurate history just before or after.[8]

One of the movies that Andrew Butler and his colleagues studied was Edward Zwick's *The Last Samurai*. In this film, Tom Cruise plays an American soldier fresh from fighting in General Custer's army against the Native American resistance. He is hired by Americans in Japan to assist the emperor in putting down a resistance movement there, led by a group of samurai. Cruise is haunted by memories of what he views as vicious massacres led by Custer. He comes to identify with the samurai and takes up their cause. The film establishes an analogy between the Native American resistance and the samurai resistance. This strengthens the viewer's sympathy for both resistance movements, and gives an American viewer a route to understand the motivations of the Japanese samurai and the peasants who follow them. Watching the movie probably changes viewers' thoughts about both American and Japanese history. Except that the men who really went to advise the Japanese emperor were not veterans of Custer's Indian Wars; they were French (see Figure 4.1). The filmmakers took this liberty with history to make a strong, clear story that would appeal to American audiences. The viewer's understanding of politics and history is a casualty, an innocent bystander.

FIGURE 4.1   *Top:* French advisors and Japanese troops in Hokkaido during the Boshin War. *Bottom:* Tom Cruise in *The Last Samurai.*

I am sure there was no harm intended in the making of *The Last Samurai*, and maybe none done. But the same techniques are used deliberately in propaganda. One flavor of propaganda presents factual material, but manipulates its presentation to sway opinion. During World War II, the U.S. Army made a series of films called *Why We Fight* (see Figure 4.2), designed to convince military recruits and civilians of the government's case for going to war. Frank Capra directed most of them, and they were made with high production values. Here is Capra recounting how these came about:

> The series was conceived in the mind of General George Marshall, then chief of staff. I had volunteered my services one year before Pearl Harbor, because I thought something might be coming up, and if I could be of any use, I'd volunteer my services....I was sent for by Marshall, and he outlined for me what he would like me to do. He wanted a series of films made which would show the man in uniform why he was fighting, the objectives and the aims of why America had gone into the war, the nature and type of our enemies, and in general what were the reasons and causes of this war and why were 11 million men in uniform and why they must win this at all costs....He wanted an orientation type of film, a series of films which would be a part of the mental training of our soldiers as to just what they were doing in uniform, and why they were called away from their jobs and told to carry a gun, and why they must win this war.[9]

Capra and his team viewed their mission as explaining the war to the recruits in order to change their opinion and motivate them to fight. By making these films, they were doing their part to win the war.

FIGURE 4.2 Frames from *The Battle of Britain*, #4 in Frank Capra's series of propaganda films for the U.S. Army.

At the same time, a group of researchers was doing their part by trying to work out how to make these movies as persuasive as possible. In 1942 a team of civilian experts in experimental psychology was assembled in Washington, D.C., by the Information and Education division of the U.S. War Department. They were headed by a 30-year-old rising star from Yale, Carl Hovland. Their main mission was to evaluate the effectiveness of media and methods for training the troops. They would work together for just 3 years, but during that period they would establish many of the basic principles of how mass media influence opinion and behavior.

Hovland's research branch aimed a whole volley of experiments at the Capra films. Capra himself seems to have been only dimly aware of this research; here is his recollection:

> There was an evaluation made of these films by the research department of the Army as to exactly what their effect was on the thinking of the soldiers. I know of one instance in which they took the film *The Battle of Britain*, which showed the time when Britain was being bombed and undergoing its worst year, and they took it to an island in the Caribbean where there were soldiers

stationed who would be stationed there for at least a year, and they questioned these soldiers, through a questionnaire, through trick questions, to find out their attitude on Britain, before the film was shown. Then they showed the film to half of the soldiers, and then went back six weeks later and re-questioned the soldiers, including those that had seen the film and those who had not, to see if attitudes on Britain had changed. They found a marked change in attitude among the soldiers that had seen the film. So this in a way showed that the messages of the films were getting across, and I must say that as far as we know, soldiers liked to see these films. They liked them very very much; because they were presented in dramatic form by professional moviemakers.[10]

Capra is clear that the goal of the films was to influence the attitudes of the incoming soldiers, and that he thought that the craft of the filmmaker was a valuable tool in this endeavor. But the research effort involved in evaluating its effectiveness was more extensive than he appreciated. The whole nation was being mobilized for war, and the draft was bringing essentially an entire generation of young men into the military. This meant that massive numbers of new recruits were being shown these movies and were available to be studied. One of Hovland's experiments involved 1,400 recruits. Each of the men first filled out a questionnaire asking factual questions about the battle and probing his opinions about the British role in the war. A week later, 700 of them saw the movie. Then, they filled out the question-naire again, either another week later or nine weeks later.

As Capra recollected, the data showed that his film was doing its job: The soldiers learned facts about the battle, and became more confident in and favorable toward their British allies. But these effects evolved over time. Memory for the facts was greatest early on and decayed with time—this is typical. But changes in opinion were all over the place. Some of the film's effects on the troops' attitudes peaked early, but most grew over time. Hovland and his team called this the "sleeper effect." At first, a message doesn't appear to be having much impact, but over time its impact grows and grows. Hovland started asking why this happened. Most memories, like the memories for facts here, decay over time. Why did opinions not behave like this?

The scientists proposed a few possible explanations for this effect. The most interesting is a dissociation between memory for the movie's *message* and memory for the *messenger*. For example, suppose you are one of those recruits. You've just been drafted, pulled away from your family and job, and placed at risk of life and limb. The army is spending 12 hours a day trying to get you physically and mentally ready to fight, and you know it. You might be a little skeptical of anything "they" say, and this would apply to the Capra movie. At the same time, you are reading the newspaper and talking to your friends as you go through this common experience. Suppose the movie is effective in allowing you to build a rich, vivid model of the events of the film and of the conclusions advocated by the film's narrator and subjects. After a week, when you think about how you feel about British fighting pluck, you might bring this model to mind and be somewhat persuaded. But at the same time you might discount its influence because you also remember the source. But after 9 weeks, what happens? Well, if you built a rich model while watching the movie, you probably will still have a good memory for the events depicted by the film and the conclusions it put forward. But you might have lost a lot of the information about the *source* of that model. You might not be sure whether these were events you read about in the news or discussed with trusted friends. You might be less skeptical and give the events and conclusions more weight in forming your opinion. *Bingo*—a sleeper effect![11]

When we remember something, how do we determine the source of that memory—whether it was something we saw, heard about, or just imagined? If we were told about it, how do we keep track of whether the source was nonfiction or fiction, reliable or unreliable? These are the sorts of questions that have occupied much of the career of Marcia Johnson, a cognitive psychologist at Yale University.[12] Over the years, a pretty complete story has emerged. When you try to remember, you bring up information in many different formats: words and concepts, visual and auditory impressions, emotional tone, and the products of the thoughts that you had when you experienced the original events. You put all this material together when you try to determine where a memory came from. If you dredge up a lot of verbal content but not much visual experience, you will be more convinced that you are remembering something you read about. If you bring up a lot of visual impressions or emotional intensity, you will be more convinced that you experienced the events.

Johnson and her colleagues have shown that we can use these tendencies to manipulate how you believe you learned something. For example, suppose you study a bunch of words and a bunch of pictures. For some of those words, the experimenter asks you to form a vivid mental image of the thing described by the word. Later, if we show you the word and ask you whether you saw it as a word or as a picture, you may falsely report that you saw it as a picture. Johnson proposes that you do this because you just retrieved a bunch of visual content—the content you had imagined when you studied the word. This suggests that the more vivid and engaging Capra was able to make *The Battle of Britain*, the more likely his recruits were to later accept its messages as part of their experience. An extreme example of this is the recent HBO movie *Game Change*, about the 2008 presidential campaign of John McCain and his controversial vice-presidential candidate, Sarah Palin. The look and feel of the movie, along with the makeup of Ed Harris as McCain and Julianne Moore as Palin, aims to match the real events as closely as possible. Watch a film like this, and good luck separating your memories for the movie from your memories of the debates and interviews you saw on TV![13]

We are starting to put together a picture of how the brain produces these effects. The first piece of this picture is working out how information in different formats is encoded and retrieved. We have already talked a bit about this in previous chapters. The visual processing areas I described in Chapter 1 are critical for encoding visual features. In Marcia Johnson's word-learning task, when these areas are more active during encoding, people are more likely to falsely remember that a word they imagined was a picture they saw. The same probably applies to the auditory cortex for hearing and the somatosensory cortex for touch. In Chapter 3, I described the role of the inferior frontal cortex and the amygdala in the experience of emotion. Activity during encoding in these areas is related to the encoding of emotional memories. When we go to retrieve a memory that has information with strong emotional associations, we may use the products of this processing to work out whether we experienced the appropriate emotional content when we encoded the memory.

The second piece of the picture is bringing together all of this retrieved information into the experience of remembering something. There is a big subjective difference between believing something to be true and feeling like you are remembering having been there. Imagine that your friend tells you, "Last Wednesday, you had cereal, milk, and a banana for breakfast." You might say, "Yeah, that sounds right," but have no particular *feel* for that event. Then, suppose your friend pulls out a picture of you with the spoon in your hand. This is a much richer, more specific cue. It might bring back a strong sense of recollection, of the feeling that you are putting yourself back into the moment.[14] That feeling is associated with activity in the inferior and medial parts of the parietal lobes. Patients with damage to these regions have trouble distinguishing between events they experienced and events they imagined or heard about.

The final piece of the source memory picture is how we put all the information and the subjective experience together to make a decision about where a memory came from and how we should use it (or not) to guide our behavior. For this piece, the prefrontal cortex is probably the key player—particularly the dorsolateral prefrontal cortex (*dorso* for "top," and *lateral* for "side"). This part of the brain is involved in lots of activities in which we have to juggle multiple pieces of information. Remember the confabulating patient I described, who mixed true memories with inferences and fantasies? He had a lesion to the prefrontal cortex. In general, people with prefrontal lesions have poor source memory. And they are probably particularly prone to propaganda.

To my mind, even more interesting than documentary propaganda films are *fiction* films that try to influence opinion. This kind of movie is not pure propaganda, but often is made by filmmakers with a dual purpose: to make a film and to change people's minds. Think of Frank Darabont's 1999 film *The Green Mile*. Set on death row in a Southern prison in the 1930s, it stars Tom Hanks as Paul Edgecomb, a sympathetic and ethical prison guard. The story itself is a fantasy: Michael Clarke Duncan plays John Coffey, a convicted murderer who appears to be gentle and harmless, and who turns out to have supernatural healing powers. Several factors work together in the film to make a case against the death penalty: Edgecomb is portrayed as thoughtful and upstanding, and he is sickened by it. One of the executions is botched and the condemned man suffers great pain. Coffey is portrayed sympathetically and ultimately proves to be innocent. Tim Robbins took up the same issues in a nonfiction release from the same year,

Dead Man Walking. Just a few years later, governor George Ryan of Illinois would cite these same points—particularly the possibility of false conviction—when declaring a moratorium on executions in his state.

A great example from around the same time as *The Battle of Britain* is Alfred Hitchcock's *Saboteur* (not to be confused with his earlier film, *Sabotage*). The film starts in an airplane factory in Southern California. A Nazi saboteur blows up the factory and frames a worker, Barry Kane (played by Robert Cummings). Kane goes on a cross-country adventure to clear his name and figure out who really did it. He eventually uncovers a conspiracy of Nazi sympathizers and confronts the bomber while hanging from the torch on the top of the Statue of Liberty. The events are clearly fictional, but the movie had a real-life agenda: to convince Americans to be vigilant against potential sabotage. The filmmakers clearly intended to convince viewers that events *like* these were going on around them, and that they had to watch out. I would bet that for many viewers the events of the film were integrated with the information they got from the newspapers and newsreels. If you were to have come back a couple months after the movie was shown and ask viewers about a factory bombing, I would bet a good number would tell you about the factory bombing without realizing they were describing fiction. That is just what makes such a movie effective as propaganda: If viewers integrate models of events in the film with their models of events in the world, then they will use the events in the film as the basis for modifying their behavior in the future. Now, *Saboteur* was made by a Hollywood studio, and I believe it turned a profit. However, it was praised for its political message as well as for its filmmaking. Here is *Time* magazine's review in 1942:

> A melodramatic journey from coast to coast shows Hitchcock at his best. It gives movement, distance and

a terrifying casualness to his painful suspense.... These artful touches serve another purpose which is only incidental to Saboteur's melodramatic intent. They warn Americans, as Hollywood has so far failed to do, that fifth columnists can be outwardly clean and patriotic citizens, just like themselves.[15]

What can we do to avoid being affected by this sort of propaganda? I asked Andrew Butler this, and he wasn't very optimistic:

I don't want to say that it's impossible. You could not watch the films but that's not a very satisfying answer. Potentially the best thing to combat it, especially for things you care about, is to watch the film but to educate yourself about the correct information that refutes the misinformation and about the broader history. The more you learn the more "accurate" history the more that helps you, at least potentially, avoid falling prey to these misconceptions.[16]

Their experiments also suggest a couple of strategies that are modestly effective in limiting later influence: giving a very specific warning that the movie might contain bogus information, and correcting students when they initially accepted the bogus facts. Those two interventions reduced the effect of the misinformation.

It is not just our models of particular historical episodes that are affected by fiction. We also learn a lot about the world by watching fictional movies and reading fictional stories. *The Black Swan* is presented as a clearly fictional film, but watching it teaches you a lot about the practice of ballet. When *Moby-Dick* was published, none of Herman Melville's readers confused it with news reporting. But it was praised for its vivid descriptions of open-sea whaling, a career to which most readers of the time had no direct exposure.

You can see the effect of fiction on world knowledge in the lab. One great example comes from a pair of psychologists at Duke University, Beth Marsh and Lisa Fazio. They were interested in whether people *could* keep incorrect "factual" information in a fictional story separate from facts they had learned elsewhere. First, they warned participants that fiction writers sometimes take liberties with the facts in order to tell a better story. Then participants were given a set of stories to read and instructed to watch out for factual distortions. Some of the stories contained statements that were true. For example, a story about sailing might include the following bit of dialogue: "This here, this is a sextant and it's the main tool used at sea to navigate via the stars." Alternative versions of the story contained bogus statements: "This here, this is a compass and it's the main tool used at sea to navigate via the stars." After reading several of these stories containing a bunch of true statements and a bunch of bogus statements, participants took a general knowledge test that asked about the statements in the stories, and also about other facts that were not mentioned.[17]

Now, if you happen to be a sailor or a naval history buff, you know what a sextant is and you would probably answer this question correctly, whichever version of the story you read. But on average, the facts Marsh and Fazio chose were ones that people get right about two-thirds of the time. When their participants read a story with the *true* statement in it, this pushed their performance up to about 75%. But when they read a story with the *bogus* statement, this pushed performance down to 50%. So, whether true or false, the readers incorporated the information from the fictional story into their fact base. If you were lobbying Hitchcock to make *Saboteur*, this is just what you would want to hear. Audience members may well pick up the events and facts from the film, making them more vigilant in watching out for real sabotage.

Here's what I find most vexing about all this: The more you find yourself lost in a good book or movie, the less able you are to sort out fact from fiction. The psychologist Richard Gerrig and his colleagues use the term *transportation* to describe this experience. Transportation is the feeling of leaving your current circumstances behind and vividly experiencing the events of a book or movie. The more you are transported, the harder you have to work to resist the influence of the fictional world on your beliefs and attitudes. Deborah Prentice, Richard Gerrig and Daniel Bailis described it this way: There is an old idea, most associated with the poet Samuel Taylor Coleridge, that when we get lost in a story we engage in "willing suspension of disbelief," setting aside the immediate world in favor of accepting the fictional one. Prentice and her colleagues say this is dead wrong: When we experience a story, our default is to accept what it tells us as true. We have to do extra work to override that default and question what we are reading. Rather than needing will to *suspend* disbelief, we have to engage in a willing *construction* of disbelief in order to keep the story world from infecting our real-world beliefs and attitudes.[18]

How can we resist importing information from unreliable sources? Once you know that this can happen, can you be more vigilant about keeping important factual information separate from fiction and resisting propaganda? It's harder than you might think. In some conditions of their experiment, Marsh and Fazio gave their readers very explicit warnings that authors take liberties with the facts, and that the stories might contain false information. They succeeded in making their readers a little paranoid—but not better at telling fact from fiction. After getting a warning like this, readers tended to answer "no" to all the knowledge questions, but they rejected true answers just as often as they weeded out the fakes. It did not matter whether the warning was given before they read the stories or after. The only thing that worked a bit was to ask the readers to tell the experimenter every time they caught a bogus fact *while reading*. If they called out the misstatements as they happened, that allowed them to better resist their influence later.

Don't get me wrong; it is a great thing that from movies and stories we can learn about strange parts of the world, about subcultures and skills and technologies that we lack the time, money, or ability to experience in real life. And great storytellers embed rich troves of true information in their made-up stories. But as we have seen, storytellers also sometimes get it wrong. Worse yet, they sometimes get it wrong on purpose to manipulate us. It sure would be nice to be able to resist importing events and facts from fiction unless we meant to.

Control over which pieces of information you accept is in part a matter of keeping track of the information's source. For example, say you think back to the first Gulf War and remember that a group of Shi'ite prisoners escaped through Iran with the help of renegade American soldiers. If you can remember that the source of this event was not the evening news but was the ending of *Three Kings*, you could decide not to treat that as a fact.

Some of us are better than others at remembering information sources. Young children have a lot of trouble with it. Older adults have more trouble than those in their 20s and 30s. This means that these groups are at greater risk for being manipulated by media. My colleague Larry Jacoby described one type of scam in which difficulty with memory for sources leaves older adults more vulnerable.[19] A con artist calls up an elder at home and collects as much personal information as possible. The con artist then calls back a couple of weeks later and starts asking questions based on the first conversation. If the victim doesn't seem to remember the first call, the con artist says something like, "About that check we discussed—we received it, but you wrote it for $1,200 and you only owe us $950. Just send us another check for $950, and we'll destroy the original check." In fact, no check was previously discussed and none had been sent. But if the victim is unable to correctly identify the source of the information, he or she is likely to go ahead and send a "new" check in. Larry went on to show that older adults perform systematically differently from younger adults in a series of laboratory versions of this scam. When older adults try to make decisions based on remembered information, they are more prone to being influenced by information that is right in front of them. Marcia Johnson's lab has also shown in a range of source memory tasks that older adults have a harder time than younger adults.[20] So maybe Mark Twain had it right when he said "When I was younger I could remember anything, whether it happened or not; but I am getting old, and soon I shall remember only the latter."

My intention in relaying these stories of propaganda, confabulation, and scams is to develop further the point we introduced in the last chapter: Whether we experience events in real life, watch them in a movie, or hear about them in a story, we build perceptual and memory representations in the same format. It does not take extra work to put together experiences from a film with experiences from our lives to draw inferences. On the contrary, what takes extra work is to keep these different event representations separate. Often it's not too much work, because events we have lived through tend to elicit different kinds of information than events we have watched. If I have a memory of a bike race that doesn't bring to mind breathing hard and sweating, chances are it's one I watched rather than pedaled in. It may be easier to keep memories of movies and reality separate when I can reason out the source of my memory. If I have a memory of skydiving, but I know I have never jumped out of a plane, chances are I watched it on-screen. But in some cases, such as when information from the movie is plausible and similar enough to information from real experience, and if enough time has gone by, we all stand at risk of becoming confused.

Why are we built this way? I think we are optimized to build representations of events that allow us to function effectively, and most of the time there is no particular need to sort out the source of our memories. Did I see a grove of apple trees over that hill, or did my cousin tell me about it? If I'm hungry, it doesn't matter much so long as the information is accurate. If this analysis is right, then our ability to build event representations vicariously could well be an adaptation. If you can program event representations into me by telling me a story (or drawing a picture or showing a movie), then that saves you the trouble of hiking me up over the hill to see the fruit. The prehistory of oral culture supports this: Many human civilizations developed traditions in which important information was passed down as stories, chants, and songs. These were augmented by carving and painting. When humans invented written language, the ability to program others with models really took off; movies are another extension of that. By living vicariously, we can construct memories on the cheap that we can use to get around in the world.

■ Twenty Random Nouns

The following words were generated using the website http://watchout4snakes.com/CreativityTools/Random Word/RandomWordPlus.aspx.

I asked it for nouns of medium complexity, and edited out ones that might be confusing.

For each word, imagine the thing it names and try to think of a memory from your life involving that thing. The words are all nouns. However, many words have both noun and verb senses. For example, if the word were *rock*, I would want you to think of something heavy on the ground, not what your high school garage band used to do.

inspector
melodrama
chipping
cavern
speedometer
spar
watercolor
clasp
imperialism
blacklist
invoice
treadmill
saffron
malnutrition
counselor
grotto
toothache
lily
fawn
pirate

5 ■
The Dark Side

Columbia County, New York, is on the east bank of the Hudson River a couple of hours north of New York City. It is weekend getaway country—farmer's markets, soft-serve ice cream, and bed and breakfast inns. In 1960 a team of psychologists led by Leonard Eron interviewed the entire third grade population of Columbia County: 875 kids. They conducted long interviews in their homes, and they asked them *a lot* of questions about themselves and their friends, including a bunch of questions about their TV viewing habits: How much TV did they watch during the week? Over the weekend? What were their favorite programs? They also asked the kids a bunch of questions about their behavior and that of their friends: Who pushes and shoves other children? Who takes other children's things without asking? Who starts a fight over nothing? Who says mean things? They asked the parents about all of this too. Between the kids, their friends, and their parents, the researchers got a pretty good picture of each child's TV viewing habits and social behavior.

Once they had boiled down all the data, Eron's team focused on whether there was any relationship between the amount and kinds of TV programs the children watched and their behavior. They found that for boys, there was a correlation between their preference for violent TV shows and their aggressive behavior: Those boys whose favorite TV shows were violent were more likely to be the class bully.

A natural conclusion is that watching violence on TV made the boys behave badly. But it would be premature to jump to that conclusion. There are two very plausible alternatives: It could be that boys with aggressive personalities preferred violent TV shows more than other boys. In other words, it could be that bad TV doesn't lead to bad behavior, but that it's the other way around. A second possibility is that there was something different about the environments of those boys who displayed more aggressive behavior and watched more violent TV shows, something that caused both of those effects. Perhaps they came from less stable homes, in which they saw more examples of bad behavior and also had more opportunity to watch TV shows that were not appropriate for kids?

Ten years later, the researchers came back to try to sort it out. They were able to locate 427 of the original group. They asked again about what they liked to watch, and asked again which kids behaved aggressively. Their logic was this: Causes have to precede their effects. So, if TV habits were causing aggressive behavior, then TV viewing at a young age should predict aggressiveness at an older age, after accounting for aggressiveness levels when they were young. On the other hand, if violent TV show viewing was only an effect and not a cause, then once we knew how aggressive the kids were in third grade, knowing about their TV viewing should not help our ability to predict their later aggressiveness. The pattern of data strongly supported the idea that the earlier viewing of violent television programs led to aggressive behavior later. Those boys who had preferred violent shows as third graders now were rated by their peers as being more aggressive young men. This was not accounted for by their aggressiveness as third graders—TV viewing added predictive value above and beyond their aggressiveness in third grade. Moreover, kids who behaved aggressively in third grade were *not* more likely to watch violent TV when they were 19. Here's what this means: Imagine you met two third graders, Jake and Jack. Jake and Jack show equal amounts of aggression as third graders, but Jake watches a lot more violent TV. Come back at graduation, and Jake will be acting badly more often. This pattern suggests it was specifically the early TV violence that caused the later aggressive behavior.[1]

Another 11 years later, the research team returned again. Now the boys were 30 years old, and some had gotten in trouble with the law. Sure enough, those with criminal records tended to be the boys who had reported watching violent TV shows when they were 8 years old. The boys who, like Jake, had spent more time with violent screen images grew up to have more trouble with violence. They were convicted of more and more serious crimes, were likely to abuse their spouses and children, and had more traffic convictions. Again, it wasn't *current* TV preferences that predicted their behavior, but what they had reported watching 22 years ago.[2]

I find the adult data particularly striking because they had to overcome a pretty big sampling bias: Boys and men who get in trouble are harder to interview, so they were more likely to be left out of the later samples.

This is just one sample of kids. I picked it because the studies are so evocative. But there is a large mass of scientific data looking at the relations between media violence and real violence. In 2003, a panel of leading researchers was commissioned by the American Psychological Society to review the evidence. Here are the highlights of their report: In the lab, exposing kids to violent TV shows or movies makes them more likely to exhibit aggressive behavior, including physical violence. Out of the lab, individuals and groups of people who watch more media violence are more aggressive. If you follow children over time, those kids who watch more violent media when they are younger are more aggressive as they grow up. The researchers' conclusion: "The scientific debate over whether media violence increases aggression and violence is essentially over."[3]

As a scientist, when I hear that there is an association between a putative cause and an effect, the question that jumps to my mind is, what's the mechanism? In the case of violent media and real violence, there is evidence for at least three mechanisms that can cause long-term effects.[4] One is *observational learning*, which is just the technical term for getting the idea to try something because you saw someone else do it. Observational learning is important in lots of situations. For example, as I write this, I just returned from my first visit to Turkey. Traveling in a new place entails learning all sorts of things about how to get around: How do you use the buses or subways? When is it safe to cross the street in busy traffic? How do you pay at the grocery checkout? You might find some of the answers from a good guidebook, but I usually learn most of this stuff by watching the locals. That is observational learning.

Movies and television are fertile ground for observational learning. What people learn can be good for them— or not. On the one hand, when *A River Runs Through It* came out in 1992, thousands of people got the idea to try fly fishing. On the other hand, a generation of Americans learned how to smoke a cigarette from watching Bacall and

Bogart on screen, and got hooked as a consequence. In much of the world, watching movies and TV for entertainment provides abundant opportunities for ideas on how to injure and kill people—six-guns in westerns; pistols in crime dramas; rifles and machine guns in war epics; hands, feet and knives in martial arts films. And a typical modern media diet vastly overrepresents the frequency of violent acts, from fistfights to shootings, which gives viewers the idea that these actions are more typical and have fewer consequences than actually is the case.

To illustrate, I want to provide some examples—but first I need to emphasize that these are *examples*, not *evidence*. Single cases tell us virtually nothing about cause and effect in general, and any given act of violence has multiple causes. With that caveat, let me describe one tragic example that illustrates the mechanism of observational learning. On Monday, March 30, 1981, John Hinckley Jr. attacked President Ronald Reagan as he left a Washington, D.C., hotel. Hinckley injured Reagan and three others, causing grave permanent brain damage to press secretary James Brady. Hinckley committed this act to impress the actress Jodie Foster, with whom he had been obsessed since seeing her in the 1976 Martin Scorsese film *Taxi Driver*. Hinckley had stalked her for years and watched the film 15 times. In the movie, Travis Bickle (Robert de Niro) attempts to assassinate a politician to impress Iris (Jodie Foster). Before and during the trial, Hinckley stated that the movie gave him the idea that assassinating a famous figure would impress and endear him to Foster. In a letter recovered after the shootings, he wrote, "I will admit to you that the reason I'm going ahead with this attempt now is because I just cannot wait any longer to impress you. I've got to do something now to make you understand, in no uncertain terms, that I am doing all of this for your sake!"[5]

John Hinckley Jr. was criminally insane. On June 21, 1982, he was found not guilty of the shootings for this reason.[6] Watching *Taxi Driver* did *not* cause his mental illness. And no one could have predicted that the film would have led Hinckley—or anyone else—to copy the actions it depicts. But if he had not seen the movie, would he have gotten the idea to try to assassinate someone? Once people have an organic mental illness, the way it plays out depends on their environment, including the ideas they are exposed to. Perhaps if the media landscape were less violent, Hinckley's obsessive thoughts would have manifested in a different, less destructive fashion.

Observational learning depends on particular pieces of information that we see and remember. We are aware of the ideas we absorb this way. There is another kind of social learning that happens outside of conscious awareness. This is a form of habit learning, and it may be another mechanism by which violent movies can make people violent. When we interact with other people, or watch interactions, we learn about how people behave in different situations. Suppose you go to a bar and see a guy—perhaps a bit under the influence—bump into another guy and spill a drink on him. In the real world, the most likely outcome is that the guy who spilled apologizes and the guy who got spilled on says, "Don't worry about it." In a minority of cases there might be hostile words exchanged. Very rarely would this escalate into a fight. Each time you see an interaction like this, you learn a little about what is likely to occur in such situations. But in the movies, a spill followed by an apology does little to drive the plot forward or to provide visual interest. So, if someone spills a drink on camera, this is usually the opening of a fight scene. When you watch this sequence over and over, what you are learning is that accidents provoke aggressive behavior. Over time, when you find yourself in such a situation, you may be primed to interpret others' actions as aggression, or to behave aggressively yourself. This is not necessarily deliberate or conscious. It is more like the habit of putting on your turn signal when driving.

The idea here is that watching screen violence puts you in a mode to interpret ambiguous actions as aggressive, and maybe to act with aggression. Part of this response involves cranking down the brain systems that are adapted for thought and deliberation—if you're in a fight, you don't want to be caught standing around ruminating when the fists start flying. There have been just a few brain imaging studies looking at brain responses to screen violence, and most of these involved video games. However, so far the data do suggest that exposure to violence on screen affects our brains' systems for controlled thinking. These changes often involve the prefrontal cortex. This part of the brain is important for exerting restraint, and it is the last major part of the brain to come online during development—you can see its structure changing through childhood and all through the teens.[7] More research needs to be done, but it is not unreasonable to guess that things that affect the prefrontal cortex will have larger effects if they happen while this structure is still developing. This means that children and adolescents may be at more risk of harm from some of the things that adults use their prefrontal cortices to cope with.

A third mechanism linking violent movies to real violence is desensitization. When you see something over and over again, it usually starts to have less of an effect. Do you like spicy food? If you do, you probably started out eating milder stuff. At first, salsa from Chi-Chi's might have seemed pretty fiery. But after a few evenings hitting the chimichangas, the effect was not as strong. You found yourself trying the special hot sauce. Then you got into piri-piri and kimchi, and next thing you know you're eating raw habaneros right off the vine. (Well, maybe not...) That's desensitization. The same thing happens with emotional responses, including your emotional response to violence. For most of us, witnessing a violent event is intrinsically aversive. When you see someone get hurt, your pulse races, you start to sweat, and you feel uncomfortable. Your autonomic nervous system is getting ready for fight or flight. You are also experiencing a "virtual" pain response; this is another example of the mirror rule we talked about in Chapter 1, and it involves some of the same brain circuitry as your response to real pain.[8] One of the things that stops us from acting on our violent impulses is that when we start to do so, we experience this aversive response.

But if seeing people getting hurt becomes a regular part of your existence, these responses get damped down. That is desensitization. It is one of the hallmarks of living through a war or a natural disaster. Ishmael Beah, in his memoir *A Long Way Gone*, describes his first few experiences with war violence and atrocities as acute stressors. When the first victims streamed into the village in which he was staying, he writes, "I felt nauseated, and my head was spinning. I felt the ground moving, and people's voices seemed to be far removed from where I stood trembling."[9] He became sick when he saw his first dead body up close: "I vomited and immediately felt feverish."[10] But after repeated exposure, Beah describes little response as he kills a defenseless prisoner for a training exercise: "The corporal gave the signal with a pistol shot and I grabbed the man's head and slit his throat in one fluid motion....I dropped him on the ground and wiped my bayonet on him. I reported to the corporal, who was holding a timer."[11] Beah's memoir traces a frightening trajectory of habituation with tragic, dehumanizing results.

Desensitization is an adaptive response—firing up the fight-or-flight response takes a lot of energy and can actually damage the nervous system if it happens too often.[12] But the cost of this adaptation is that it weakens one of the brakes on aggressive behavior. People who are desensitized to violence don't experience as much of this aversive signal, and so they may be more likely to act out when they find themselves in a threatening situation. In Beah's case, he reports that his trainers fed the desensitization process using sleep deprivation, indoctrination, and drugs. They also used violent movies: "We watched movies at night. War movies, *Rambo: First Blood, Rambo II, Commando,* and so on, with the aid of a generator or sometimes a car battery. We all wanted to be like Rambo; we couldn't wait to implement his techniques."[13]

This can be seen in miniature in the lab. In 1982, Margaret H. Thomas published the results of a study in which male college students came into the lab and watched 15 minutes of television. Half of them watched a violent crime show; the other half watched an exciting but nonviolent program about horse racing. They then did a problem-solving task with a person they could not see in the next room. As part of the task, they were instructed to deliver electric shocks to punish their partner for lapses in performance. (In fact, no shocks were delivered.) This is exactly the sort of situation that should lead to an aversive physiological response in the person delivering the shock. The researchers measured the students' pulse rates to see how big this physiological response was. Those who had watched the crime drama had pulse rates that were 4 to 11 beats per minute lower than those who had watched the horse races. They were responding less to the shock situation. (They also delivered slightly more shocks, but this was not a reliable difference.)[14] Over time, acute effects such as this accumulate, and violent situations that would have provoked a strong aversive reaction no longer do so.[15] This potential process is hard to catch in the lab: first, because it takes time, and second, because manipulations that would produce large changes are unethical.

But cumulative effects of desensitization have been studied in miniature in the lab. In one recent experiment using video games, an international team led by Youssef Hasan had people play one of six videogames over 3 days in the lab. All six were fast-paced, exciting games, but three were shoot-em-ups and three were nonviolent vehicle-racing games. After each game play session, participants performed a task in which they had to press a button as quickly as possible when a target appeared. They were told they were competing against someone in the next room, and that on each round the winner could blast the loser with a loud sound—a mix of things like fingers scratching a chalkboard, dentist drills, and sirens. (In fact, they were competing against a computer; nobody got blasted.) Those who played the violent games set the sound blasts to longer and louder settings than those who played the racing games, and this difference grew across the three days of sessions.[16]

Case closed? Not quite. There have been other studies using similar methods that have found similar results, but there also have been studies that found no effects. In one published in 2013, participants first watched violent or nonviolent television programs, and then clips showing acts of violence. The researchers were interested in whether viewers would report less empathy for the victims in the final clips after watching violent TV. For half of the participants, the final clips showed real news footage; for the other half, the final clips were fictional film violence. For neither group did the researchers find that watching violent TV produced less empathetic responses.[17]

Does this null result mean we should suspect that desensitization doesn't really happen? No. Conflicting results are standard fare in science. Sometimes they happen because one laboratory or the other didn't "do the experiment right." Maybe the crime show in the first experiment was really dull, and that made viewers petulant. Maybe the empathy measure in the third study wasn't sensitive enough or didn't really represent the feelings that produce aggressive behavior. Sometimes conflicting results reveal other variables that exert important influences.

Perhaps media violence produces desensitization only with some groups of viewers or only with real-time interaction. The way we sort out these kinds of questions is by collecting results from many studies and looking at the broad patterns. The gold standard in reviewing scientific findings is a technique called *meta-analysis*. In a meta-analysis, the researcher conducts an unbiased search of the literature using databases of published articles, and uses statistics to combine findings across studies. This wrings as much information as possible from the data, but, more important, it helps prevent the researcher's biases from creeping into the analysis. In fact, there have been a number of large meta-analyses on this topic, and they provide clear and strong support for the effects of media violence on aggression.[18]

A smaller recent meta-analysis, restricted to studies from 1998 to 2008, investigated a couple of factors that could inflate estimates of the size of the effect.[19] One is the "file drawer" problem: Studies that find null results may have a harder time getting published so they get dumped in the researcher's file drawer. Another is the "third variable" problem: In correlational studies, a missing variable that wasn't measured in the study could be responsible for the relationship. This study did find evidence for both of these factors. I talked to one of the study's authors, Chris Ferguson, who also coauthored the study that failed to find an effect of violent TV on empathy. I asked him what he thought was the true magnitude of the relationship between media violence and aggression, and here's what he said: "I think by and large the overall effect is zero. We're really wasting a lot of time worrying about this. This is really a culture war phenomenon, not a scientific phenomenon."[20] But even taking the possibility of publication bias and third variables into consideration, I believe the much larger meta-analyses make too strong a case. I asked Brad Bushman, who has coauthored a couple of the large meta-analyses and also was part of the teams that did some of the experiments I just described, and he reminded me that there are essentially zero studies that find violent media reduces aggression, there are a whole lot that find violent media increases aggression, and the soundest and largest meta-analyses report very consistent effects.[21]

In short, we know that people—kids in particular—who watch violent movies and TV become more aggressive. It doesn't look like this is a case of the aggressive kids choosing the violent shows. It looks more like the shows are causing changes in the kids' behavior and shaping who they become as adults. There are several mechanisms that could produce such changes, and there is laboratory evidence for these mechanisms. All in all, it is a pretty strong case.

Does this square with what you have read or seen in the news? Brad Bushman and his collaborator Craig Anderson decided to take a look at this. They gathered all the news reports they could find about media violence from 1950 to 2000 and coded what each concluded. Some basically said there was no effect, a few said there was clearly a substantial effect, and many were in the middle. They also analyzed the scientific results from 1970, when this research began in earnest, to 2000. They found a disturbing disconnect between the accumulation of scientific evidence and the news media's perception. From 1950 to 1970, news reports did track the research, though not perfectly: The news reports shifted from being, on average, pretty close to the fence, to a wishy-washy endorsement that there was an effect. But from 1970 on, as the evidence that media violence is bad for you has gotten stronger and stronger, the news reports have stalled out—they have stayed right where they were.[22]

What is going on here? There is a helpful analogy between the effects of media violence and the effects of smoking.[23] One reason it took so long to convince the public that smoking was a serious risk for cancer is that news outlets—particularly live media such as television and radio—strive for balance. This is mostly a good thing; it helps us as listeners and viewers to be critical. But suppose one of the two sides represents the strong scientific consensus, and the other represents a small minority? It can be hard to convey this in the fast-paced world of TV news, and if the program brings on one person to represent each side, the result can look much more balanced than it actually is.

A second reason is that it can be hard to get a sense of which effects are important. In the analysis I described earlier, most of the studies found correlations between media violence and real aggression of around 0.1 to 0.3, with the mode being around 0.2. Is that big or small? One way of putting it is that such a correlation accounts for only about 4% of the variability in aggressive behavior. When you put it like this, the relationship sounds pretty weak.[24] Researchers concerned about these effects have noted that a correlation of 0.2 is almost as strong as the relationship between smoking and lung cancer, and is stronger than the HIV risk reduction associated with wearing condoms. The medical comparison has been vigorously disputed, with skeptics noting that smoking causes illnesses other than cancer, and that medical outcome variables are often more directly tied to practical consequences than are the outcome measures in psychological studies.[25] Notwithstanding these critiques, I think the effect sizes are defensible—and I think there is a larger point about small-looking effects: Statistically small effects can be important. We're used to thinking of causes as all-or-none: If A, then B. But lots of causes in the medical and social world are not deterministic but probabilistic. It would be very strange to suppose that the movies we watch would *completely* determine our behavior. Of course we are not robots programmed by our screens. The rest of our lives matter, and even if we have training that disposes us to behave badly, we can overcome such tendencies if we work at it. (In Denzel Washington's *Antwone Fisher*, the driving theme is the title character's struggle to overcome a trained-in tendency toward aggression.) But small effects are real effects, and even small effects can make a big difference. Add them up over millions of viewers, and you have the potential to substantially increase levels of aggression and violence in society.

A third reason it may be hard to convince people that violent media are bad for them is this: They may not like hearing that something they enjoy is bad for them. And finding that smoking or violent movies is bad for you might invite policies that restrict what we can consume. This sort of thing gives many of us the heebie-jeebies. Particularly in the United States, the threat of restricting our personal freedoms taps into a deep vein of resistance.

Finally, there are large industries with a vested interest in preserving the status quo. The Dove Foundation, based on industry surveys, concludes that film studios favor R-rated movies because they believe them to be more likely to succeed financially.[26] The film industry has both artistic and commercial reasons to resist the consensus scientific conclusion, and has deep pockets to promote an alternative view. The social psychologist Jonathan Freedman addresses this in the opening of his book on media violence and aggression. Freedman has not conducted research in this area, but he has followed the research for decades and written the only two significant scientific reviews rejecting the conclusion that watching violent movies can make you more aggressive. The second of these is a book published in 2002. Freedman is admirably transparent in describing his connection with the motion picture industry. As he describes in the opening of the book, he was approached by the Motion Picture Association of America to update his previous review and expand it to book-length format. Most of us in psychology and neuroscience spend significant amounts of time seeking funding sources for our research and scholarship, so this must have been a pleasant surprise! He agreed to take on the review, with a strict firewall between his work and the funders—they would have no control, nor prior review, of the book. This is all as it should be, and although this arrangement is not ideal, I think we can be confident that Freedman was not directly influenced by his funders. What the industry money *did* do in this case is select one voice from the scientific community—a discrepant one—and give it a megaphone.

In this book, Freedman provides descriptions of a large number of studies investigating the relationship between media violence and aggression. When positive results are found, he raises methodological concerns that throw those results into doubt. When positive results are not found, he emphasizes these findings. In the end, Freedman concludes that the data do not support a causal connection between media violence and aggression. The book covers a large number of studies and is slow going, but I think it is worth reading for anyone with a serious interest in this topic.

So why doesn't the scientific community agree with Freedman's conclusion? The book has two major flaws when it comes to scientific reasoning. The first problem is that it uses unsystematic verbal description to summarize the findings rather than quantitative methods. The only quantitative conclusions presented are a few tallies of positive and negative findings, and in those cases the descriptions of the methods used to compute the tallies are too vague to be repeated by another scientist.

A second problem with Freedman's method is that he treats null results as evidence against the hypothesis that media violence causes aggression. What's a null result? A result that could plausibly be due to chance. Suppose I take a coin and flip it in the air 10 times, half of the time while standing on my left leg and half of the time while standing on my right leg. Say the left-leg flips produce 3 heads and 2 tails, and the right-leg flips produce 3 tails and 2 heads. Would we be safe concluding that standing on one's left leg makes it more likely to flip heads? Of course not. We would attribute those differences to chance. Whenever we set up an experiment, we have to pick a procedure for deciding whether an effect is "real," or might be due to chance. Psychology is typical of experimental sciences in that it is conservative in the way it sets up its experimental designs and statistical procedures. As a field, we long ago decided that missing a real effect was a less serious error than falsely accepting a bogus effect as real. When an experiment passes this conservative threshold, we call this a *statistically significant* effect. This conservatism has an important consequence for reasoning about null results: It means null results don't tell you much. The way we set things up, a null result could mean there really is no effect there, or just that you missed it this time. If you run a hundred experiments testing for a relationship between media violence and aggression, and find a statistically significant effect half the time or even a third of the time, with few significant results pointing the other direction, that is very strong evidence that the effect is present. This is precisely the situation that Freedman describes, yet he concludes that the presence of null results should weaken our confidence. Professor Freedman is a statistically sophisticated scientist, so it is a bit surprising that he reaches this conclusion. I think that this is exactly the sort of situation where a quantitative meta-analysis would be helpful. As I read the book, I think his view is that the well-conducted studies tend to find null results, and the studies with problems tend to find effects. Without a means to cumulate results across studies, a few null results from well-conducted studies can seem very compelling. Coding all the studies for quality and factoring this into a meta-analysis would have been a great help in coming to a sounder conclusion.

In sum, the data provide strong evidence that consuming violent media increases aggression. What are we to do? My first concern is just to get the facts right. I believe that in order to make informed decisions about what to watch ourselves, what to show our kids, and what if any restrictions to place on the entertainment market, people need to hear the straight story. Scientists and reporters need to make clear that there is overwhelming evidence that watching violent TV shows and movies leads people to behave more aggressively. (At the same time, it is important to acknowledge the limitations of the data where they exist.) There is still a lot to learn about how aggression develops and what factors moderate influence on aggression, but the basic question "Does consuming violent media increase aggression?" is settled. People need to know this.

What does all of this say for policy? This is a hard problem. Consider violence, where the potential negatives are clearest and most potentially destructive. On the one hand, I would not want to live in a world in which violent acts were banned from movies any more than I would want to live in a society that banned the color blue. Many of my favorite films are pretty violent: *Angel Heart, Reservoir Dogs, McCabe and Mrs. Miller,* and *Blade Runner,* to name a few. As we saw in Chapter 5, emotionally extreme situations in movies allow us to exercise parts of our brains that—we hope—are rarely pushed so hard in real life. They allow us to vicariously experience strong emotions, threatening situations, and risks in a safe context that we can step out of at will. And for many artistic projects I believe that violence plays a legitimate and vital role.

On the other hand, at least when it comes to media violence, I am not so keen on the world we live in right now. Media surveys show that there is a *lot* of violence on TV and in the movies. A survey in the 1990s found that 61% of TV shows portrayed violent acts—and the highest proportion was in children's shows. Of the top-grossing PG-13 films of 1999–2000, 90% contained violence. I strongly support filmmakers' individual rights to choose when and where to use portrayals of violence in their work. And it could be that all of these statistics reflect thoughtful artistic decisions about violent acts that are integral to the work— but I doubt it. The industry itself has at times agreed with me on this. Back in 1993, a group of entertainment industry luminaries testified to the U.S. Senate about violence in TV and movies. There was a strong consensus that media were too violent. Here is Jack Valenti, who was president of the Motion Picture Association of America (MPAA, the people responsible for determining the movie ratings) at the time: "Let me state, up front, my response to this hearing. I agree with Senator [Paul] Simon that there is some gratuitous violence in some TV programs. I believe that creative programmers and broadcasters have a responsibility to their fellow citizens and co-inhabiters of this free and loving land to try, as best we can, to reduce gratuitous violence wherever it exists in our programs."[27]

In part, the answer to the policy question depends on your politics. If you are a hard-core libertarian, it does not much matter whether violent movies make people more prone to violence. It is up to the people who create movies to decide what to depict, and up to viewers and parents to decide what to watch. This is the position that Valenti took in 1993: "These are matters which do not fit within government or laws or Parliament-planted restrictions. A creative story-teller, in this land, tells a story the way he or she chooses and the only coercion constitutionally available to force a change in that choice is within the individual creator, and no one else. The First Amendment, the least ambiguous clause in the Constitution, is very clear on that point."

This leaves it to the media industry to take responsible voluntary action, and to viewers and parents to make smart choices. In the same testimony, Valenti pledged that the industry would voluntarily address the problem of violence in movies just as it had addressed issues such as racism, smoking, seatbelt use, and drunk driving. But here's the problem: since that testimony, not much has changed. A 2003 article summarized the situation for prime-time television like this: "For the past 30-plus years violence was found in 60% of prime-time network programs at a rate of 4.5 acts per program. Television violence is a pervasive thematic element. Thus, whether a light, moderate, or heavy viewer, most people encounter some violence when watching."[28]

If you are more open to state control over media, you might support state controls on media depictions of violence. In the United States, the strongest controls on depictions of violence applied to broadcast television. These have weakened over time and become less relevant as the world has moved to cable, satellite, and Internet distribution of movies. In 1930, the motion picture industry adopted the "Hays Code," which dictated what you could and could not show on screen. It was most restrictive where sex was concerned, but also specified that special care be taken with topics including arson, guns, brutality, murder, branding, and rape. (The full list is in Wikipedia and is worth reading. It also includes "excessive or lustful kissing.") In 1968, this system was replaced by the MPAA movie rating system. These are the G, PG, PG-13, R, and NC-17 ratings we all know. The rating system has had a quasi-legal status, albeit a weak one. For example, the MPAA may determine that due to violence a movie will be rated R, which means that children 17 and under cannot view it in a theater without being accompanied by an adult. However, as with the TV restrictions, this rule is becoming less relevant given the new distribution systems. I do not see new, stronger legal regimes coming on the horizon.[29]

What about self-regulation? I do hope that by getting the data out there, we can help filmmakers think about the balance of violence and aggression they use in their work. I firmly believe there is a role for depictions of violence in art and entertainment, just maybe not such a prominent one as we currently have. The film industry, despite commitments to take this problem seriously, has not been effective in addressing it. What options does that leave us? I think the most promising is public education. These efforts should focus on children, for two reasons. First, the science says that kids are susceptible to the long-term effects of exposure to violent movies. Second, kids are much less able than adults to evaluate the content and effects of media for themselves.

I do think that public education efforts can be supplemented by the judicious application of good regulation, aimed not at restricting freedom of expression or choice but at providing accurate information in a perspicuous form. The current movie rating system does not provide parents with good guidance as to the age appropriateness of a movie. We can do better. For example, as I write this, the movie *X-Men: First Class* is just opening. Here is the MPAA rating: "Rated PG-13 for intense sequences of action and violence, some sexual content including brief partial nudity and language." Now, let's look at the website commonsense-media.org, which is run by a nonprofit group that has been developing media ratings for parents. The reviews are prepared by the group's staff and consist of numerical scores shown with graphics and a couple of paragraphs describing potential issues for younger views. In the case of *X-Men: First Class*, the age-appropriateness graphic provides more detailed information, along with a color code: green (safe) for 12-year-olds and older, orange (iffy) for 10–11-year-olds, and red (not appropriate) for 8 and younger. The content rating, which ranges from 1 to 5, gives this movie the following scores: 4 for violence and consumerism, 3s for sex and language, and 2s for positive messages, positive role models, and drinking, drugs and smoking. Parents and educators can post their own reviews as well. This is information in a form that parents can use much more easily.[30]

Thinking about the labeling of movies like this suggests an analogy: Stories are food. We "ingest" films, taking them in through our eyes and ears. We "digest" them, creating memories and altering our psychology by learning. The stories we tell each other around the campfire are like the fruits and vegetables we buy at the organic farmstand—artisanal, unique, and largely free of artificial intensifiers. Hollywood movies are like commercial prepared food—tricked up using the latest technology to maximize response. In much of the world, the majority people take most of their sustenance from commercial food. Because commercial food is complex and can have major effects on health, it is important for consumers to be able to make informed choices about it.

By this analogy, I do *not* mean to suggest that the farmstand is always good or that the prepared food shelf is always bad. When local tomatoes are out of season, I'll take high-quality canned tomatoes over fresh for almost all my cooking. I might use them to make a sauce to serve over a really good factory-produced dry pasta (which works better than fresh pasta for lots of cooking applications). Commercial food preparation provides us with items that would be virtually impossible to make ourselves: soy sauce, chocolate, and malt whiskey, to name a few. My point is that commercial food preparation—and commercial story preparation—are much more complicated than small-scale organics, and so we need good information about what we are getting.

There is a further feature of commercial food preparation that fits this analogy perfectly: Natural properties of foodstuffs are altered and amplified to push our evolutionary buttons. Manufactured foods are often heavy in simple sugars and fats. Why? Because humans evolved in an environment where resources for metabolic energy were scarce.

Sugar and fat are rich sources of energy. Thus, we are adapted to prefer these tastes. Commercial food preparation techniques allow manufacturers to exaggerate the sugar and fat in prepared foods, and consumers like it. The end-point of this trend is candy. Candies are foods that make a highly effective appeal to our evolved preferences for energy-dense foods.

We have seen in the previous chapters that people digest movies using a set of perceptual and cognitive mechanisms that evolved for getting around in the real world. Storytelling, books, music, theater, and movies all leverage those mechanisms. Movies are like processed food in that a complex manufacturing process is applied; this gives filmmakers a lot of control over how movies look and sound in the same way that food manufacturers are given a lot of control over how foods smell and taste. Filmmakers get direct feedback from the box office about what sorts of perceptual experiences attract audiences. As a result, I suspect that films made in a commercial context are very well adapted to appeal to our evolved perceptual and cognitive mechanisms. Some features of stories are exaggerated and amplified: speed, emotion, violence.

By this analogy, we could think of an action movie as a piece of candy—adapted to appeal to evolved processing capacities, amplifying some flavors out of proportion to what occurs in less processed foodstuffs.

Should we cut candy out of our diets? Regulate its distribution? I don't think so. Candy tastes great, and it is fine in moderation. But at the same time, we have an interest in promoting a balanced diet. Too much of any one thing leaves you starved for other nutrients. Kids in particular need help evaluating and regulating what they watch. In short, we need good information about the "nutritional content" of the media we consume.

Before I quit with the analogy, I want to use it to call attention to one gap in our knowledge: When it comes to food science, we have pretty good theories about why, say, fat and sugar are so attractive. Our bodies need calories to run. Fats and sugars have lots of calories. Calories were hard to come by in the environment in which we evolved. Theories about what particular features of movies are so appealing are nowhere nearly as developed. It's not like we have a biological need to watch explosions or car chases in the way that we need to ingest calories to run our bodies. This is where I think my colleagues and I have a lot to learn from the movies. Let's watch what people seek out. It may tell us a lot about the situations for which our brains evolved and the strategies those brains developed to survive. As we turn to Part II, I'm going to adopt this strategy frequently. I think that psychology and neuroscience have a lot to contribute to filmmaking—but I think that movies have at least as much to give back.

Intermission

Remember when movies used to have intermissions? *Lawrence of Arabia* has great intermission music, and when I saw *Reds* as a kid, there was a good long intermission that gave you time to get up and stretch your legs. Why don't we do that anymore? For one thing, really long movies are rare these days. For another, it could be that theater owners don't want to give up time that could be allocated to showing more movies and selling more tickets. (But if you had a long intermission people would buy more popcorn!) Well, movies may not have intermissions anymore, but this book does. And this is it—a brief pause between Part I and Part II.

In Part I, I focused on the experiences we have watching movies—what it's like to build models in our heads of events depicted on the screen and to remember them later, how movies make us laugh and cry, how they teach us things and influence our behavior. In Part II, I'm going to take you behind the camera and show you how movies trick our brains to produce the illusion of a rich world of motion, depth, and color from a series of still pictures flashed on a screen. We'll see again that the way in which movies work makes sense if we keep in mind that our brains weren't built for movies but for dealing with real problems in real life.

In this section, we'll start with the illusion that gives *movies* their name: the illusion of motion. We'll move on to look at how film editing works in the mind and in the brain. We'll see how filmmakers play tricks on our perceptions and our memories—and why that's a good thing. Finally, I'll indulge in shameless speculation about how movies might change in the future.

So stretch those legs and grab some more popcorn. Here comes Part II.

PART II

The Tricks That Make Movies Work

6 ∎
Action!

The opening of *Mission Impossible 2* shows Tom Cruise moving up a cliff wall in the desert of the American Southwest. As we watch him climb the face, the camera swoops around him. Cruise hangs, swings, jumps, and pulls his way to the top of the escarpment. As he comes to rest, a helicopter whizzes in the air and flies toward us. It fires a missile, and we track its path as it embeds itself in the red stone. The missile does not explode; instead, we see Cruise's hand remove the tail of the missile, revealing the message with his next assignment. Off and running. Without a word and with barely a sound, the sequence is designed to grab you and draw you into the film with movement—the climbing figure, the racing missile, the swooping arc of your own point of view. We don't call them "movies" for nothing.

Of course, a modern movie has a lot going on: It usually will include a soundtrack with dialogue, sounds of the environment, and a musical score. It will probably be in color, and may project separate images to the two eyes to increase the sense of depth. It probably tells a story, introduces you to interesting characters and involves you emotionally in their fates. It may terrify you or make you laugh or cry. But first and foremost it *moves*. The fundamental difference between movies, pictures, books, and music recordings is that movies create for us the illusion of a world of moving objects.

But, as we all know, in a movie nothing actually moves. A movie is a succession of still images, usually projected but perhaps viewed on a cathode ray tube, LCD screen, or the organic LED display of a smart phone. If we didn't know better, we might think that trying to transmute still pictures into a moving world would be as doomed as the alchemist's dream of turning lead to gold. Yet quite easily there it is—suddenly there's a man jumping from a plane or a child smiling. We call them moving pictures, but why do they move?

A compelling—but incorrect—explanation can be traced back to a presentation by Peter Mark Roget at a meeting of gentleman scientists in London in 1824. Roget was a down-on-his-luck physician, depressive, and obsessive list maker. He is best known to us now for his *Thesaurus*. But on this occasion he was interested in neither medicine nor words. He was presenting a short paper to the Royal Society giving a detailed analysis of a visual illusion. As he described it, "A curious optical deception takes place when a carriage wheel, rolling along the ground, is viewed through the intervals of a series of vertical bars, such as those of a palisade, or of a Venetian window-blind. Under these circumstances the spokes of the wheel, instead of appearing straight, as they would naturally do if no bars intervened, seem to have a considerable degree of curvature."[1]

Roget offered an explanation of the curvature illusion that came to be known as *persistence of vision*. He suggested that when one flash of the wagon wheel reaches the eye, it stimulates it, forming a mental image of the parts of the spokes that are visible through the gaps in the fence. As the wheel moves forward and turns, a different part of the spoke is visible, stimulating a new mental image. If the wheel is spinning fast enough, the parts of the spoke that can be seen through the slat will trace a curved path, and if they are fused together, the spoke will appear curved. Roget's paper was one of the earliest scientific investigations of how successive images presented to the eye interact.

At about this time, the salon society of Europe was having a ball with toys based on visual illusions. This was the era of the *thaumatrope*, the *phenakistascope*, and the *zoetrope*—toys that created visual illusions by rapidly presenting a series of pictures. The thaumatrope was the simplest—just a disc with a picture painted on each side that could be spun rapidly. When the disc spins, the two sides alternate, and the images fuse nicely. For instance, if you were to paint a cardinal on one side and a birdcage on the other and set the disc spinning, you would see the cardinal in the cage (see Figure 6.1). The images in a thaumatrope did not appear to move, but they visually fused. The phenakistascope produced the illusion of movement. This device showed a series of images painted on a disc. When the disc was spun, you could see each image through a slit as it passed by. The most popular subjects were simple repeating movements—say, a horse galloping or a girl waving (or a couple dancing, as in Figure 6.2). The zoetrope improved on the effect by putting the pictures on the inside of a cylinder with slots just above the pictures. If you put your eye to a slot and spun the cylinder, you would see the successive frames on the other side of the cylinder appear to move. Here, in its simplest form, is the transmutation of still pictures to motion.

At the same time, Daguerre and others were developing technologies to capture images from life. Photography

FIGURE 6.1 Johnny Depp spins a thaumatrope in Tim Burton's *Sleepy Hollow*.

rapidly caught on and became popular as portraiture, entertainment, and documentation. In 1872, an English expatriate photographer named Eadweard Muybridge, of San Francisco, was commissioned by Governor Leland Stanford of California to capture on film the stride of his prized racehorse, Occident, at a full gallop. Stanford was interested in resolving a dispute about whether, when a horse galloped, all four of its hooves left the ground at the same time. Muybridge set up 24 cameras in a row, triggered by triplines, creating the first known photographic motion record.[2] A few years later, the French physiologist Étienne-Jules Marey invented a camera that could create a series of exposures on a single photographic plate,

FIGURE 6.2 A phenakistascope disc created by Eadweard Muybridge.

allowing him to study the precise movements of birds in flight. These motion studies were quickly adapted to the zoetrope and the other motion toys. But photography and motion really came together with Thomas Edison's invention of a camera and display device using celluloid film. Edison's *kinetoscope* advanced a strip of celluloid photographic film containing a series of pictures in front of a lens and peephole, allowing the viewer to watch a film up to about a minute long. Within a couple of years, the Lumiere brothers in France devised a film projector that had all the familiar elements in place: film on a reel, an illuminating lamp, a shutter, and a projecting lens. That basic scheme ruled the screen for a century.[3]

As this technology was maturing, people tried to understand how it worked, and they thought about Roget's illusion of the wheel behind the fence. Roget was not actually particularly concerned with the perception of motion. Remember, he reported that the *shape* of the spokes was distorted; he made no claims about how the wheel came to appear to move. In fact, the illusion he described can be seen best when the wagon wheel appears not to be turning at all. But others at the time *did* apply the image fusion idea to motion perception, offering it as an explanation for why the phenakistascope and the rest worked. According to this explanation, successive images are fused by persistence of vision, like when a single frame of film is exposed twice and the result is an image that superimposes information from the two exposures. By 1926, film historians had incorporated this idea into the standard accounts of how movies work. But it turns out the visual persistence story is only half right, and the half that is correct does not explain anything about why moving pictures move. Let's start with the part that is right but not relevant: the fusion of rapidly presented images.

There is now very good evidence that the brain's response to a visual stimulus persists long enough to fuse with another image at 24 frames per second. (This evidence didn't come along, however, until well after Roget's time.) One great example is a study conducted by George Sperling in the 1950s. Sperling was a PhD student at Harvard, and this work became one of the more famous PhD theses in perceptual psychology. Psychologists had previously observed that after a briefly flashed picture, viewers could report about three of the objects in the display. Sperling suspected that their visual system actually had information about much more of the picture, but that the information decayed so quickly that it was gone before they could report much of it. To test this, he showed his subjects pictures of three rows of objects, and asked them to report not the whole picture, but only one line of it. Which line to report was cued with a tone presented just after the picture was turned off: If you heard a high tone, you were to report the top row; a middle tone meant report the middle row; and a low tone meant report the bottom row. If the tone was presented immediately, Sperling found the reports were just about perfect. By the time one second had passed, they were much worse. From this we can infer the existence of a neural pattern that maintains a lot of visual information, but only for a brief interval: visual persistence.[4]

Since Sperling's work, there have been neural recording studies that corroborate this finding. We have vision because cells in the retinas of our eyes are sensitive to light. A photon of light is focused through the lens of the eye and hits one of these cells, causing a chemical change that leads a neuron to fire. Those neurons project to other neurons within the retina, which project to neurons in a nucleus at the base of the brain called the lateral geniculate nucleus, which in turn projects to the visual cortex at the back of the brain. When the retina is stimulated, activity reverberates throughout these neurons for a very brief period—about 80 milliseconds. Visual persistence again.[5]

So, what is wrong with this as an explanation for why movies move? Now we come to the half that is wrong: fused images are not moving images. Think through the supposed explanation provided by the persistence of vision account. Suppose we print two frames of a movie on clear plastic, lay the pieces on top of each other, and hold them up to the light. The result is not a moving image but a collage. Persistence of vision happens, but it is not sufficient to explain the appearance of movement.

Worse yet, we can see motion without any image fusion. Suppose you take two tiny lights and place one beside the other. Then, darken the room and stand back 10 feet or so and have a friend turn on one of the lights. You wouldn't be able to tell whether it was the left or right light that was on, even after looking at both lights repeatedly. Then, suppose you had your friend turn on one light, then turn it off and the other one on at the same time. You would definitely see motion despite the fact that the change in position was too small to detect![6]

The real story of how we perceive movie motion is much stranger and more interesting than the visual persistence story. To understand it, we will need to explore a bit more of the visual system. Visual signals originate in the retina, are passed through the lateral geniculate nucleus, and then project to the visual cortex. In the cortex, visual information processing is distributed across a collection of a few dozen different brain regions. We are intensely visual creatures, and a large portion of the backs of our brains are sensitive to visual signals.

Information processing in the visual brain is organized according to the three principles I described in Chapter 1. First, it is made up of *maps*. Nearby locations in the world are represented by nearby cells in the visual cortex. Second, visual brain regions are *specialized*, each performing a different function. Third, the regions are organized *hierarchically* in levels, with each level receiving input from the previous level, and providing feedback to that level. Higher levels represent more abstract features of the world. To explain why movies move, I'm going to need to take you on a tour of part of the visual system. Hold on, here we go.

Figure 6.3 shows the anatomic locations of some of the key anatomic players in human motion perception. The first part of the cortex to receive visual input is the primary visual cortex, or V1. V1 is most sensitive to local changes in brightness. The boundary between a bright region of the image and a dark region is called a *brightness contour*. For example, at the moment, I am looking out my window at a courtyard. The edges that delineate the black doors from the white walls produce strong brightness contours, as do the light leaves of a bush against the dark shadows or the light bricks against dark paving stones of the floor. Brightness contours are critical for perceiving the location and orientation of

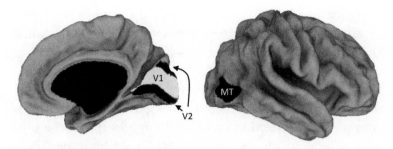

FIGURE 6.3 Two views of the brain's right hemisphere, highlighting three visual areas. The left image shows a medial view, as if you were looking at the brain from the left with the left hemisphere cut away. Area V1 is highlighted in white, area V2 in black. The right image shows a lateral view, as if you were looking at the brain from the right, with areas MT and MST highlighted in black (labeled "MT").

objects, because the edges of objects usually produce big local brightness changes. Most V1 cells respond selectively when there is a change in brightness in a particular location in the image. Each V1 cell cares about brightness contours at one particular location in the image, and nearby V1 cells care about nearby locations. In other words, V1 implements *maps* of brightness contours. But V1 also already represents information about motion, because V1 cells respond when brightness contours change over time. If a bird hops in front of the white wall, this creates a brightness contour at a particular location. Cells in my V1 map that respond to contours at that location and orientation will start firing. If the bird takes another step, the brightness contour will stimulate a new set of cells. In addition to cells that respond to the first configuration and cells that respond to the second, there are also cells that respond to the *change* from the first configuration to the second. Changes such as this are the basic elements of visual motion.

The processing of brightness contours and their changes is refined somewhat in V1's primary target, called secondary visual cortex, or V2. But the brain's real motion specialist is area MT, a little further up in the visual processing hierarchy. (MT has a next-door neighbor, called MST, that has similar properties and is also important for motion perception.) Individual cells in area MT respond selectively when something is moving at a particular location in a particular direction at a particular speed. For example, one collection of MT cells might fire if the bird were to hop to the left. As the bird kept hopping, these cells would stop firing and a new set would start. If the bird turned and hopped back, none of these would fire; instead, new sets with a different directional tunings would fire.

The firing of MT cells is closely related to our conscious perception of motion. One compelling piece of evidence comes from studies conducted by William Newsome and his colleagues at Stanford. They were able to electrically record from small groups of MT cells while a monkey performed a difficult motion discrimination task. The monkey looked at a field of moving dots. Some of the dots moved randomly, but others moved coherently all in the same direction. The monkey's job was to report which way the coherent-moving dots were going. If *all* the dots are moving coherently, this is really easy—but if you crank the number of coherently moving dots down to 10% or so, the task becomes fiendishly difficult. Newsome and his colleagues set up the task so the monkeys could do it but they were working hard most of the time. They found that particular clusters of cells in MT responded when the dots were moving in a particular direction—in other words, MT implements maps of motion direction. But they still weren't sure this was what *caused* the monkey to perceive motion. To test this, they did something that was a real tour de force: Using the very tricky stimuli, they electrically stimulated small groups of cells in MT while the monkey did the motion discrimination task. For example, they might find a group of cells that responded to rightward-moving stimuli and then stimulate these cells while the monkey looked at a stimulus that had only a small percentage of rightward-moving dots—or maybe even *no* rightward-moving dots, just randomly moving dots. When they stimulated, the monkey became more likely to respond "right."[7] Therefore, stimulating that group of cells caused the monkey to believe it was looking at rightward motion.

So, MT is important for perceptual judgments about motion. But what does MT contribute to the *experience* of motion—what it feels like to see motion? We can start to get a sense from the reports of people with a rare condition called *motion blindness*. Motion blindness occurs when one suffers a brain injury that selectively affects MT and nearby regions. Here is a description of one patient's experience with motion blindness:

> In May 1980 a 43 year old female patient, L.M., arrived at the Neuropsychological Unit of the Max-Planck-Institute for Psychiatry in Munich, Germany....L.M. reported that looking at objects in motion made her feel quite unwell. The explanation she gave sounded rather odd. She claimed that she no longer saw movement; objects which should move, as she well remembered, now appeared as "restless" or "jumping around." Although she could see objects at different locations and distances, she was unable to find out what happened to them between these locations. She was sure that objects did not move, but appeared as "jumping from one position to the next, but nothing is in between." Because of these difficulties she avoided streets, busy places, supermarkets and cafés. Traffic had become very frightening; she could still identify cars without any difficulty but could not tell whether they were moving or stationary....She reported substantial difficulty in pouring fluids into a cup or glass, because the tea, coffee or orange juice appeared "frozen like a glacier."

As you can imagine, this deficit made it difficult for L.M. to get around. Worse yet was the lack of understanding she initially faced. Until she made it to the neuropsychological clinic, her doctors had never heard of this condition and seemed to think she was making it up. Her friends were puzzled by the fact that she avoided looking them in the face; this was because she was irritated by the way their lips seemed to "hop up and down." It is as if, for L.M., all the individual frames of a movie were perceptible, but the *motion* was missing. This gives us a hint that motion is not just the result of a sequence of shapes and colors.

When tested in the lab, L.M. could discriminate red from green and diamonds from circles as well as a typical person could. She could recognize faces and objects, even when shown in unfamiliar views, without any trouble. She could identify the location of objects quite well by pointing or by looking. However, on many measures of motion perception, she was profoundly impaired. She was unable to report the direction of a dot moving in her visual periphery, a task that a control subject performed perfectly; in fact, she often failed to report seeing the dot at all. When she was asked to report the speed of a moving object, she always judged it as moving slowly, and her estimates increased only slightly when the object was moving fast enough to sweep all the way across her visual field in a couple of seconds.

When she was first admitted, the doctors discovered that L.M. had suffered a stroke; a blood clot had cut off circulation to part of the back of her brain. Brain scans later revealed that L.M. had a large lesion affecting MT and nearby areas on both sides of the brain. A decade later, L.M.'s impaired motion perception had not improved, though she had developed ways to cope with it.[8]

From L.M.'s case, it seems clear that some parts of her brain—MT in particular—are specialized for processing motion information. It is important to note what is *not* happening here. One plausible way to recognize motion would be to first build up a representation of the visual shapes and then match up the corresponding shapes over time. This fits the intuition that an object and its motion "belong" together. One could imagine that L.M. retained an intact shape processing pathway, but that the part of her brain that did the matching up had been taken out by her stroke. But that is not what is going on. The matching explanation is ruled out by another sort of neurological patient; these are patients with *agnosia*, the inability to recognize objects. Here is a description of John, a patient with such a disorder:

> [John] trained to be an aeroplane pilot and spent the initial part of the Second World War stationed in France with the R.A.F....In 1981 John's life changed dramatically. He was taken ill and had an emergency operation for a perforated appendix. Post-operatively, he suffered a stroke....The damage was in the region of the posterior cerebral artery, affecting the occipital lobes at the back of the brain.[9]

It soon became clear than John had acquired a serious visual processing deficit. His wife wrote to his doctor:

> He is totally colour blind and also seems to have no visual pictures in his memory. He cannot tell the difference between different leaf shapes or differentiate between flowers and leaves in the garden, which prevents him from enjoying his favourite hobby of gardening. He can still not recognize even me by sight, and if waiting for me outside a shop, will look blankly or perhaps, uncertainly, at me until I begin to speak. He does not see pictures and cannot describe the subject matter of those we have had in the house for years.[10]

But despite his inability to recognize objects by their color or shape, John's motion processing was intact; in fact, he was able to use it to cope in some situations:

> Generally, I find moving objects much easier to recognize, presumably because I see different changing views.... For that reason, the T.V. screen enables me to comprehend far more of an outdoor scene than, for example, the drawings on my living room walls which I have known for a lifetime, but now cannot recognize.[11]

So, L.M. can see shapes perfectly well but cannot see motion. John can see motion but not shape. Putting these facts together leads to an important conclusion: It cannot be the case that motion perception requires comparing representations of objects' shapes over time. L.M. shows that shape perception is not sufficient for motion perception, and John shows that it is not necessary. This conclusion, strange though it may sound, fits in well with data from experiments using nonhuman animals and with functional imaging studies in humans. Those studies suggest that MT is not very sensitive to shape. MT takes information about local contours that is computed by V1 and V2, and processes it to extract changes in those contours over time. Thus, L.M.'s motion processing deficit probably arose because the MT circuits that implement those dynamic change detectors were damaged. Other visual areas that sit below MT take the local contour information provided by V1 and V2, and process it to extract information about shape. In John's case, the grouping of local visual features necessary to recognize objects was impaired.

A really important point here is that you don't need to compute shape to recognize that a local contour is moving. You can see this, for example, when you see a field of grass blowing in the wind or a river covered with floating leaves in the fall. You don't need to be able to resolve the individual blades of grass or floating leaves to perceive the motion vividly and accurately. Your motion perception system operates mostly on the little bits of contour at the edges of the grass or leaves, and doesn't need to connect those bits up into objects to do its job.

We are now in a position to explain why moving pictures *really* move. The real answer is that thaumatropes, zoetropes, and modern movies all stimulate cells that respond to changes in brightness contours, just like real motion does. The visual system has no need to fuse two visual images because it does not build up a representation of motion by comparing objects in fused images. Rather, it responds directly to local changes in visual contours. If you stimulate MT's contour change detectors in a way that corresponds to real movement, the movement will look real.

Why does motion look wrong if the frame rate is too low? Because of a conflict between MT and other parts of the visual system. If the frame rate is too low, MT cells won't register motion very well, but other parts of the visual system are registering the change in position. This conflict generates the sense that things look strange. How fast does the frame rate have to be to fool MT? It turns out this depends on how fast things are moving. Each MT cell, like each V1 cell, responds to only a small part of the visual world. That is called the cell's *receptive field*. To look okay, the frame rate needs to be fast enough that the moving object remains in an MT cell's receptive field for a few frames. If objects are moving slowly, a slower frame rate will work because an object will still have several frames to stimulate an MT cell. But if an object is moving fast, it will skip over the MT cells' receptive fields without stimulating them adequately, and the illusion of motion will break.

We can estimate how fast the frame rate needs to be from the size of the receptive fields of MT neurons. Hold your thumb out at arm's length. The most selective MT neurons only respond to motion within a region smaller than your thumbnail. These are found mostly in the fovea (the middle of your visual field). Other MT cells, in the periphery, respond to motion with an area wider than your hand. For the motion to look right, the frame rate has to be high enough so that a moving contour will spend a couple frames in the thumb-sized receptive fields. Suppose I film a movie of someone walking by on the other side of a wide street. That is about a quarter-thumb per second. If I shoot the film and play the movie at 10 frames per second, it will stimulate a detector in the fovea for 10 frames, providing plenty of signal to drive the cell. But suppose I film a car driving right in front of the camera. That is about 12 thumb-widths per second. If I play this back at 10 frames per second, the object moves more than a thumb's width with each frame, which is too large a distance to stimulate the cells in the fovea. But if I increase the frame rate to 24 frames per second, this is probably sufficient for the faster object's motion to look right. Twelve thumb-widths per second is pretty fast; things moving that quickly almost look like a blur when we see them in reality. So that is probably fast enough for film to work nicely. In short, at 24 frames per second, by the time we get to MT, the motion signals we get from a movie are little different from the motion signals we get from real life.[12]

But do the small discrepancies left over matter? Some filmmakers think so. As I started writing this chapter, director Peter Jackson was filming *The Hobbit*—at 48 frames per second. Why did he feel the need for speed? Here is his answer: "There is often quite a lot of blur in each frame, during fast movements, and if the camera is moving around quickly, the image can judder or 'strobe.' "[13] Is he onto something here? I confess to a bit of skepticism. There *are* individual differences in the distribution of receptive field sizes; perhaps he has exceptional vision. Or, it could be that *The Hobbit* was able to take advantage of a higher frame rate because Jackson filmed in 3-D. That means that for each frame, slightly different images are being presented to each eye to increase the sense of depth. MT is also responsive to stereoscopic depth, so it is just possible that this increases your sensitivity to motion glitches. But if I were a theater owner, before I outfitted my viewing chambers with new projectors, I would want to see an experiment or two showing that the viewers actually can see the difference!

Luckily, there are data that answer exactly this question, thanks to a research group at Sony led by Yoshihiko Kuroki. This team built a really cool apparatus to compare real motion to motion sampled at different frame rates. They constructed a screen and projector connected to computer-controlled motors, which allowed them to show an image and *physically* move the screen with the image projected on it. The apparatus could also show moving images in the normal way movies work, by successively changing the projected image by small amounts without changing the physical position of the screen. This way, they could move an object perfectly smoothly by moving the screen, or move it in jumps by showing a movie of the object moving. The edges of the screen were covered so that viewers couldn't tell whether they were watching real movement or a movie. The participants were asked to track objects traveling at various speeds, judge the blur and jerkiness of the image, and judge the depth of 3-D objects. For all the measures, they found that performance with sampled motion improved up to about 240 frames per second, at which point it was pretty much as good as real motion. The biggest increase came between 60 and 120 frames per second. So, even though the lowly 24 frames per second is pretty good, we *can* see improvements out to frame rates 10 times faster!

It also turns out that the effects of frame rate can depend on other features of the visual display: how much contrast there is between the lights and darks, how long each individual frame is exposed for, how big the moving features are, and which direction we are moving our eyes. Our sensitivity to the benefits of these higher frame rates must depend on the combinations of these features that occur in real movies—and there has been precious little research using these sorts of stimuli. I asked vision scientist Andrew B. Watson how high a frame rate was likely to make a difference for your average viewer. He has developed the most comprehensive model of how video processing affects your experience. Watson estimated that for typical theater fare, a system that can capture and display at 120 frames per second is probably as good as we need.[14]

(Of course, none of these tests of detectability and acuity tell us what we should *prefer*. It may be that a super-fast frame rate will allow me to make more accurate judgments but will look "too real" or be objectionable in some other way.)

If you are a fan of old silent movies, you might have a couple of objections at this point. "But wait! Why do some old movies flicker if their motion signals are indistinguishable from those of real motion?" Because brightness is processed differently than motion. In fact, we often experience global changes in brightness with no motion whatsoever: for example, when someone turns on a light. Think of a strobe light. Start by setting it to run very slowly, say one cycle per second (1 Hertz). At this rate you will see a series of distinct pulses of light. Speed up the rate to about 5 Hz and you will see flicker. Keep speeding up the rate and the flicker will fuse into a continuous light. The strobe is still going on and off, just too quickly for your global brightness tracking system to detect. The same thing is happening whenever you stand under a fluorescent bulb. (This is why failing bulbs can produce an irritating flicker; as the bulb dies, its rate can drop.) The rate at which the individual pulses fuse into a continuous light is called the *critical flicker fusion rate*; its exact value depends on the brightness of the bright and dark phases, but under normal movie viewing conditions it is not more than about 50 Hz.

So does this mean that we need to show 50 frames each second to create flicker fusion? Not quite, because the motion threshold is lower than the flicker fusion rate. Early film technologists came up with an ingenious solution to take advantage of this discrepancy. In most film projectors the shutter actually has three apertures. The shutter turns one revolution each time the frame is advanced. The new frame is exposed once, then covered up and re-exposed two more times. So, even though the frame rate is 24 frames per second, the flicker rate is 72 frames per second—well above the flicker fusion rate.

In fact, probably few people still alive today have *really* seen a movie presented without a double or triple shutter. If you remember seeing flickery old movies (I do), probably what you are remembering is a shot within another movie that was intended to *look* like what an audience would have seen in the early days of film projection.

Another potential objection to my explanation about why moving pictures move: "Last time I really saw an old movie, the motion did look jerky and unnatural. If 16 frames per second is fast enough to produce good motion, why would that be the case?" The answer to this one is much simpler: Because you probably saw those movies played back too fast. Most of the classic silent films of the early 1900s were filmed at 16 frames per second. However, once industry standards moved to 24 frames per second, many projectors were built without the ability to play back at that rate. So, you probably saw many of these films sped up by a factor of 50%. No wonder they looked funny! Thankfully, the digitization of early films is largely taking care of this, allowing viewers easily to experience these works as they were originally intended to be displayed.

While we are clearing up confusions, let us take on one more: "Why doesn't each frame look blurry as it speeds by behind openings in the shutter?" Here is one reasonable guess: "The shutter exposes the frame so briefly that the motion of the film behind the aperture is negligible." Reasonable, but it turns out it's wrong. To make a projector that worked this way, the frame would have to be exposed for only a very brief moment during each cycle; the rest of the time the shutter would be closed. This would produce a very dim image and a great deal of flicker. So here again, the early film inventors came up with solutions that were exceedingly clever. If you look carefully at a film projector, you will see that, in fact, the film does not move continuously past the shutter. Instead, it is pulled forward while the shutter is closed and then held still while the shutter is open. The projectionist leaves a loop of slack between the reel and the cog mechanism to allow this jerking and holding to happen 24 times per second without tension on the reel of film. If you are old enough to have watched 16 mm films in elementary school, you may remember some of the peculiarities that can arise when this system goes awry. If the synchronization between the mechanism for advancing the film and the one for opening the shutter is broken, then the image *does* move and look blurry. And if the alignment between the cogs and the shutter goes out of whack, then you will see the bottom of one frame and the top of the adjacent on each exposure instead of an intact image.

While we are talking about the genius of early film technology and its vicissitudes, let me mention something: All of what you have just read about film technology is undergoing a revolution. We are coming through a wrenching transition of the film medium from chemistry to computer science. From before 1900 through the 1980s, the life cycle of a feature film was almost exclusively analog. The cameras used celluloid film, which was physically cut, printed, and duplicated. By the early 1990s, digital recording and editing played an important role in the soundtracks of most major films, and digital special effects were increasingly prevalent, but the primary means of creating a visual image was still to expose a piece of film to light. By the early 2000s, digital projectors were available that rivaled—and quickly exceeded—the fidelity of film projectors. Theater owners began making the switch to digital. At the same time, digital video cameras had taken over from videotape in the consumer market and were quickly making inroads in broadcast television. But most feature filmmakers found the resolution still inadequate for large-screen exhibition. This has now changed. Digital cameras are now available that can capture images with resolution exceeding that of all but the largest film formats, and the new cameras allow photographers to manipulate exposure durations and frame rates with greater flexibility than film ever afforded. In a few years, shooting analog film will be a deliberate anachronism, like filming in black and white is now. One consequence of this transformation is that the flicker problem largely goes away. Digital projectors do not need to blank the screen while the film is advanced. Instead of going dark each time the frame changes, each pixel simply changes to its new value, and the overall brightness of the display does not change much during the transition.[15]

So that is how movies move without moving. Movie projection is finely calibrated to produce a visual illusion. With simple instruments an engineer can easily detect the difference between real continuous motion and the sequence of still pictures in a movie. If our visual system were just a little bit sharper, today's movies would look like a flickering jumping mess. Knowing how moving pictures work, it is not hard to imagine an alternative version of us, a sort of perceptual superhero, who would look at a movie screen and see not motion, but a slide show.

For us as we are, projecting a series of images, each showing the world 1/24th of a second later, will almost always produce a good perception of motion. This is necessary for movies to work. But not every new frame in a film corresponds to a moment 1/24th of a second after the preceding frame. Just as important as what happens within a continuous clip is what happens when two clips are spliced together. When the early filmmakers filmed one shot, stopped the camera, filmed another shot, and then played back the results, they saw something that had perhaps never been seen before by human vision: one full-field moving image instantaneously replaced by another. They saw a cut. And so, now we're going to cut to cuts.

7 ■
Cut!

A cut is the simplest way to join film shots. Early in the development of film, an editor would cut the film with a scissors after the last frame of the first run of the camera, and again before the first frame of the second run of the camera. The two ends were then joined together with tape. When you ran the result through a projector, the audience would see continuous motion: The first strip would be followed by an instantaneous transition to the second strip. The film strips were called *shots* because they resulted from pointing a camera at something and running it—*shooting*. *Cuts* got their name from the act of cutting the film to join the two shots. *Splice* would actually make more sense, but that term never caught on.

The earliest films had no cuts. They were mostly single continuous shots—and they were pretty short. The early films of Edison and the Lumiere brothers were usually under a minute long. But composing films from multiple shots quickly gained hold. *The Great Train Robbery*, released in 1903, used cuts heavily.

By 1924, editing machines were replacing hand editing. These allowed the editor to view shots in motion and also frame by frame, to precisely select edit points. The next major transition was to "nonlinear" editing systems that used a videotape representation of the film stock. This allowed the editor to make a long list of decisions about cuts, preview the results, and make changes before the machine actually cut into the film. Today, almost all editing is done using digital representations, and edits are infinitely revisable. Even movies that are shot on film (an increasingly rare event) will be digitized for editing.[1]

One of the earliest filmmakers to explore the potential of cutting was Georges Méliès, a Parisian magician. Interest in Méliès has renewed thanks to Brian Selznick's book *The Invention of Hugo Cabret* and Martin Scorsese's film *Hugo* based on Selznick's book. As a young man, Méliès was inducted into his family's shoe factory business, but he left as quickly as possible and became a successful magician. When the Lumiere brothers exhibited their *Cinématographe* projector in 1895, he tried to buy one. When they turned him down, he designed and built his own combination camera and projector.

Méliès made a series of films in which he used cuts to make objects appear and disappear or transform. He made most of his cuts by a technique even simpler than splicing: He would stop the camera in mid-action, rearrange the props and actors, and then restart the camera. For example, *The Magician* (made in 1898) begins with Méliès in a wizard costume pacing a room. He waves his arm and—*CUT*—a table appears (Figure 7.1). A twirl of the fingers, and—*CUT*—a box appears on the table. He leaps into the air toward the box and—*CUT*—it disappears. In the remaining time of about a minute, the magician transforms into a clown and then a classical Greek sculptor, chases his

FIGURE 7.1 Georges Méliès conjuring a table in *The Magician* (1898).

disappearing statue around the set, and then is kicked off-screen by a soldier who appears out of thin air.[2]

Méliès mostly used cuts to create effects: Objects and people appeared and disappeared, grew whiskers and lost them, jumped from place to place. Later in life, he described what he was doing as an extension of his stage shows, keeping to the visual style of the theater and using the new medium to create fantastical effects that would be difficult or impossible in a live performance. From 1895 to 1912 he made over 500 films, and they were shown all over the world, but by 1912 the craft had become big business and Méliès became perhaps the first independent filmmaker to be edged out by the big studios.

Méliès thought of cuts mostly as a special effects device. It did not take long, however, for filmmakers to explore how cuts could be used to tell a story in a new way. In Russia, Sergei Eisenstein and Lev Kuleshov were intensely concerned with how adjacent shots were combined by the mind when a cut occurred. They termed this process *montage*, and argued that it is the fundamental property of cinema. Montage can overcome distance in space and time: If a shot of a woman opening a door cuts to a shot of her walking down a set of steps, we as viewers join these and interpret the sequence as if she walked out of the building and down the steps, even if the first shot was filmed in a studio lot in California and the second shot was filmed in Toronto months earlier. Eisenstein and Kuleshov also proposed that montage can combine abstract concepts. In Eisenstein's *Battleship Potemkin*, after a ship's officer is thrown over the side by the mutinous crew, there is a cut to a screenful of squirming maggots, then to a card that read (in the English version), "He's gone to feed the fishes." Eisenstein intended that the oppressing officers be connected with maggots in the mind of the viewer.

To test these ideas, Kuleshov conducted a series of informal experiments that became quite famous. Here is his description of one:

> In 1916–1917 . . . the then famous matinee idol, Vitold Polonsky and I had an argument. . . . Emphasizing that, however one edits, the actor's work will invariably be stronger than the montage, Polonsky asserted that there would be an enormous difference between an actor's face when portraying a man sitting in jail longing for freedom and seeing an open cell door, and the expression of a person sitting in different circumstances—say, the protagonist was starving and he was shown a bowl of soup. The reaction of the actor to the soup and to the open cell door would be completely different. We then performed an experiment. We shot two such scenes, exchanged the close-ups from one scene to the other, and it became obvious that the actor's performance, his reaction of joy at the soup and joy at freedom (the open cell door) were rendered completely unnoticeable by montage.[3]

In a later version illustrated in Figure 7.2, a shot of the actor Ivan Mozzhukhin is preceded by a shot of a steaming bowl of soup, a corpse in a coffin, or a beautiful woman. When audiences saw the soup and then the actor, they described his expression as hungry. When they saw the

Figure 7.2 Recreation of Kuleshov's montage demonstration.

coffin and then the actor, he looked sad. When they saw the woman and the actor, he looked lustful. Kuleshov reported that in each case, the audience complemented the actor's subtlety and force of expression.[4]

This effect created the foundation for a school of film-making based on the unique ability of film cutting to juxtapose arbitrary scenes. The classic films of Eisenstein are probably the place where this is worked out most fully. But you see it regularly in commercial film and TV. A particularly clear example is Alfred Hitchcock's *Rear Window*. James Stewart plays Jeff Jeffries, a news photographer who has been immobilized by a broken leg that he suffered while trying to get a shot. Bored, he sits in his apartment and looks out at the neighbors in the courtyard through his long lens. As he watches, curious events unfold in the apartments across the way. Here is Hitchcock describing what he was after:

> It was a possibility of doing a purely cinematic film. You have an immobilised man looking out. That's one part of the film. The second part shows how he reacts. This is actually the purest expression of a cinematic idea....In the same way, let's take a close-up of Stewart looking out of the window at a little dog that's being lowered in a basket. Back to Stewart, who has a kindly smile. But if in the place

of the little dog you show a half-naked girl exercising in front of her open window, and you go back to a smiling Stewart again, this time he's seen as a dirty old man![5]

In Méliès, we see cuts used to create visual illusions. In Eisenstein we see cuts used to create new meanings from disparate elements. Both techniques are alive and well today. But most cuts in narrative films are less fancy—they just keep the story going. The typical pattern is illustrated in Figure 7.3. You start with a medium or long establishing shot showing a few characters in a setting. You then cut to a closer angle as the scene continues. The camera moves along with the action in a continuous *tracking shot*, or with a series of close and medium shots. As the characters engage in conversation, the camera adopts positions over the shoulder of the character being addressed so the

FIGURE 7.3 Establishing shot and following tracking sequence in Charlie Chaplin's *Modern Times*.

audience can see the speaker in close-up. All of the clips following the initial establishing shot are meant to depict an ongoing scene that is continuous in time and space. The cuts that join these clips are called *continuity edits*.

The amazing thing about continuity edits is how invisible they are. Try a little experiment: Pick a simple scene in a film and count the cuts from one major scene break to the next. You may get a hint right here that something is going on, because most people find this harder than they expected. Now, show the scene to a few friends. *After* they watch, ask them to estimate how many cuts there were. Chances are their estimates will vary quite a bit and, on average, be low. A cut is a massive visual change—why do we sometimes miss it?

To work this out, let's take a look at the tasks our visual system has to do for us. Of course, it needs to recognize the objects in front of us: to figure out where those objects are; to recognize where we are standing and where we are heading; and to read the facial expressions and body movements of our friends, family, and coworkers. All true, but these are just particular facets of a larger functional role: Vision (as well as hearing and the other senses) exists in order to allow us to act. The simplest organisms have mechanisms to respond to their environment: Plants turn toward the sun, and plankton paddle toward where nutrients are more concentrated. Our sensory systems do much more, but they are still coupled to our motor systems and they still serve the purpose of allowing us to act adaptively.

To understand the workings of the visual system, people have developed several metaphors over the years. One popular metaphor imagines vision working as a digital camera—taking information from the eyes and constructing a representation in the head that is stored as if on a hard disk and updated when the visual world changes. This is a metaphor with a grand history in Western thinking; it goes back at least to the pre-Socratic philosophers. (They referred to stone tablets rather than hard disks, but the workings are the same.) It is an intuitive and sensible way to think about seeing, and it is a metaphor I find appealing and easy to understand.

The only trouble is that it is wrong. First, the camera metaphor is passive. If I am trying to hit a ball with a bat, taking pictures of it with a camera does me no good. I need information about where the ball is in a format that can drive my arms. Second, the camera metaphor is backward-looking. It is about recording what the world used to look like, whereas vision to control action has to look forward. I need a representation not so much of where the ball was, or even where it is right now, but of where it will be when it comes to the plate. Third, the camera metaphor suggests that vision constructs a single representation that lives in one part of the brain, whereas real visual representations are fragmentary, specialized, and distributed. So, rather than think of vision as a passive picture-making process, think of it as *active, predictive,* and *distributed.*

As the human visual system evolved and became more complex, it developed multiple, different mechanisms for controlling action. The actions that we perform guided by vision span a range from the fast and simple to the deliberative and complex. At the fast and simple end, think of ducking a flying frisbee or reaching for a cup. At the deliberative and complex end, think of deciding which sandwich to choose from a refrigerated case in a cafeteria or plotting a course with a map. We saw in Chapter 1 that once visual signals are relayed from the eye to the brain, they diverge to multiple brain areas with different jobs. These brain areas are coupled to each other, to the other sensory systems, and to the parts of the brain that control action.

Back in Chapter 1, I briefly described the major division within the visual system: the breakdown into the dorsal and ventral visual streams. Let me remind you, and say a little more. The dorsal stream is specialized for controlling fast and simple *actions*. It is built to guide your body right now, to allow you to respond quickly to things in your immediate environment. Area MT, the motion specialist, is part of this stream. The dorsal stream can quickly construct representations of objects' location and shape, in formats that are useful for interacting with those objects. If you were to have a stroke that affected areas in the dorsal stream, you would likely find it hard to reach for objects guided by vision. You might be perfectly able to identify a coffee mug in front of you, but you would find the attempt to pick it up a clumsy and frustrating process.[6]

The ventral stream, on the other hand, is specialized for visual *thinking*—for recognizing objects, for categorizing configurations of objects, for problem-solving. It includes areas that are sensitive to color, texture, and shape, and even to complex conjunctions of these features. Neurons in parts of the ventral stream respond selectively to particular kinds of things—say, cats versus dogs. Some of these neurons even respond selectively not just to particular types of objects but to particular objects—Fido versus Spot. If you were to have a stroke that affected the ventral stream, you would be at risk of developing a deficit in recognizing objects from vision. Unlike a patient with a dorsal stream lesion, you might be perfectly able to reach for the mug and pick it up, but you might have a hard time saying what it was until you got your hands on it and could feel its shape rather than just see it.

You can imagine that these two visual streams play pretty different roles in controlling what we do. We use our dorsal streams for moving around fluently in the world, for grabbing things and placing them accurately. We need them to walk around smoothly, to wield tools, to do things like put on clothes and feed ourselves without making lots of clumsy mistakes. We use our ventral visual streams for figuring out what is out there, for forming conceptual representations of the objects and people in our world that allow us to plan how we might interact with them in a moment or later.

Let me be careful here not to overstate the independence of these two systems. I do not wish to give the impression that there are two different visual brains trapped in your head acting independently. There are a lot of connections between the two systems, and most of the things we do to our eyes and brains affect both systems. But considering the dorsal and ventral streams has an important lesson: Don't think of vision as a passive process of taking what comes in from the eyes and trying to extract information from the signal. Instead, think of vision as an active process by which the dorsal and ventral visual streams try to solve problems to guide action.

You can tell that vision is an active process when you just look at someone's eyes for minute or so while they have a conversation or shop for groceries. They are constantly moving their eyes and their heads in order to point the fovea of the eye—the high-resolution part—at different parts of the world. These movements can be driven both by the dorsal stream and by the ventral stream. Most of the eye movements are quick jerking jumps, called *saccades.* Smooth, slow eye movements are much less frequent; they occur only when you are tracking a moving object.

Watching someone's eyes also shows the importance of prediction in vision. If there is a noise at the door, our eyes jump to the door—anticipating that there will be something important to look at there. A flash of light in the corner of our visual field produces the same result—we don't have the resolution to figure out what it is, but our visual system predicts that it may be important and moves the eyes to a position where they can gather more information. Eye movements to sights and sounds happen very fast, and they are probably controlled by the dorsal visual stream and more primitive parts of the brain. But other sorts of predictive eye movements are likely controlled by the ventral visual stream. For example, if you are sitting at the table and someone says, "This could use some salt," you likely will make a saccade to the salt shaker, anticipating that they will reach for it.

So, I want you to let go of the camera metaphor for visual perception. Let me give you another metaphor. Imagine that the visual stimulus is a patient in a hospital with a mysterious illness, and the mechanisms of visual perception are a team of medical staff trying to treat the patient. The radiologist collects one batch of information; the hematologist collects another batch of information; the primary care doctor and the nursing team collect yet other batches of information. They all talk to one another and take actions to produce more information. They also pass information to the surgeon and the pharmacy, who take additional actions. The medical team is a distributed, active system, where information is specialized in different parts of the team. This is a lot more like how the visual system works; each component of the visual system builds a partial representation that captures just the features that are relevant for the job it is doing. The whole system is coordinated and actively doing things to explore the visual environment.

It is hard to let go of the camera metaphor—most of us feel like we have a complete, picture-like representation of the visual world in our heads. But if we can let go of that false metaphor, we can start to get an understanding of how cuts work.

Cuts work because they hide in the gaps in our visual toolkit's analysis of the visual world. Our visual tools are sensitive to some things and not others, and they are more sensitive sometimes and less sensitive at other times. If a cut happens when our visual toolkit is busy doing other things, or if it is camouflaged such that there is no tool in the kit that is sensitive to the disruption it introduces, it might well go unnoticed.

But there is one instance when our eyes are really not sensitive: when they are closed. We blink on average 15 to 30 times per minute, and when we do, our eyes actually close for a pretty long time—several 10ths of a second. The active nature of our visual processing means that there is some consistency to when we blink: We tend to blink after a burst of cognitive work. Blinks might not be frequent enough to hide most cuts, but there is another visual lapse that might even be better than a blink: a saccade. Remember saccades? They are the fast, jerking eye movements we make as we explore our visual worlds. Saccades happen much more frequently than blinks— 3 to 4 times per second. And though our eyes don't actually close, they are effectively out of commission for about a 1/12th of a second while the eye is moving. With our eyeball jerking from one position to the next, any signals from the retina would be too noisy to be useful, and in fact the brain cuts off the input from the eye during this period. Between blinks and saccades, we are functionally blind to the world about one-third of our waking moments! Perhaps filmmakers intuitively—or deliberately—hide cuts at the places people are likely to blink. The film editor and director Walter Murch, in a probing book called *In the Blink of an Eye*, proposed that good film editors synchronize their edits with the places their audience is likely to blink. If so, maybe this works to hide the edit?[7]

If this trick is going to work, we would need to be confident that most people were blinking and moving their eyes at about the same time so the cut could hide there. For blinking, a recent experiment conducted by a team of researchers at the University of Tokyo suggests this is actually true. In this study, people's blinks were recorded while they watched an episode of *Mr. Bean*, watched a landscape scene, or listened to a chapter of a Harry Potter audiobook. When people watched *Mr. Bean*, they did tend to blink at the same times—more so than when they watched a landscape scene or listened to someone read a story. And they did tend to blink around the cuts, just as Murch predicted. So far, things are looking pretty good for the idea that blinks hide cuts. But there is a problem: When they blinked at a cut, it was on average about half a second *after* the cut. That's too late for the blink to be hiding the cut. More likely, the blink was a reaction to the cut.

There is a little bit of evidence that viewers tend to make saccades at similar times while watching movies (I will describe some of it in the next chapter), but we don't actually have good data on this point. We do have good evidence as to whether saccades coincide with cuts, from a study by Tim Smith and John Henderson. They did this work while Tim was studying for a PhD with John at the University of Edinburgh. They asked people to try their best to identify cuts while watching a set of scenes from commercial films. The viewers' eyes were monitored the whole time. For the most part, the answer they got was like the answer for blinks: Yes, there is a bit of an uptick in saccades, but it occurs about a quarter second *after* the cut. So, most of the time the eye movements are, like the blinks, probably a reaction to the cut rather than a place it can hide.[8]

The Smith and Henderson study also explored whether blinks and saccades are effective in hiding cuts. If they were, one would expect that when people miss cuts, they would be more likely to have blinked or made a saccade. Surprisingly, this was pretty much not the case.[9]

I think there is something deeply right about the idea that cuts are like blinks or changes in eye movements. But it is *not* that editors place cuts at those points when people tend to blink or move their eyes. Instead, it is that we are used to being briefly deprived of visual input on a regular basis by blinks and saccades, as we shift our gaze and our attention from one part of the world to another. Doing so gives us answers to our visual questions. As long as movie cuts mimic the experience of losing visual input for a moment and then returning to find a visual question answered, things look "right." This offers a partial explanation for why cuts are easily digested. But we don't have good evidence that blinks or eye movements actually hide saccades, so it is still a bit of a mystery why so many cuts go unnoticed. Are there other mechanisms at work here?

Probably. Eye blinks and eye movements are not the only ways our visual systems actively acquire information to guide action. The perceptual psychologist Julian Hochberg has written that perception involves forming "visual questions" that the visual system seeks to answer.[10] For example, suppose I see a red ball roll behind a bush. Will the ball come out the other side? This is a visual question. My visual system may configure itself to discover an answer by moving my eyes to focus on the other side of the bush, in which case it would make a saccade. But it may also make purely internal adjustments. For example, it may increase its sensitivity to red things. Visual questions are closely tied to predictions—the visual system anticipates the most likely outcome and configures itself accordingly.

One particularly powerful way of generating visual questions is with the human gaze. We are built to keep track of what other people are looking at—for highly social creatures such as us, this is critical for figuring out what other people are doing and coordinating our actions with them. If you put your face in front of an infant as young as 3 months, the baby will follow your eyes and look where you are looking. As adults, we find it hard not to focus our attention where someone else looks. We do this even when we are doing hard visual tasks where we know we would be better off ignoring others' gaze.[11]

So one sort of cut may work this way: Something in the movie generates a visual question. Cut. The next shot gives the answer to the question. Figure 7.4 provides an example from *Ferris Bueller's Day Off*: In the top frame, Alan Ruck is looking in disbelief at something. What is it? That's a visual question. We cut to the odometer of his father's illicitly borrowed Ferrari (bottom frame), showing that car has been driven hundreds of miles, a fact his father is sure to discover. This answers the question.

There is one more perceptual mechanism that likely plays a powerful role in making continuity edits easy to digest and hard to detect: *masking*. Masking refers to the increase in difficulty in detecting one sensory change when it is accompanied by lots of other sensory changes. For example, imagine that you are a waiter at a fancy

FIGURE 7.4 Visual question and answer in *Ferris Bueller's Day Off*.

restaurant and the diner closest to you drops a napkin. That would be easy to detect—at a truly posh place, the napkin would never hit the ground. Now, instead suppose the diner knocks over a glass of wine, dousing someone's plate, staining the tablecloth, *and* drops the napkin. You would be much less likely to detect that the napkin had fallen. We would say that the spill masked the dropping of the napkin. Masking can be literally simultaneous—the spill and the drop at the same time—or the spill could precede or follow the drop by a moment and still generate effective masking.

The effects of masking on visual detection can be dramatic. In one experiment, people looked at pictures of everyday scenes, such as the couple dining in Figure 7.5. After 3 seconds, one of the significant objects in the scene

FIGURE 7.5 Masking a change in a picture. If the "mudsplashes" blink on at the same time, the large change in the railing can be very difficult to see.

From O'Regan, J. K., Rensink, R. A. & Clark, J. J. (1999). Change-blindness as a result of "mudsplashes." *Nature*, 398, 34.

changed—for example, the railing in the figure. The viewers knew there would be a change and were watching for it. Every 3 seconds the pictures switched back and forth. These changes are easy to detect when we look straight from the picture on the left to the one on the right in the figure—everyone gets it on the first try. But if the experimenters added a brief "mudsplash" right at the moment the bar moved, it made the change much more difficult to detect. When objects that were not central to the scene were moved, as in the example in the figure, only about 10% of viewers were able to find the change the first time and about 30% still hadn't found it after 48 seconds! This was *not* because the mudsplashes covered up any of the change. As you can see in the figure, they were carefully constructed so that they never covered the changing object.[12]

Magicians have known about visual masking for hundreds of years; it is the basis of most sleight of hand tricks. At the same time the magician waves her handkerchief with her left hand, her right hand is palming the coin. The puff of smoke can hide the conjurer's appearance or disappearance even if it doesn't cover her up. Now consider Figure 7.6, which shows a cut from the end of *Skyfall*. James Bond rigs his family home to explode by running a fuse to a stack of compressed welding gas canisters. The last frame before the cut shows the fuse burning down. Cut to an exterior view just as the explosion goes off.

Smith and Henderson tested the effect of exactly this sort of masking in their cut detection experiment and found it worked like a charm: Cuts in which a moving action continued across a cut were the hardest type of cut to detect. These were missed altogether almost one-third of the time; and when they were found, it took viewers 25% longer to respond.

Let's pause a moment and take a tally. There are at least three mechanisms in our visual system that could account for part of why continuity edits work. The first is literal

FIGURE 7.6 Big visual changes can mask cuts. *Top:* Toward the end of *Skyfall*, Bond has rigged his family mansion to explode. The fuse is burning down toward one of the tanks. *Bottom:* Immediately after the cut to the exterior, the house goes up.

blindness—cuts hiding in blinks or saccades. This probably works well when it happens but so far the data do not show that it happens very much. The second is visual questions. These probably work pretty well, but the evidence is not too strong. The third is visual masking. This works well and probably happens often. It would be really nice to know better how frequently each of these things happen across different sorts of movies. Quantitative data are scarce at this point—but we have a wealth of knowledge implicit in the practices and writings of filmmakers. Books on film show that filmmakers know these visual mechanisms like old friends, though they may not talk about them quite the way scientists do.

One rule of thumb is *cutting on action*. This rule says that whenever possible, you should cut in the middle of a movement and match the action before and after the shot. The first shot might show a woman starting to reach for an umbrella. She turns her body and extends her arm. Cut. In the next shot, her arm is in motion as she is picking up the umbrella. Cutting on action is a straightforward application of visual masking. The sensory changes that occur when we cut from one view of the woman to the other are masked by the motion of her body following the cut.

Film editors recommend that a match on action shot preserve the *direction* of motion from the first shot to the second. This probably provides an additional benefit beyond masking: It reduces the change in visual motion that happens at the cut. If the first shot shows the woman's body and arm start to move to the left, and the motion continues in that direction in the second shot, there is less of a visual feature to detect.

Film editors also have found a trick to make cuts smoother and less visible: Overlap a couple of frames such that the first frames of the new shot repeat the time covered by the end of the old shot. Why does this work? We're not exactly sure, but Art Shimamura and his colleagues at the University of California at Berkeley have demonstrated that it *does* work. One possibility is that it gives the visual system time to make up for the disruptive effects of masking. Another possibility is that it reduces the distances that objects jump across the screen during the cut.[13]

A final rule of thumb is called *eyeline match*. This rule says that if a character looks off-screen, you can cut to the location that she or he was looking at. This is a type of visual question and answer, as illustrated with the odometer sequence in Figure 7.4. Eyeline matches were discussed by film writers from early on, and in explicitly psychological terms. Here is Hugo Münsterberg writing in 1916: "A clerk buys a newspaper on the street, glances at it and is shocked. Suddenly we see that piece of news with our own eyes."[14] You can see how this relates to our earlier discussion of visual questions and visual answers. An eyeline match works because it raises a visual question—what is he looking at?—and then answers it. It also leverages our powerful tendency to follow others' gaze, which I described a little while ago.

A special case of eyeline match is *shot/reverse shot*. This is one of the standard ways of editing a dialogue scene. The film cuts back and forth between the speakers. Here, the dialogue plays a big role in synchronizing the cuts, and may play a role in masking them as well. This reminds us of an important point: Sound and vision work together to make cuts less or more noticeable.

In short, people who work on films know a lot about how vision works. You do not need to know jargon like *masking* and *saccade* to exploit the mechanisms of active vision, but over the generations filmmakers have figured out some of the same things as psychologists and neuroscientists, working by trial and error rather than by experiment and theory. This is *not* just common sense. Here we really have to avoid succumbing to the illusion that we have direct access to how our perceptual systems work. The camera metaphor is intuitive and seductive, much more so than the medical team metaphor. The fact that vision is distributed and active can be hard to wrap your head around. Experiments like the mudsplashes study are particularly helpful in avoiding that illusion, precisely because they conflict with the camera metaphor. Continuity edits are so effective because they capitalize on the discrepancy between the camera metaphor and how our visual systems really work— we think that our brain is like a person looking at a set of pictures taken by our eyes, but what really happens is more like a bunch of specialists each zooming in on a different aspect of the data.[15]

So far, we have been tripping along as though cuts always "work," and asking how they do so. But some cuts *don't* work. Sometimes a cut sticks out like a sore thumb. One sort of failed cut is the *jump cut*. In a jump cut, an object appears to "jump" suddenly from one place to another. At the beginning of Alfred Hitchcock's *Psycho*, there is a jump cut that is all the more jarring because Hitchcock and his collaborators were such masters of editing. As the opening credits roll, the film starts with a helicopter shot of the skyline of Phoenix, Arizona. The shot zooms in on a hotel, and fades quickly to a shot framing a window of one of the rooms (Figure 7.7, *top*). As the camera continues to approach the building, there is a cut to another view of the window from a different angle (Figure 7.7, *bottom*). At this point, the window appears to jump from left to right, turning slightly at the same time.

Why do we perceive jumping in a jump cut? To explain, I need to distinguish between two kinds of motion illusion. The kind of motion perception I described in Chapter 6, *short-range apparent motion*, is indistinguishable to the brain from real motion. As we learned, producing it requires that the displacement in space from frame to frame be small enough to fool the cells in all our brain's visual areas. Figure 7.7 depicts a different kind of motion illusion, *long-range apparent motion*, which is the sort of quasi-motion that you see when you look at one of those green "walk" lights on the street with two pictures that alternate. You can see it as moving, but at the same time it does not look as though the intermediate positions between the two poses are actually ever are shown. Another example is an old-fashioned theater marquee. The even and odd lights alternate, which gives the impression that they are moving each time they switch, but at the same time it does not really look as though the lights actually pass through the spaces in between.

FIGURE 7.7 Jump cut in the opening of *Psycho*. As we cut from the shot pictured in the top frame to the shot pictured in the bottom frame, the window appears to jump over and turn slightly, as indicated with the arrow.

Why do theater marquees and jump cuts look funny—like motion and not-motion at the same time? Because different parts of the visual system are giving different answers as to what they detect. Remember area MT, the motion specialist? The cut illustrated in Figure 7.7 stimulates MT just like a moving object would. So MT is signaling that the contour at the right of the window is moving, as indicated by the arrow in the figure. But to other parts of the visual system, this cut produces a very different response than real motion. In Chapter 1, I described areas V1 and V2, the earliest parts of the cortex to respond to visual signals. These areas respond with exquisite sensitivity to the position and orientation of visual contours. If you look at the path shown by the arrow, you can see that there is not much contour information along it in either frame: In frame 1, the bricks give a weak contour signal; in frame 2, the shadow gives almost no contour signal. No contour, no response from V1 or V2. So, at the same time that MT is signaling that a contour has moved on the path of the arrow, V1 and V2 are failing to detect any changes in the contours there. This discrepancy is probably what makes long-range apparent motion appear different to us than real motion. Jump cuts happen when a contour in the last frame before a cut is close enough to a contour in the first frame after a cut to stimulate MT, but not close enough to match up in the rest of the visual system. In terms of the hospital analogy, it's as though the radiologist is reporting a big lump but the hematologist doesn't see anything abnormal in the patient's blood tests. Something funny is going on.[16]

The brain's motion specialists are not very sensitive to shape or color. This can lead to some pretty fancy apparent motion tricks, as illustrated in Figure 7.8. Objects undergoing long-range apparent motion can appear to change color, size, or even shape. Long-range apparent motion can produce the sensation of movement in depth as well as in the plane of the picture. (This one is tough to illustrate in a book.)

Knowing how long-range apparent motion works tells us a lot about the circumstances under which jump cuts will and will not occur. For a jump cut to happen, you need to have contours in the old and the new shot that are close enough to be linked by the motion sensitive parts of the brain, but far enough apart so that other parts of the brain can detect the mismatch. This suggests a set of strategies

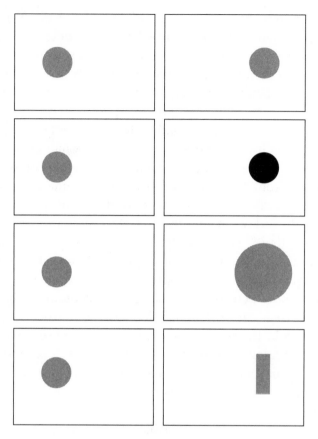

FIGURE 7.8 Long-range apparent motion. For each pair of pictures, if the left picture were replaced by the right picture you would have the sensation of motion. The top image produces the sensation that the circle is jumping back and forth. For the remaining pairs, the object appears to change brightness, size, or shape in mid-motion.

for avoiding jump cuts. First, if there are no contours, there will be no jump cut. In *Rope*, Hitchcock hid cuts by ending the first shot as the camera panned through a shadow and then beginning the next shot still in shadow. The frames on either side of the cut are then pure black. If you cut from black to black, not only is there no jump cut but effectively there is no cut at all. In *Eternal Sunshine of the Spotless Mind*, Michel Gondry hides a series of cuts in exactly the same way: Jim Carrey is frantically searching a streetscape as his perceptions are being altered by memory-revision technicians. Each time he turns, the buildings, people and vehicles have been tweaked—all without an apparent cut. Gondry pulled this off by panning the camera in front of a light pole in the extreme foreground and cutting whenever the pole filled the frame.[17]

What about if a movie cuts from a dark night sky to bright blue morning sky? Here, there is definitely a cut but there will not be a jump because neither frame has much contour. Cuts like this, with little contour on either side of the cut, are rare. Much more frequently movies cut from one shot with a lot of contour to another shot with a lot of contour. In this case, what the filmmaker needs to do is to make sure that most of the salient contours are far enough apart not to jump. This ought to be the most common way to avoid jump cuts.

Filmmakers figured this out long ago. It is codified in one of the rules of thumb written down in film school textbooks: When you cut within a scene, move the camera by at least 30 degrees. By doing so, you ensure that objects present in both shots move enough to avoid producing long-range apparent motion.

Before we finish out discussion of jump cuts, I need to say one more thing. So far, I have been describing jump cuts as if they are a bad thing. For most filmmakers most of the time they are: They are noticeable and jarring, and divert the audience's attention from the story being told on the screen. But, depending on the filmmaker's goals, this could be a good thing. The director Lars von Trier makes heavy use of jump cut sequences, which, for me, produces a sense of tension combined with a sense that time is passing quickly. For example, in *Dancer in the Dark,* von Trier tracks Björk using a floating camera with jump cuts every few seconds. This generates a feeling of time passing strangely, and a sense of disorientation. In music videos, one kind of jump cut became a visual cliché in the 1980s: Film the band walking toward the camera, and drop intervals of about a half a second at a time, so that the band members seemed to be jumping forward as they approach.

Cuts are not the only way to get from one shot to the other. If you have a laptop, it probably came installed with video editing software that can implement a whole menu of shot-to-shot transitions—mine has 20 different options! The most significant are fades, wipes, and iris effects. Some of these acquired particular meanings in the early history of film, when they were used frequently. In a *fade*, one image gradually transitions to another. On the first frame of the fade, the image is 100% composed of the old shot. Halfway through, the old shot and the new shot are superimposed. At the end, the frame is 100% the new shot. If one of the shots is a black screen, you can fade to or from black. A fade often indicates a major scene break—a change in time, space, or both. In a *wipe*, an imaginary line moves across the screen, and behind it the old shot is replaced by the new shot. A wipe often is meant to show that the new shot depicts action at the same time as the old shot. In an *iris out* effect, a black screen transitions to a shot by exposing first just a point at the center of the screen and then expanding out in a circle. This can be used to begin a major section of a film; the reverse can be used to end it. (This was popular in American silent films.)

Fades, wipes, and iris effects are all more complex and more noticeable than cuts. They may work in part because they capitalize on things our visual system does naturally, but they probably require experience with film to comprehend. I do not think anyone has done the experiment, but my hunch is that if I were to ask you to try to spot edits in film, fades, wipes, and iris effects would all be very easy to catch.

Joining multiple camera shots is the basic act of constructing a film. But I also need to mention that there are other ways of making films. Directors sometimes eschew editing, using stage direction and other techniques to tell the story. A shot that lasts a long time and tells a lot of story without cuts is called a *long take*. The phrase *long shot* would make sense, except that the term already has a meaning in film lingo: a shot filmed from far away. (Worse yet, it has another meaning entirely in horse racing.) Film nerds go crazy for long takes. One of my favorites is Orson Welles's famous opening to *A Touch of Evil*. The shot is a technical *tour de force*, utilizing a camera mounted on a crane on a dolly to follow the action through a complex nighttime city crowd scene. The action opens with a close-up of a bomb being armed. The bomber runs to a car, places the bomb in the trunk, and runs off. A couple climbs into the car, pulls into the boulevard, and is stopped by a traffic cop at the corner. Now, we see another couple crossing the street and walking up the cross street. It's Charlton Heston and Janet Leigh, the leads. As they walk, laughing and talking, they pass hundreds of people, half a dozen goats, and two vendors with carts before coming to the border checkpoint. The car catches up with them again as they talk with the border guard, then drives out of the shot again. The first cut in the film happens about 3½ minutes in, cutting to the car as it explodes.

That shot, and a bunch of other long takes, are referenced in the opening of Robert Altmann's *The Player*. As Fred Ward walks in and out of the shot, chatting up other characters, they trade recollections of *Touch of Evil*, *Absolute Beginners*, *Rope*, and *The Sheltering Sky*. Characters and vehicles come and go, and the camera zooms in and out. As the sequence goes on, you realize that it itself is a highly technical long shot making use of exactly the techniques to which the dialogue pays tribute.

The extreme end of long takes is the film without actual or apparent cuts. Alfred Hitchock's *Rope* came close. The film makes extensive use of camera motion but has only 10 apparent cuts. Another 10 are hidden by darkness, but he had to retain 10 visible cuts so that the projectionist would know when to change reels.[18]

By 2002, when Alexander Sokurov released *Russian Ark*, digital cameras allowed one to film a 99-minute feature film in a true single shot. He took advantage of this in audacious fashion: Set in the Hermitage museum in St. Petersburg, the film includes a cast of 2,000 actors and extras in period costumes and three orchestras. It was filmed with a camera mounted on a device called a Steadicam, which allowed the camera operator to walk from room to room and up and down the stairs with minimal bumping and jerking. Both *Rope* and *Russian Ark* were widely praised by film critics and audiences. *Russian Ark* was marketed aggressively as a spectacle, and the mobile camera draws attention to how the film was made as it sweeps and glides through the castle. But I have been surprised by how many viewers report that they never had noticed that *Rope* was effectively one long take. It shows that the right filmmaker can tell a story without making use of the cut—which was exactly Hitchcock's point.

So far, I have emphasized that cuts work partly because they capitalize on what your visual system was built to do. You experience brief visual discontinuities frequently, when you blink, when you saccade, or when you walk down the street and a van zips by in front of you. But I also have emphasized the important sense in which cuts are something utterly new in the evolutionary history of our species. In a cut, a big piece of our visual field can be instantaneously replaced with something completely different. Do we have to learn how to handle such changes?

One recent study suggests that the answer is mostly "no" but with a dash of "yes." Sermin Ildirar was a Turkish filmmaker and scientist visiting Stephan Schwan at the Knowledge Media Research Centre in Tübingen, Germany. She had family in a village in the mountains of Turkey who had little exposure to television or movies. She knew there were other villages nearby where there was absolutely no TV. She and Schwan designed an experiment to look at how people who had never seen a cut respond the first time they saw one. They did not want to use Hollywood movies, because if the villagers saw them differently, it might be due to the strangeness of the actions shown on the screen. So they filmed their own simple short films in one of the villages using locals as actors. The movies were a few seconds to a couple of minutes long and included a few cuts. Then Ildirar hiked up into the mountains and set up her laptop to test the villagers. Would these people even describe the pictures on the screen as depictions of actions that took place someplace else at a different time? No problem there. Would they be able to describe what was taking place both before and after the cut, or would they be disoriented by the cut and have trouble describing the subsequent shot? Again, no problem. Where they *did* have trouble was in describing how the shots related to each other.

Consider the following sequence: When the film begins, a medium shot shows a man approaching the door to a house, from a point of view in the yard. Cut. The next shot is taken from the doorway and shows the door opening; the camera then pans into the house. You or I would probably describe that by saying something like "The man walks up to the house, opens the door, and steps inside." The villagers said things like "He opened the door but I didn't see him anymore." They described the content of each shot accurately but often didn't seem to think of the shots as related in the same way that experienced viewers would. Familiar actions helped, leading to more standard descriptions, but even so, about half of the descriptions were not the sort you or I would be likely to give. Schwan and Ildirar speculated that when one sees cuts for the first time, the depiction of familiar actions helps viewers to learn how the cuts work and what they mean. I think this explanation is probably right on target.[19]

Our brains have not evolved appreciably since movies were invented—but movies have evolved like crazy. One thing that has changed is the frequency of cutting: Shots have gotten shorter. One factor is the relatively low resolution of broadcast television. Because it is hard to make out a face in a medium shot on TV, directors and editors tend to use more close-ups. Instead of keeping two or three actors on the screen, they cut among them, which pushes up the frequency of cuts. TV commercials tend to have lots of cuts both because of the need to use close-ups and because they only have 30 or 60 seconds to tell their story. These practical considerations have interacted with cultural and stylistic factors. In the 1980s music videos popularized a fast cutting style that continues to influence TV and film editing. The film researcher Barry Salt carefully analyzed editing in 340 films released from 1912 to 2000, focusing on films through the 1950s and from the 1990s. The mean length of a shot in his 1950s films was 11.2 seconds; by the 1990s it was down to 5.6 seconds. In action sequences it is now not unusual to cut every second or two.[20]

It's not just that the rate of cutting has increased; the rhythm of it has changed too. We know this from a recent study by James Cutting. (A perfect name for studying film editing!) Cutting, together with Jordan DeLong and Christine Nothelfer, analyzed films from 1935 to 2005 taken from five genres: action, adventure, animation, comedy, and drama. They wanted to know how the timing of each cut was related to the timing of the cuts that preceded it. At one extreme, imagine that on each frame of the movie you randomly decided whether to cut or not with some fixed probability. A viewer would have no way of predicting when a shot was going to end from how long it had gone on. At the other extreme, imagine that each shot in the movie was of exactly the same length. As you watched the film you could learn to predict exactly when the next cut was coming. Of course, real films are in between—there are long takes and short takes mixed up together. Cutting and his colleagues discovered that more recent films tend to be constructed so that a long take is more likely to be followed by another long take, and a short take by another short take. This is especially true of action films. Why this trend? Cutting and his colleagues suggest that movies are evolving toward this structure because attention waxes and wanes in the brain with a similar structure. Possibly this feels natural because it mirrors how we naturally experience events.

At the same time that movie-editing practices have been adapting, perhaps to fit our brains, our brains are shaped by the experience of watching cuts. I do *not* mean that that natural selection is shaping the genes that build our brains to make us better movie watchers. Evolution by natural selection is much too slow a process for this to happen. What I *do* mean is that our brains are shaped not just by our genetic endowment but also by our experiences, and particular forms of experience can have profound impacts on the sorts of brains we wind up with. Think of learning to drive or learning to read. These are tasks that people practice regularly over long periods of time, and they result in perceptual skills that nondrivers and nonreaders do not have. Drivers learn to coordinate visual input with hand movements to control the wheel, foot movements to control the accelerator and brake, and eye movements to monitor for relevant information from traffic signals, pedestrians, and other cars. They can do these things much more quickly than nondrivers and can do them without much conscious attention. Readers execute a tightly choreographed ballet of eye movements simply to scan across a page of text, and are for the most part altogether unaware. In both cases, the right way to think of this is as a perceptual skill—a new way of looking—that is learned by extensive repetition just like a golf swing or knitting. When we learn a skill like this we reshape our brains to produce a new coordination of our sensory organs and the muscular and neural processes that control them.

Most Westerners these days have massive amounts of experience watching movies and TV. You know the statistics: The average American between 8 and 18 watches more than 4 hours of television a day.[21] For most of us, watching moving images is the equivalent of a part-time job. The average adult therefore has a *lot* of practice processing cuts. This means that processing film editing is a perceptual skill like the perceptual skills we acquire when we learn to drive or learn to read. We saw that novices can basically do it, but with extensive experience I believe we acquire perceptual routines that change our visual abilities and habits. This could be good or it could be bad—we don't really know because there are not a lot of data. The effects probably are not huge because if they were we would be able to see them without doing experiments. But I would bet that if we *did* conduct the right experiments, we would find that people who have a lot of experience watching film editing see the world a little differently from those who do not. Recent studies of video game players show that people who play games based on hand-eye coordination have better visual attention and some kinds of mental imagery abilities.[22] It could well be that a lot of practice watching cuts improves your ability to bridge visual information across discontinuities. This could produce improved performance in situations in which there are lots of moving objects temporarily blocking your view, or in which you have to look around a lot and put a larger picture together.

Watching cuts also could well hurt our ability to do some kinds of real-world visual processing. Continuity editing is designed to feed you the right visual information at the right time. If a dialogue scene is filmed with a series of over-the-shoulder shots, you do not have to shift your gaze from speaker to speaker. Instead, the relevant visual information is placed right in front of you with each cut. Does this sort of experience make it harder for us to guide our own attentional systems and our own eyes when there is no editor there to do it for us? What about these changes in the rate and predictability of cutting? How do they affect our perceptual systems? One concern is that faster and faster cutting makes it harder to process information that is not carved up into bite-sized chunks. Critics have even speculated that watching a lot of fast-paced video can give a child attention deficit disorder. Again, I think that if the effects were huge, we probably would have detected them without a formal experiment. Moreover, even if someone is watching screens 4 or 5 hours a day, this still leaves a lot of hours in which vision has to operate in its normal way.

So where do we stand? Does watching moving pictures make you visually stupid? Or can it turn you into a star athlete of visual perception? On the one hand, we can be reasonably confident that movies *are* reshaping our brains. Any skill that we practice regularly over long periods does so. It is possible that the consequences of this reshaping for our perceptual systems are truly significant and we just haven't noticed yet. In Chapter 5 we saw that some parts of our psychology *are* significantly influenced by the media we practice on and that people *have* noticed. But for basic perceptual processing I suspect that practice with media does not produce dramatic changes; rather, that the range of media experience most people have now has modest effects on our perceptual abilities. Of course, this could all change in the future. If stereoscopic (3-D) projection or interactive movies become ubiquitous, we might develop a whole new set of perceptual skills. It is possible that these new skills will impact our mechanisms of seeing and thinking even after we leave the theater.

8 ■

Bottlenecks, Spotlights, and Chunks

In this chapter, we are going to turn from the moment-by-moment illusion of motion to the larger scale structure of movies. Today's films are imposingly complex artifacts. The early nickelodeons displayed short sequences of grainy monochrome images at 16 frames per second; modern films are shot in high-resolution color at a frame rate of at least 24 frames per second, often higher. For a modern film, the visual signal alone conveys at least 1.8 billion bits of data per second. (A bit is a single on/off, zero/one value.) So, exhibiting *Spider-Man* (121 minutes) takes about 13.3 trillion bits. If each one of those bits were a ½-inch piece of popcorn, they would wrap around the earth more than three times.[1]

Our peripheral sensory organs—eyes, ears, and skin—can handle this massive amount of data. When the late Steve Jobs raved in 2010 about the "retina" display on Apple's latest iPhone, he was referring to this sensitivity. He claimed that the resolution of the phone's screen was so high that when you held it up, the screen could display visual changes finer than your eye could see. (This was not quite correct, as it turned out.)[2] Digital movie production is getting close to that resolution for typical projection situations. This means a *lot* of pixels, because a movie screen takes up much more of your visual field than a phone screen. Our visual systems must be sensitive to *some* of this exquisite detail, or else we would all still be watching nickelodeons.

Which brings us to a paradox: Despite the huge capacity of our sense organs, the processing load that our central nervous system can handle is really quite modest. When you look at your TV or your computer, does it *feel* as though you are processing every little pixel on the screen? For most of us most of the time, the answer is "no." Instead, we seem to inhabit a world consisting of a modest number of objects and events. The question then is, how is the vast data stream that impinges on our sense organs transformed to something that is tractable for our central nervous system and that corresponds to our subjective experience of the world? This question has a two-part answer: (1) a lot of what happens in our sensory fields is filtered out before it even gets to the central processor, and (2) what does get through is radically reshaped, so that what our brain represents is not billions of pixels but something much more modest and much more useful. Both of these mechanisms evolved to deal with the complexity of sensory stimulation in real life. Movies hijack those mechanisms, taking advantage of the shortcuts that our perceptual systems use in order to control where we attend, what we see, and how we remember.

In psychology there is a name for the selection and squeezing and reshaping of sensory data: *bottleneck*. One of the first scientists to invoke the idea of the bottleneck was the psychologist George Miller, in a famous 1956 paper called "The Magical Number Seven, Plus or Minus Two."

Miller showed how, across many different situations, our capacity to apprehend seems to be limited to about seven items.[3] For example, if I flash dots briefly on the screen and ask you how many were presented, you will probably be quite accurate up to about seven dots. However, if the number is eight or nine, or higher, you will likely start to make mistakes. Psychologists since Miller have suggested the bottleneck is even tighter—current estimates are about four items.[4] But it's not the exact number that is important; any reasonable number is smaller than the base of the bottle. How does our nervous system squeeze inputs down through the bottle's neck?

Part of the answer is that comprehension is selective. Most of what our sense organs encounter is processed at only a very superficial level. This is a smart strategy because it preserves resources for more thorough processing of those things that are important—as long as we are picking the *right* things to focus on. We perform this sort of selection on just about every dimension of experience. One dimension that is especially salient and relatively easy for scientists to study is space, so let's start there.

Most of the time you are attending to one and only one region of your spatial environment. A good metaphor for this is the *spotlight*. Think of your favorite prison-break scene—in *X-Men 3*, for example. As the escapees run for freedom, the spotlight sweeps the yard from the guard tower. You know a lot about the small area covered by the light, but everything else is dark and fuzzy. You can make the spotlight more diffuse, or maybe even split it in two, but then it is not as bright. When we watch movies, we depend on attention's spotlight to select the relevant visual information. First, it selects the screen itself and filters out the rest of the room. Theater designs help: Lighting is low, the colors are dark, and there is usually a black border around the edge of the screen; but they are not perfect—most theaters have bright exit signs and floor lighting for emergencies. The screen may be big, but at typical viewing distances it still fills only 20–25% of the width of your visual field. Watching a movie at home is usually a bit worse: The screen is much smaller; and often objects, lights, people, and pets clutter the room. If you watch on a tablet computer or phone, it's even worse. Yet most of us are perfectly happy to watch a movie on a TV or an even smaller screen. This works because our spotlights emphasize the region of interest and deemphasize the rest.

The spotlight works not just to select the screen at the expense of the rest of the world, but also to select regions within the screen. Movie watching depends critically on this as well. If the director can predict where you are attending, he or she can focus resources on making sure the attended part of the frame looks perfect and not worry so much about the rest. Think of early movies that relied heavily on painted backdrops, and of movies from the 1990s when computer-animated augmentation became popular. When *Jurassic Park* was released in 1990, it was heralded for the herds of computer-generated dinosaurs tromping across the screen. One dramatic shot shows a herd of gallimimus—an ostrich-like herbivore—being chased by a T. rex. It is a spectacle, no question—but look closely. If you focus on any one of them, the creature won't look so great. The animation technology was stretched to its limits, and the movements and rendering of each individual gallimimus is actually pretty clunky. The film works because your spotlight is on the people at the center of the action. For shots in which your spotlight lingers on a dinosaur, the filmmakers devoted massive effort to render the creature in convincing detail, combining computer-generated animation with animatronics and doing a lot of work by hand.[5]

To keep our attentional spotlights focused on useful places, humans have evolved an exquisitely tuned set of mechanisms of which we are largely unaware. But, like many areas of brain function, we can get hints about how these mechanisms work by considering cases in which they fail. One such case is *neglect*. Neglect is a neurological disorder that often occurs after a stroke affecting the back of the brain just in front of the visual cortex, particularly areas on the right side. People with neglect have a hard time focusing their spotlights on the side of space opposite to the lesion—so if I were to suffer a right-hemisphere stroke, I would likely neglect my left side. Patients with neglect might eat only the food on the right side of their plates, leaving the left untouched. If asked to copy a picture, they might draw a rich image on the right but only a few squiggles on the left. At first you might think the person was blind in one visual field. However, if enough external support is provided, say by pointing, the same patient would reveal perfectly good vision on the affected side. This shows just how important correct focus of the spotlight is: If we can't attend to something, we almost might as well be blind to it.[6]

So how does the spotlight become focused in the right place? An analogy may help here; I'll try one that is silly but picturesque. Think of your spotlight mounted on a tower so that it has a panoramic range. Now, imagine it is being pulled on by a dozen different ropes, each held by a trained monkey. Each monkey is responding to a different aspect of the situation, so they may all wind up tugging in different directions. One monkey is obsessed with features of the environment that are distinctive; this is called *visual salience*. Things are visually salient when their visual features contrast with those nearby. For example, a red apple in a pile of green apples is salient, as is a vertical golf club in a display of horizontal clubs. So whenever there is a salient color or orientation, this monkey is going to tug its rope to pull the spotlight over to that location. Visual salience can often make an object seem to "pop out" of the display, giving the subjective sense that it is immediately and automatically the focus of attention. Frank Miller's *Sin*

City is filmed mostly in stylized black-and-white tones with high contrast, emulating the visual style of the graphic novels on which it is based. When occasional elements are rendered in color—the flasher on a police car, a woman's dress, a pool of blood—they almost jump out of the screen. Experimental data back up this phenomenology: When people are asked to search for visually salient features, they are often quite fast and little influenced by the number of other objects in the display.

While one monkey is driven by visual salience, another is obsessed with whatever features are relevant to your current task. For example, if you're watching an airport TV, the screen is small and there is a lot of distraction. The task-driven monkey is desperately trying to keep your spotlight on the TV screen. If you were watching the climactic soccer scene in John Huston's *Victory*, one of the monkeys would be trying to keep the spotlight focused on the ball because it's important for understanding what is happening.

There may be other monkeys pulling for other reasons. If you are trying to find a face in a crowd scene in *Reds*, you might adopt a deliberate strategy of searching left to right and top to bottom. We can think of this as another monkey that you have trained to pull your spotlight on a particular path. So what happens when some of the monkeys are pulling their ropes in one direction and another set is pulling in the opposite direction? Scientists aren't quite sure yet how this conflict gets resolved. This is a fascinating question. But the important thing is that everyone more or less agrees that visual salience, task guidance, and deliberate strategies interact to direct the spatial spotlight.[7]

Spatial selection is important enough for humans and other animals that there is a fair bit of specialized circuitry devoted to it. One particularly important brain area is the posterior parietal cortex. This is a large region near the back of the brain on the upper (dorsal) side. Just below it lies the posterior part of the temporal lobe. The area at their juncture is the place where brain injury produces the neglect syndrome described previously. The posterior parietal cortex interacts with structures in the midbrain, buried beneath the cortex, to coordinate the focusing and shifting of the spotlight. One particularly important piece of the posterior parietal cortex is in medial parietal cortex: the part of the cortex that wraps around to the middle of the brain in either hemisphere. Recent studies suggest that part of the medial parietal cortex is essential for detecting when a shift in focus is needed—whether you are shifting from left to right or vice versa, or even shifting from vision to hearing. Once this part of parietal cortex signals to initiate a shift, interactions between it and the midbrain coordinate to select the new target of attention.[8] Here's one way to think about it: The medial parietal cortex is like a monkey whose job is to watch for when its compatriots need to start tugging on their ropes. It gives a call, all the other monkeys start to pull, and the spotlight lands in a new spot.

All of this happens fast and often without much awareness. Controlled experiments show that the spotlight can be refocused within a couple of hundred milliseconds. But the spotlight of attention has a fascinating additional feature: It is tightly tied to the movements of the eyes. Here's why: Your brain is constantly trying to keep the most sensitive part of your eye, the fovea, pointed at the most important part of your visual world. This is a hard job because the fovea is small and the important stuff often keeps moving around. When a salient or important stimulus occurs, the typical sequence is that you make a rapid shift of attention to its location and initiate a rapid eye movement (called a saccade, discussed in the previous chapter) shortly thereafter.[9] This maximizes the amount of information you can obtain about the objects to which you are attending. Parts of your posterior parietal cortex and midbrain that control shifts of attention are also tightly coupled to regions that control movements of your eyes, which are located more anteriorly in the parietal lobe and in the frontal cortex, on the lateral surface near the top.

Filmmakers have known from the beginning how important it is to direct the viewer's attention and how powerful a medium film is for doing so. In recent years, that craft knowledge has been supplemented by data from the laboratory. Uri Hasson and his colleagues observed viewers while screening Jim Sheridan's *In the Name of the Father* (see the three frames at the top of Figure 8.1). They measured where viewers looked; the most popular spots are marked with white outlines.[10] Almost everyone is looking at the same locations: the faces of the characters doing the talking and the hands of the character playing air guitar. This result is typical. If you were to look out from behind the screen at a theater playing a blockbuster and could make out the audience's eyes, you'd see them shifting across the screen almost as though they were being operated by remote control. The bottom row suggests the role that the filmmaker plays in coordinating attention: It shows five frames from an unstructured video shot at a park in Brooklyn, with eye gaze data superimposed. The

FIGURE 8.1 Most frequent gaze positions for frames in the film *In the Name of the Father* (*top*) and an unstructured film (*bottom*). Eye gaze is tightly controlled in former, but there is still some gaze alignment in the latter.

Adapted from Hasson, Vallines, & Heeger, 2011, with permission.

agreement among observers is pretty good, but nowhere near as high as for the commercial film.

The spatial spotlight, then, accounts for an important part of how sensory information becomes squeezed through the central bottleneck, but it's not the whole story. Sometimes information that is right in the spotlight still gets left behind. In a now-famous experiment, Dan Simons and Chris Chabris asked Harvard undergraduates to watch a video of two teams passing a basketball.[11] One team wore white shirts and the other black, and the viewers were asked to count the number of bounce passes and aerial passes of one of the teams. At 44 seconds into the video, a woman in a gorilla suit walked right to the middle of the frame, stopped, pounded her chest, and walked off. The balls were passed literally right around her, so it's very likely that most viewers' spotlights fell on her at least once, yet fully 46% of the viewers failed to notice. This phenomenon is called *inattentional blindness*. The features of the gorilla are quite available and salient, but viewers didn't process them. This is *not* a case of spatial selection, because the gorilla features overlapped spatially with the basketball features.[12] Here, the spotlight metaphor doesn't capture what is happening; a better metaphor is a sieve. Depending on the size and shape of the holes in the sieve, different particles get through.

In short, part of how you beat the bottleneck is by being selective. When you watch a movie, your visual system selects *where* to pull information from, and also *what* sort of information to pull.

Selection is part of the solution to the bottleneck, but it can't be the whole story. Let's go back to the *Spider-Man* example. Suppose my attentional spotlight filters out 90% of the visual environment and my central processors have to cope with only the remaining 10%. In terms of the low-definition TV signal, that is still 1.3 trillion bits—enough to string popcorn from Manhattan to Madagascar.

That is still much more than the central processors can handle. Moreover, such a representation is not even very useful. It doesn't tell me how many objects there are in the spotlight or what they are, let alone what they are doing or what it might mean. To truly beat the bottleneck, our nervous systems need not just to select but to recode the information into a compact and useful format. A second critical component, therefore, is *chunking*.

Chunking is intuitive if we think about how it works in space. Shine a spotlight from my office window in St. Louis and you might light up a tree or two, a couple of cars, and maybe a person walking. Spatial chunking consists of two operations. One is dividing the scene into the important parts and the less important stuff in between. The important parts are usually called *figure* and the rest *ground*; the process is called *figure-ground segmentation*. The other operation is segmenting the figure into objects and parts. More on that in a minute.

Figure-ground segmentation is one of those scientific problems that sneaks up on you. The notion of figure and ground is immediately intuitive, and for the most part all of us would agree as to what is the figure and what the ground in any natural scene. But that doesn't mean we know how it works. If you stopped somebody on the street and asked, "Hey, why is it that we can pick out the figure in a picture from the background?" he or she might launch into an answer without hesitation...and then trail off. "Well, it's the, um, important stuff...it just sticks out...it's better defined?...brighter?" Then your interviewee would probably give up. It turns out that lurking below the sense that figure-ground segmentation is simple and intuitive there is a lot of complexity. Table 8.1 contains the most current list I know of the features involved in segmenting figure from ground.[13]

The other spatial chunking mechanism, *part segmentation*, groups regions within the figure into objects and their

TABLE 8.1 Principles of Figure-Ground Segmentation

Principle	Description
Surroundedness	If one region surrounds another, the enclosed region is perceived as figure.
Size	Other things being equal, smaller regions are perceived as figure.
Orientation	Regions that are straight up and down or right and left tend to be perceived as figure.
Contrast	Regions whose brightness contrasts more with that of the surrounding area are more likely to be seen as figure.
Symmetry	Symmetrical regions are more likely to be perceived as figure.
Convexity	Whenever you have a curved edge, you have an "inside" and an "outside." The inside is more likely to be perceived as figure.
Parallelism	Regions with parallel edges are more likely to be perceived as figure.
Meaningfulness	Regions whose shape corresponds to a meaningful object are more likely to be perceived as figure.

Source: Adapted from a description by Stephen Palmer.

parts. Part segmentation simplifies our spatial world by chunking it into a set of discrete regions and treating the space within each region as being qualitatively identical. To illustrate, here's a quick geography quiz:

1. If you were to travel due south from Detroit, Michigan, what is the first country other than the United States that you would encounter?
2. Which is farther west, San Diego or Reno?
3. Which is farther north, Rome or New York?

If you look at the answers at the end of the chapter, you'll see that our knowledge of geographical space is subject to

some pretty strong distortions, and these arise from chunking in our spatial memory. Distortions such as these illustrate that chunking entails giving something up—we lose
information about the exact locations of objects by treating
a contiguous region as one thing. Sometimes, these examples show, this operation can lead us to the wrong answer.
However, more often the chunk is enough. If you need to
guess which of two cities is farther north or west, most of
the time the locations of the chunks to which they belong
are enough to do the job.

Film and television producers take advantage of the fact
that we chunk space into regions and have trouble holding
on to the details of exact locations. Movies are usually made
by filming scenes in different outdoor and indoor locations
that are selected for how they look rather than where they
are really located. Viewers can accurately track which location is which, but often have little idea where things are
within each setting, or of how someone would get from one
to the other. To get a feel for how sketchy your spatial memory is, try this: Pick a favorite scene from a movie you have
on DVD—ideally one you have watched a few times. Close
your eyes, imagine yourself at a particular location on the set,
and try to point to the critical characters and objects around
you. It's amazing how bad people are at this. One study
selected people who were addicted to the TV series *ER*. On
average they had watched about 70 episodes. When the
experimenters tested their ability to point to easily recognized locations on a set, they did just slightly better than they
would have if they had been blindfolded, spun around, and
pointed at random. They were no better than people who
didn't watch *ER*.[14] This means the filmmakers can select or
construct settings that look the way they want without worrying about how those settings relate to one another in space.

There are exceptions, though. Some narratives are set
in environments that are small enough that the characters

regularly walk from one setting to the other on-screen. You might think this would allow viewers to build up a coherent and accurate representation of the relations between the settings over the course of a feature film or multiple episodes of TV. If so, producers ought to be in trouble because it is cost prohibitive to construct an office building to film an office comedy or build a school to film a school drama. The TV series *The X Files* built up a devoted, even obsessive, fan base over nine seasons from 1993 to 2002.[15] Many episodes included scenes set inside and around the J. Edgar Hoover FBI Building in Washington, D.C. In the third episode of season 6 ("Triangle"), the producers staged a sequence of long takes that followed Special Agent Dana Scully through several floors of the building. They thus were forced to create large connected spaces, knitting together rooms that previously could be represented by unconnected sets. The result is surely not consistent with the previous representations of these spaces—which in fact were not consistent with one another.[16] However, the episode played effectively for its target audience; the *X-Files'* dedicated fans failed to detect the producers' conspiracy to remake the show's spatial environment. As long as the chunks were basically the same—the same offices and hallways—how they were connected was not important.

The assembly of spaces and their relations to one another is an area of great recent progress in neuroscience, and what we have learned fits well with the behavioral phenomena and the movie examples I just gave. A lot of the most exciting data have come from electrical recording studies in rodents. Rats are terrific for studying spatial navigation—they are highly spatial animals, and they are smart so they can learn complex navigation tasks quickly. By recording electrical signals from single neurons in the brains of rats as they moved around, researchers have learned how space is represented, particularly by a set of structures on the bottom surface of the cortex, in and around the hippocampus. Perhaps the most basic component of spatial representation found using this method is the *head direction cell*. As the rat moves around, a particular grid cell fires only when the rat is facing in one direction. If you imagine a rat wandering a rat-sized football field, one cell might fire when it faces the home team's goalpost, whereas another fires when it faces the visitors' bench. Head direction cells are *not* compasses—in each space they pick on a salient set of axes and represent direction relative to these; the axes may not be consistent as the animal moves from room to room. Head direction cells were initially found in an area called the post-subiculum, just behind the hippocampus. They have since been found in other areas.

The second key component of the spatial representation is the *grid cell*. When the rat first emerges onto the football field, grid cells divide the space up into a rectangular grid. Think of it as covering the field with a regular pattern of tiles made of a few different colors. Each cell would fire when the rat was standing on one particular color. Grid cells are thought to work by putting together information from the head direction cells with information from other areas that keep track of how many steps the rat has taken. Grid cells are found mostly in a piece of the cortex adjacent to the hippocampus called the entorhinal cortex. The most complex piece of the spatial representation was actually the first one discovered: the *place cell*. A place cell responds selectively when the rat is in a particular location in a cage or maze. Place cells don't care which direction the animal is facing or moving, just where it is. They form a mental map of the space. Place cells probably build up their representations from the inputs of grid cells and head direction cells. As you might imagine, head direction cells, grid cells, and place cells are all much easier to study in the rat than in you or me. But there is now a bit of evidence that the system works similarly in humans. (You may remember that in Chapter 2, I described human functional MRI studies of the *parahippocampal place area*. This area is immediately adjacent to the hippocampus and tightly connected with it. Human electrical recordings find that cells in this area respond to views of landmarks, and find evidence for place cells in the human hippocampus. And as I write this, a new study has just reported finding grid cells in several areas of the human brain.)[17]

Together, head direction cells, grid cells, and place cells provide a reasonably high fidelity representation of current location and heading. A key feature of these cells is that they all remap shockingly quickly when an animal enters a new space. As the animal explores a new space, the head direction cells pick out a new conceptual "north," the grid cells form a new grid, and the place cells quickly specialize to span it. When the animal moves from one room into another, things more or less reset. This is consistent with the geographic and movie memories we just considered. This system provides a relatively high fidelity representation of the immediate environment, but different spaces are only loosely related to one another. When we want to navigate over large distances, we have to deliberately attend to spatial relations that are not automatically tracked by this system—and we almost never do this when watching a movie.

To sum up, real space is continuous in all directions, but when we go to the movies we usually are shown a set of discrete settings whose spatial relations to one another are haphazard. This works because our perception and memory of space relies heavily on qualitative, categorical representations. How we think about a particular location depends on its location in a spatial hierarchy: A room is in a hospital, the hospital is in a neighborhood, the neighborhood is a in a city, the city is in a state...Within a setting we may keep track of some continuous information about the locations of people and objects, but even this sort of information is hierarchical and sketchy. Film doesn't need to give us more information about space because we wouldn't use it even if it were there—our nervous systems would simply chunk it away.

If chunking in space has a big impact on our experience of movies, chunking in time probably has an even bigger one. What do you do when somebody asks you about a movie you just saw? A big part of your response is likely to be a list of the events—the temporal chunks—that made up the film. Just listen to "bob the moo," a frequent poster on the movie review and information site imdb.com, reviewing Francis Ford Coppola's *The Godfather*:

> Michael Corleone returns home from the war for his sister's wedding [*event*]. However his return coincides with the beginnings of a war between the main families [*event*] sparked by the marketing of drugs [*event*]. Michael's involvement in the family business increases [*event*] when his father is the victim of an assassination attempt [*event*] and Michael wants to kill the two men responsible [*event*] before going to Italy for a year to lay low [*event*]. When Michael's brother Sonny is murdered [*event*], Michael returns home to take control of the family and clear up the war [*three events*]![18]

And it's not just amateurs recounting events. Pauline Kael's *5001 Nights at the Movies* is an encyclopedia of capsule reviews. Many—though not all—contain brilliantly condensed plot synopses. She wrote the following about *All My Sons* (1948): "Edward G. Robinson is the money-hungry industrialist who ships a batch of defective airplane-engine cylinders to the Air Force, blames his partner for the crime, and causes one of his sons, an aviator, to commit suicide out of shame." I count three events in this sentence. Or, writing about *Dial M for Murder* (1954), she says "Ray Milland is the suitably suave husband who hires unsavory, penny-dreadful Anthony Dawson to kill his rich, unfaithful wife, Grace Kelly; he then calmly goes out for the evening with her lover, Robert Cummings. The unexpected happens: the wife dispatches her would-be assassin with scissors, so the determined husband goes to work to make the murder look premeditated." Four events over two sentences. Finally, here is *Mr. Smith Goes to Washington* (1939): "When the young Senator's illusions are shattered, he stages a filibuster, defeats the villains, and re-establishes the whole government on a firm and honorable basis." I count four events in a single sentence. Kael's ability to condense and distill the events from a stream of frames is part of what made her a towering figure as the *New Yorker*'s movie critic for 24 years.[19]

You might object that movie reviews—amateur or pro—are special. After all, there is a whole set of conventions that have built up around this particular genre, and perhaps the genre norms simply specify that one of the things the reviewer does is summarize the plot. A quick look at everyday talk would convince you otherwise,[20] but even better is probably to look at expert storytellers: novelists. Chapter 3 of Stieg Larsson's *The Girl Who Played With Fire* starts with this workmanlike description of a set of events:

> Salander woke at 7:00 am, showered, and went down to see Freddy McBain at the front desk to ask if there was a Beach Buggy she could rent for the day. Ten minutes later she had paid the deposit, adjusted the seat and rear-view mirror, test-started it, and checked that there was fuel in the tank. She went into the bar and ordered a *caffé latte* and a cheese sandwich for breakfast, and a bottle of mineral water to take with her. She spent breakfast scribbling figures on a paper napkin and pondering Fermat's $(x^3 + y^3 = z^3)$.[21]

Even a masterful thriller like *The Girl Who Played With Fire* includes hundreds of paragraphs of simple linear event descriptions such as this one.

When novelists *do* veer from straightforward event descriptions, they do so for emphasis, as when James Joyce tried to put down in words Leopold Bloom's stream of consciousness for a waking day in *Ulysses*. In *The Mezzanine*, Nicholson Baker stretched out an escalator ride to fill a whole novel. Chapter 1 begins, "At almost one o'clock I entered the lobby of the building where I worked and turned toward the escalators, carrying a black Penguin paperback and a small white CVS bag, its receipt stapled over the top."[22] The final chapter, a single paragraph, consists of the protagonist stepping off the escalator and waving to a maintenance man, who waves back. By stretching out a brief and mundane trip up an escalator over 15 chapters, Baker played against the usual prominence of event descriptions that we usually see in novels.

It is my view that this habit of description is no accident. I think we synopsize to our friends because to do so is an elemental part of the experience of watching a movie. When we experience a continuous run of film, I believe our brains are frantically chunking the continuous visual and auditory signals into meaningful events, and that later it is those chunks that we remember. What's the evidence?

Drop in at my laboratory in St. Louis any given day and we might sit you down in front of a computer, turn on a movie, and give the following instructions:

> What I want you to do is to mark off the behavior of the person you'll be seeing into units that seem natural and meaningful to you. There are no right or wrong ways to do this; I just want to know how you do it. You should mark the units by pressing the button when, in your judgment, one unit ends and another begins. It is very important that you press the button exactly when you

believe one unit ends and another begins. Please be careful not to press in the middle of a unit, and try to be as accurate as possible.

If you are like most of our participants, you'll look at us funny. You might ask, "Well, what's a unit?" We'll tell you it's whatever intervals seem meaningful to you. "How do I know if I got it right?" We'll try to reassure you that there is no right or wrong answer. We'll let you practice for a couple minutes and then set you loose on some longer movies—4 to 8 minutes of a woman making a bed or fixing her breakfast or a man doing dishes or laundry. That's it.

This task, which was originally developed by the social psychologist Darren Newtson, is blindingly simple and a little bit odd. But it produces rich and regular data. If we ask a person to segment a movie on two separate occasions, the data from the two sessions will be quite similar—even if the sessions are separated by a year or more. If we ask two different people to segment the same movie, their boundaries will be similar as well.[23]

Temporal chunking, like spatial chunking, is hierarchically structured. The smaller chunks group together into larger chunks. Just like with space, this hierarchical organization structures our memory. Edward Lichtenstein and Bill Brewer from the University of Illinois demonstrated this when they showed viewers movies of a man writing a letter or setting up a slide projector, and then asked them to describe what had happened. Viewers were better able to remember events that were higher in the hierarchy. For example, in the letter-writing film, "signs letter" was recalled more frequently than "puts down pen"; and if they did recall the lower level action, they were quite likely to also mention the higher level one. In some versions of the film, Lichtenstein and Brewer had the actor alter the order of actions so that a lower level action was performed before the higher level unit of which it would normally be a part (for example, taking out an envelope in the middle of typing a letter rather than as part of the mailing unit). These out-of-place events were often remembered as having occurred within the higher level unit in which they "should" have happened.[24] We can see hierarchical chunking not just in memory but also in perception. In our lab we sometimes ask viewers to segment movies twice, once to identify fine-scale units and another time to identify larger scale units. The boundaries of the larger scale events tend to line up with boundaries at the finer scale, suggesting that people are grouping the fine-scale events into larger structures.[25]

We think that chunking in time happens for the same reason as chunking in space: because the full unchunked signal is too much for our brains to handle. The exact mechanisms are still being discovered, but here I will give you my best current guess as to how it works. As we watch a movie, we build up a representation of the current event, a chunk that captures "what is happening now." We use this representation to predict what is going to happen next. For example, in *The Maltese Falcon*, once I see Humphrey Bogart pick up a telephone, I probably set up a "phone call" chunk. Based on what I know about phone calls, I likely predict he will dial and then talk. If the context were different, I might set up a "fight" chunk, and predict that he will hit someone over the head with the phone rather than dial it. I want to emphasize that none of this prediction is conscious or deliberate—it happens fast, automatically, and in the background. Having set up a chunk like this allows my perceptual system to select what information will pass through the bottleneck. If the event is toothbrushing or shaving, then it is probably not important to carefully code the birds outside the window or the number of steps the actor takes to the sink. By setting up a toothbrushing chunk, I tune my attentional filters to select information relevant to toothbrushing. So, one form of efficiency is selecting *what* information needs to be processed further. A second form of efficiency is selecting *when* to process more heavily. As long as things are predictable, the system can take it easy and perform less sensory and perceptual processing, just enough to maintain my current event model and maybe tweak it a little bit. But what happens when Bogart finishes talking and hangs up? Now my phone call chunk is out of date and is likely to lead me to make bad predictions. I need to update. At this point we think the processing system ramps up, letting more information through the bottleneck in order to construct a new event chunk. Once this happens, the system can relax and go on as before.[26]

That's a nice story, but how can we know whether processing fluctuates over time in this way? One challenge is that the segmentation task I described—and any other task we might try—changes the very processing we are trying to study. In physics this is called the *observer effect*, and a famous version of it is Heisenberg's uncertainty principle. (Heisenberg showed that it is impossible to measure both the position and velocity of a quantum particle relative to arbitrary position, because it is necessary to give the particle some sort of push in order to measure it.) In psychology this problem is called *reactivity*. How can we measure changes in processing over time without affecting that processing?

In my lab in St. Louis we have tried to get around this problem by combining functional MRI with a trick of experimental design. fMRI enables us to directly measure changes in brain activity over time, solving half of our problem. However, we still have to be clever in our use of the fMRI recording in order to work around the observer effect. For example, suppose we were to ask you to perform the segmentation task in the scanner, and suppose we were to observe large changes in your brain when you pushed the button.[27] How would I know which components of the brain changes were related to the mental processes that were always going on in your brain—the ones that might be the updating of your event chunks—and which were related to the extra stuff I had asked you to do? Making a decision to press a button is pretty simple, but it still produces large, vigorous changes in brain activity. How could we measure activity related to ongoing chunking without the button-pressing activity getting in the way? This is where the experimental design trick comes in: First, you simply lie in the scanner and watch a few movies. *Then*, we explain the task and ask you to watch the movies again and segment them. (Usually, this takes place outside the scanner.) We take your own boundary judgments and apply them to your brain data, going back and asking what was happening during the initial viewing at those points in time that you later told us were event boundaries. The fMRI data are uncontaminated by the button-pressing task because you weren't doing it—in fact, at that point you had not even heard of it, so you could not have been covertly performing the task.

When we first tried this, we were nervous. What if we recorded for an hour from each of our participants and found nothing? It wasn't hard to imagine this being the outcome. Remember how much information there is in a film clip. Imagine all of that signal blasting through the brain and producing all sorts of responses. Pulling out the one piece that had to do with chunking events might have been like finding a needle in a haystack. Moreover, what if people saw the movie quite differently the second time, and so their event boundaries when they pressed the button differed from the ones they had experienced the first time through? But that wasn't the way it turned out. Instead, we found evidence that brain activity in a number of regions in the cerebral cortex started to increase a few seconds before the event boundary, peaking right around the boundary, and then decreasing.[28] For the first time, we could see a piece of the mechanism of segmenting the stream of consciousness without interfering in that mechanism's operation.

The particular brain areas that showed this pattern were suggestive. They included a collection of areas in the back of the brain—in the temporal, parietal, and occipital lobes—that respond strongly to visual signals but also to other modalities including sound and touch. These areas don't do the basics of visual processing. Instead, they are involved with analyzing the more complex features of objects' spatial arrangement and motion. Motion-selective regions in particular were strongly activated. The other major focus of activation was in the prefrontal cortex, specifically a region called the *dorsolateral prefrontal cortex*. (*prefrontal* means "the front part of the front," and *dorsolateral* means "on top and off to the side). This part of the cortex is involved with holding things in memory for short durations, focusing attention in space, and keeping track of what we are trying to do at any given point in time. In the next chapter, we will consider in a bit more detail what these brain areas might be doing when we watch movies. For now, let's just say that they probably aren't critical for low-level vision or hearing, and that they are good candidates for being part of a temporal chunking mechanism.

Since that initial study, we have replicated this design with a feature film, with simple animated shorts, and with written narratives. We have tested college students and retirees. Across different kinds of movies (and stories) and across people, it is striking how consistent this response is. Whatever we are trying to comprehend, it seems clear that temporal chunking is going on and that it modulates our brains' activity in a significant way.

In movies, cuts segment time. Now we see that perceptual experience segments time too. So what is the relationship between the segmentation that a movie imposes on experience and the naturally occurring segmentation that results from normal perception? When I first started working on this problem, my hunch was that cuts would turn out to correspond to event boundaries in perception. But my colleagues in film studies quickly objected: They told me that many cuts are invisible. And not all cuts are created equal. In classical Hollywood cinema, the majority of cuts are the continuity edits I described in the previous chapter. These are edits within an ongoing scene. They can be contrasted with the edits that join sequences that are discontinuous with the previous action. Film theorists have emphasized three important kinds of discontinuity: space, time, and action. These three often change together: For example, in *Star Wars, Episode IV*, once the starship Millennium Falcon escapes the Imperial starships leaving the port on Tatooine, we cut to a view of the Death Star (a new location) some time later (a new time) as Darth Vader's forces prepare to destroy Alderan (a new action). However, it also frequently happens that one or two of these features change but not all three. In a chase scene, we may follow a set of characters through a series of locations but the temporal sequence and action are continuous. Or an edit may transition from a shot of a character falling asleep to awakening in the same location the next morning. Changes of action occur when the actors take up a new set of goals or meaningful actions. Intuitively, they correspond to what would be scene changes in a stage play—major breaks in the action.

What does it take to make an event boundary in a film? Is a cut sufficient, as I initially suspected? Or does it take a change in space, time, or action? Joe Magliano and I looked at some of our segmentation and neuroimaging data to find out.[29] We used the data from Lamorisse's *The Red Balloon*, which I described back in Chapter 2. This movie is an ideally simple case study, because the editing is workmanlike and very much in the commercial mainstream. Almost all of the edits are simple cuts rather than fades, wipes, or other fancy transitions. Joe coded every frame in *The Red Balloon* to find each edit and classify its level of discontinuity. As is typical, most of the cuts were continuity edits. A smaller proportion were discontinuous in space or time—that is, they jumped to a viewpoint that did not overlap with the setting established by the previous shots, or jumped slightly forward in time. A subset of those were also changes in action—major scene changes. For example, one of the action discontinuities occurs when a boy walks into a school building and then the camera picks up two older men walking on the street outside.

When viewers marked event boundaries in *The Red Balloon*, they were barely more likely to identify an event boundary at the point of a continuity edit than at a point with no edit at all. So a cut isn't sufficient to make an event boundary. To our surprise, even jumping to a new spatiotemporal location did not produce boundaries. But the subset of edits that switched location *and* started a new action was about twice as likely to be perceived as an event boundary.

This left us with something of a puzzle: We knew that massive amounts of visual information were changing at edits, and even more when the edit involved changing location. Yet viewers seemed oblivious to all this discontinuity, segmenting instead on major changes in action. How did this work? We had a hunch: Maybe Lamorisse and his colleagues, in editing *The Red Balloon*, provided cues that allowed viewers to bridge the discontinuities in visual form and spatiotemporal location to follow the action of the plot. If so, this would mean that viewers' perceptual systems were cued to do the work to bridge discontinuities at continuity edits, but not at action discontinuities. Could we see evidence of this bridging in the viewers' brain activity as they watched?

Remember, when two clips are edited together with a cut, every point in the image changes instantaneously. For this reason we expected that edits would activate visual cortex. Did they ever! In the primary visual cortex—the earliest cortical stage of visual processing—edits were associated with large increases in MRI signal. We also saw increases in nearby areas that are specialized for processing motion, and further decreases in some motor areas and other parts of the frontal cortex. All of these suggest that continuity edits produce a momentary intensification of the ongoing viewing experience—you must process the visual signal more thoroughly; other things that your brain does on an ongoing basis get put on the back burner for a moment. We think that the visual system bridges the visual discontinuity in the same way it would if you were to look from one place to another around a room or if a truck drove by, occluding your field of view.

For major action discontinuities, it doesn't pay for the visual system to do this bridging. Would we see evidence that the system could shut down some bridging-related activity at action boundaries? Yes. We saw a ring of areas involved in higher level visual processing in the back of the brain that showed exactly the right pattern. They included parts of the occipital lobe involved in complex visual analysis and object processing, parts of the temporal lobe involved in representing the identity and category of objects, and parts of the parietal lobe involved in representing spatial location.[30] There were plenty of areas that were highly activated at the event boundaries—there's a lot of work to be done at those times to build a representation of the new event. But these high-level visual areas effectively took a rest.

Here is what we think this means: A well-made film gives your brain cues as to how to process it. Continuity edits say, "Hang in there, more of the same coming." In response, your visual system attempts to bridge the visual discontinuity, connecting what was on the screen before the edit to what is there afterward. Action discontinuities say, "Whoa there. This is a major break. Take a breather and start from scratch." How do film edits do this? Here the data are sparse, but we can make some educated guesses.[31] One technique is to minimize the discontinuity. If the camera pans into a shadow and the cut occurs while the frame is dark, there is no discontinuity at all at the boundary. If the camera or the action being filmed is moving very fast and continues in the same direction after the edit, there is very little discontinuity. A second technique is to use an actor's eyes to direct your attention. This is ubiquitous in dialogue sequences: An actor speaks a line and looks off-screen. Cut to the character who was being looked at, who then reacts. Such sequences leverage our tendency to follow others' glances. A third technique is to establish a rhythm. If the scene alternates shot by shot between two vantage points, this encourages us to bridge the visual discontinuity between them and makes it easier to do so. Finally, sound is a powerful cue to scene continuity: If the dialogue, environmental sounds, and music continue across the cut, this is a great cue that the action is continuous. By combining these cues and probably a few others, a film can encourage the viewer to connect the shots into a unified event.

Film also has a set of tools to cue you when a new major action occurs. First are visual effects: The simplest edit is the cut; your view just clicks from one frame to another. But since the early days of film, editors have used jazzier transitions to mark major boundaries. They can fade from one clip to another, fade to black or white and then back to the new clip, wipe from side to side or top to bottom so that the new frame is revealed over the old, squeeze from the sides, or impose an expanding or contracting circular mask (an "iris") over the frame. Some of these effects are associated with a particular time or genre—I can't see an iris effect without thinking of old American silent movies, and wipes and squeezes always make me think of *The*

Brady Bunch. I believe that these more intrusive visual effects discourage visual bridging. But *The Red Balloon* and many other films get by perfectly well without them. Here are a few of the techniques they use. One is to allow the action to move off-screen and leave the camera filming the background for a few moments. Another is to cut to an establishing shot, a wide-angle view of a new location. Finally, a break in auditory continuity is probably a particularly strong cue that a new action has begun: A new musical theme or environmental soundscape tells us that a new scene is underway. My hunch is that in classical Hollywood cinema these cues are effective about 90% of the time. But I also think that sometimes we as viewers miss for a moment or two that a new action is underway. We try to bridge to the previous scene, fail, and *then* form a new chunk.

If we are really always breaking the stream of sensation into chunks, what would it be like not to do so? If the account I have given is correct, then selection and segmentation are like the air we breath—ubiquitous, surrounding, and invisible. What would a movie with no chunks look like? I am tempted to look to nonnarrative experimental films or psychedelia for the answer. For example, most of Stanley Kubrick's *2001* is told in conventional narrative. However, when Tom Bowman goes through a space warp, the audience is confronted with a 9-minute nonnarrative interlude, intercut with brief distorted views of Bowman's face and eye through his helmet. Perhaps viewers' segmentation mechanisms would shut down when confronted with this? Maybe, but my hunch is that even here most people would see substantial visual pattern changes as boundaries. To form an impression of what unchunked experience might be like, I think we need to turn to thought experiments and experiments of nature.

For thought experiments in psychology, you can't do better than William James, the turn-of-the-20th-century philosopher and psychologist, and the brother of the novelist Henry James. In addition to possessing a masterful command of the emerging scientific literature in experimental psychology, James was a brilliant writer and speculator about psychological phenomena. (A favorite quip among psychologists is that Henry was a novelist who wrote psychology while William was a psychologist who wrote like a novelist.) James wrote that although the stream of consciousness is continuous, it is jointed like a stalk of bamboo:

> We believe the brain to be an organ whose internal equilibrium is always in a state of change,—the change affecting every part. The pulses of change are doubtless more violent in one place than in another, their rhythm more rapid at this time than at that. As in a kaleidoscope revolving at a uniform rate, although the figures are always rearranging themselves, there are instants during which the transformation seems minute and interstitial and almost absent, followed by others when it shoots with magical rapidity, relatively stable forms thus alternating with forms we should not distinguish if seen again; so in the brain the perpetual rearrangement must result in some forms of tension lingering relatively long, whilst others simply come and pass.[32]

Famously, James speculated that achieving this ordered stream of consciousness requires extended learning and development. He suggested that for an infant, the world crashes in, unselected and unsegmented: "The baby, assailed by eyes, ears, nose, skin, and entrails at once, feels it all as one great blooming, buzzing confusion."[33] I think this gives just the right impression of what it might be like to experience a world without a well-functioning chunking mechanism. However, these days we don't think this is what an infant experiences. On the contrary, there is good

evidence that infants chunk experience—and movies—
much as do adults.[34]

But sometimes chunking can start to come apart in
adults who are in a position to tell us what it feels like. This
is rare, but occasionally patients have injuries that cause
the components of their experience to come unchunked.
The following excerpt comes from an interview conducted
with one of these patients by the neuropsychologist Oliver
Zangwill at Cambridge University:

INTERVIEWER: I think you also had some difficulty in
   perceiving people as units.
PATIENT: Oh, oh yes. There was a slightly different effect
   I think, that if I saw a complex object, such as a person,
   and there were several people in my field of view,
   I sometimes saw the different parts of the people as not,
   in a sense, belonging together, although... if a given
   person moved so that all the parts of him went in one
   direction, that would... tend to make him into a single
   object. Otherwise there was this confusion of lots of
   things, all of which were there, but did not seem to belong
   together.... Several of these cases of things not belonging
   together gave quite absurd results. For instance, I do
   remember one case where there was what seemed to me
   to be one object which was partly motor car, partly tree
   and partly a man in a cricket shirt. They seemed
   somehow to belong together. More frequently, however, a
   lot of things which to any ordinary viewer would be parts
   of the same thing were parts of different things.
INTERVIEWER: So it was essentially common movement that
   created these units.
PATIENT: Yes... I think that was perhaps the most frightening
   case. A common color, especially in the case of
   clothes... when there were crowds of people together for
   instance on the lawn or on the beach, also formed a

unifying thing.... The effect was much more striking when a large number of objects were on the same table... it was not obvious what belonged to what; there were a whole lot of different things and in fact sometimes they—when one only saw a small object one could hardly say anything more than one saw a colored patch... [if somebody I knew was speaking to me]... it sounds quite absurd but there were two distinct things. One was that so and so was speaking to me and I could hear and understand what he said; two, that he was standing in front of me and I could see his mouth moving, but I noticed that the mouth moving did not belong to what I heard any more than a— than one of the old talkie pictures would make sense if the voice tape had been the wrong tape for the conversation. That was absolutely quite fantastically exciting... [35]

This is a unique story, because despite this dramatic disruption of perception, the patient was lucid and able to describe what was happening to him. To me, "fantastically exciting" puts quite a brave face on things—"frightening" seems more on the mark. Not exactly the sort of experience likely to make it at the box office.

Cases like this one show us how fundamental chunking is to our conscious experience. We are going to perceive most movies most of the time in terms of chunks because we perceive everything that way, just as we are constantly performing a massive amount of selection. A movie doesn't have to do anything special to lead us to select and chunk; it's how we beat the bottleneck. But most commercial movies go further—they guide us through the bottleneck by shaping our attentional selection and providing cues to chunking in time. The result is that a film audience's chunks are likely to be much more consistent than those of witnesses to a real-life event. I believe this promotes the strong sense of shared experience that films can provide.

Answers to the geography quiz on page 207:

1. *Canada*; specifically, Windsor, Ontario: Detroit is part of the United States, whereas Windsor is part of Canada. Most of Canada is north of most of the United States and so many readers disregard it when searching for places that could be south of Detroit, but Detroit sits in a bend in the Detroit River, with Windsor tucked in just south.
2. *San Diego.* Reno is chunked with Nevada, and San Diego with California. Most of Nevada is east of most of California, but because the coastline tilts east as you head south, San Diego is in a part of California that projects east of Western Nevada.
3. *Rome.* Rome is chunked with continental Europe, and New York with the continental United States. New York is toward the north of the United States, and Rome is toward the south of Europe, so many readers judge New York to be north of Rome. However, Europe as a whole is quite a bit north of the continental United States; we just don't have reason to notice this fact very much. (The fact that Rome has warmer weather than New York may contribute to this distortion.)[36]

9 ■
Sleight of Hand

Let me tell you a story of two Dans. In 1995, Dan Levin and Dan Simons were graduate students at Cornell University. They both were studying perception and memory, and they were both interested in—and loved—movies. Levin had come to psychology after a lot of experience in acting and film. They understood all about continuity errors and how difficult they were to spot. But they had a hard time reconciling their personal experience and the anecdotes from the film world with what they were reading in their psychology textbooks. Vision was supposed to be exquisitely sensitive and memory for pictures was supposed to be really good. What was going on here? They decided to try an experiment. First, they made a short film that was—deliberately—a continuity catastrophe. The film shows a short conversation between two women over lunch. In just 30 seconds they crammed in nine major continuity errors. One woman's scarf comes and goes, the plates on the table change from red to white, food magically appears and disappears.

Some of the changes are illustrated in Figure 9.1. Even in black and white, the errors are pretty obvious when you see the stills side by side. But when the Dans showed the film to 10 college students, only *1* reported noticing any of the changes. Levin describes it like this:

> When we made the film we were thinking, "We'll make a bunch of continuity errors, some tiny ones and some big ones, and see how many people can see." We assumed they would see all the big ones—the scarf change and all that stuff. Every single change we made, we thought "Whoa, this is way too big." And then we showed it to people and they never saw any of them unless they were

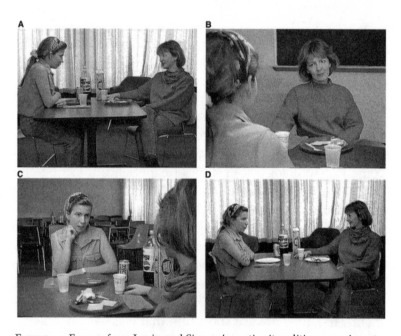

FIGURE 9.1 Frames from Levin and Simons's continuity editing experiment. Almost everyone missed the changes shown here: From 1A to 1B, the scarf of the woman on the right disappears; from 1C to 1D, the plates change from red to white and the hand of the woman on the left jumps from up to down.

From Levin, D. T. & Simons, D. J. (1997). Failure to detect changes to attended objects in motion pictures. *Psychonomic Bulletin & Review*, 4, 501–506.

explicitly looking out for changes, and then they did see one or two.[1]

What was going on here? Maybe the changes, though they seemed huge to the Dans, were too subtle. So they made an even simpler movie with the biggest continuity error possible. The film consists of just two shots and lasts only a few seconds. In the first shot, an actor is sitting at a desk working. A phone rings. The actor gets up to answer it. Cut to an angle showing the phone as the actor approaches and answers. Except that the actor in the second shot is a different person, similar in build but with different hair, different clothes, and a clearly distinguishable face. Just to be sure they were not accidentally matching the actor too well, they made eight different versions of this little short, and showed each one to five college students. Only a third of the viewers caught the change. And it wasn't that they were not paying attention—they could describe what had happened and infer why it had happened, they describe many of the objects in the room, and they could explain the path the actor had walked. What was going on here?

Was this some sort of special-purpose temporary amnesia that is specific to movies? Maybe it's a special insensitivity that you have to acquire to be able to handle cuts in film. By now you know that is probably not the right answer, but the Dans conducted another series of experiments to try to answer this question empirically. Here is my favorite: You are an undergraduate student at Harvard University, and you are recruited in the lobby of the psychology department for a quick experiment. It will just take a couple minutes, and you will get a candy bar for your time. You take the elevator to the eighth floor, and an assistant directs you to a counter. There, the experimenter greets you and gives you a consent form to read and sign. This is standard practice for participating in experiments on college campuses. The form tells you what the experiment will be about so that you can decide whether it is something you want to do. In this case, the form explains that you will experience a brief event and then be asked about it. You sign the form and return it. The experimenter ducks behind the counter, saying, "Let me just get you these forms." A *different* experimenter pops up with the forms. The forms ask you to describe everything you saw since you exited the elevator, and to mention whether you noticed anything funny. Of the 20 students who participated, only 5 indicated that they noticed the switch. So, 75% of the time, the students walked up, talked briefly with someone, and then continued their conversation with a completely different person without noticing the difference.[2] This tells us something important: Continuity errors are so easy to miss not because of something weird about cuts, but because insensitivity to these sorts of changes appears to be a general feature of our visual experience.

If cuts aren't weird, maybe they mimic visual disruptions that occur during real life. In the disappearing-experimenter study, there is definitely a disruption though there is no cut. Is that what does it? Probably not. Daniel Simons and Steve Franconeri showed that people can be blind to changes without there being any visual disruption at all. They just made the changes happen very slowly, and ensured that all the intermediate states looked reasonable. For example, you could be looking at a landscape picture with a field of grass that slowly changes from green to brown. If it happens slowly you have a good chance of missing it even though it's happening right in front of your eyes.[3]

Research in perceptual psychology has been characterizing these lapses since the early 1990s. The name for the phenomenon is *change blindness,* and it is absolutely ubiquitous. But there is a big disconnect between how we *feel* we are performing when we look at these sorts of changes and how we are actually doing. You can see the Levin and Simons video online (dansimons.com/videos.html). Now that you've been let in on the secret, take a look at the video and see how many more changes you can detect. When you look at the answers, chances are you'll be surprised by your poor performance. You can also try a version of the "mud-splashes" task that I described in Chapter 7 (www2.psych. ubc.ca/~rensink/flicker/download). The screen switches between just two versions of a picture, with a cut or a mud-splash to mask the change between versions, but you'll likely be shocked by how difficult it is.

Don't worry—this mismatch between feeling that you're doing okay and actually performing pitifully isn't just you. Dan Levin has studied it in the lab. He asked large numbers of people how they thought they would do on the continu-ity task. No matter how carefully he described the task, people radically overestimated their performance. We appear not only to be blind to lots of visual changes, but we also are blind to the fact that we are so blind. Appropriately, Dan dubbed the overconfidence *change blindness blindness*.[4]

So, why are big visual changes surprisingly difficult to detect? I think it is because we *believe* that we are relying on one brain system to detect changes, but we are *actually* relying on a completely different system. It *feels* like we are using the visual persistence system that I described back in Chapter 6, but we are *actually* using our event models. Remember visual persistence? It is the firing of the early parts of your visual system once a stimulus is removed. Visual persistence gives us a high-fidelity representation of the visual field. When we think about what it feels like to look at a scene, we are probably thinking about the repre-sentations that visual persistence provides. But visual per-sistence hangs on for only a fraction of a second, and it is completely wiped out when new objects overlap where the old objects used to be.

We *can* use the early parts of our visual system to detect changes when they are not camouflaged by the big visual disruption that a cut provides. If the woman's scarf were to suddenly appear or disappear in the middle of a shot, you would probably notice. But when it changes across a cut, all the other things happening at the same time effectively mask the change. Visual persistence is too fragile to save the day.

I think the representations we *do* use to detect changes across cuts are the event models we build of the situation. Event models, as I described in Chapter 2, persist for long enough to detect changes—for many seconds, often. And they represent the sorts of things that might change: objects, people, actions, and so forth. But models are very much incomplete and schematic representations of the world. Let's talk for a moment about how models are constructed. You start with early sensory representations that are very rich but very fragile. The attentional bottleneck filters the sensory signals down to a more manageable subset. The chunking system abstracts the filtered signals into coherent objects and events, leaving lots out as it does so. The models that result are made up of these chunks. So, models can capture only a small fraction of the information that was available in the signal, and that information is stretched and remolded by the chunking process.[5]

If a continuity error introduces a discrepancy between the model of the situation before the cut and the model of the situation after the cut, you have a better chance of detecting it. But so much information never makes it into the model in the first place! Here is where our intuitions depart from what our brains can actually do. We experience the rich representations of visual persistence, so we think we have access to them later when we go to remember. But what we actually have access to is a sketchy, incomplete model.

The sorts of continuity errors that people *do* detect tell us a lot about how this works. Say an actress playing a bit part is wearing a police uniform in the first shot, and this causes you to represent her as a cop in your model. The filmmakers can introduce continuity failures that change the style of the uniform, the buttons and medals and such, without being very noticeable. But if the uniform changes from a police uniform to a firefighter uniform, this will be more likely to set off an alert. If there is a barber pole in the shot and it changes size or color across a cut, that probably won't be noticeable; but if it changes to a copy shop sign, that could be a problem. These sorts of continuity gaps change the *gist* of the scene—what it is all about. This provides a lot of potential cues for you to detect the continuity error. For this reason, filmmakers are unlikely to make such errors and are likely to catch them before the film hits the theater.

Even for continuity errors that don't change the gist of the scene, viewers are usually by no means completely blind. In the experimenter-switch study, sure, 75% of the students missed it, but 25% caught it. What determines which switches you catch and which you miss?

The answer, I think, is that we detect changes in those features of the situation that have been incorporated into our model. Directors occasionally use continuity errors to produce deliberate effects in their viewers—disorientation or disintegration. One great example appears in *The Eternal Sunshine of the Spotless Mind,* directed by Michel Gondry. (I mentioned this one in Chapter 7.) The movie's premise is that a technology has been developed to edit memories to get rid of the embarrassing or painful bits we would rather forget. We see Joel Barish (Jim Carrey) lying on his pullout couch, undergoing memory erasure of a painful relationship with Clementine Kruczynski (Kate Winslet). We witness his inner world deconstructed as the "therapy" progresses. In one sequence, Joel and Clementine are walking up and down a street, arguing, as the memory is being edited out from under them. Gondry used a lamppost to

FIGURE 9.2 Frames from Michel Gondry's *Eternal Sunshine of the Spotless Mind*, with large, deliberate violations of continuity. The two frames are separated by about 8 seconds. Note the changes to the storefronts, the placement of the mailbox and car, and the signs on the lamppost. The figure in the left of the first frame is Clementine; the figure in the center of the second frame is Joel.

hide a series of cuts, and during each cut changed the background scenery, moved Joel's car, and moved Clementine (see Figure 9.2). These continuity errors are meant to introduce conflicts between what is in your mental model and what is on the screen, and Gondry wants them to jump out at you, contributing to the feeling that Joel's mental life is being dismantled. I certainly noticed them with higher frequency than I usually detect continuity errors, but even with these flagrant disruptions I didn't catch the majority until I stepped through the sequence frame by frame.[6]

We are not generally aware of event model updating, but our brains devote substantial computation to getting it done. Model updating is an incremental process. We saw in Chapter 2 that psychologists and neuroscientists can measure the processes of model updating by looking at behavior and brain activity while people experience events. In the previous chapter I explained that my lab has collected data suggesting that the mass of model updating happens at *event boundaries*—when one meaningful event ends and another begins.

Can we see the consequences of that updating in memory performance and in the brain? This is a question that was asked by Khena Swallow, who at the time was an exceptional graduate student completing her PhD with me at Washington University.[7] Khena wanted to know whether, when we experience a boundary between events, we update our visual memories and thus lose access to some of the information we had loaded up. First, she had to find movies that didn't have too much dialogue, that had lots of objects coming and going so we could test visual memory, and that would not be too familiar to our undergraduate participants. It took the better part of a year scouring the cinema of the world and pilot testing, but she came up with a terrific set. The films that made the cut: *Mr. Mom* and *One Hour Photo* (USA), *3 Iron* (Korea), and *Mon Oncle* (France). She then asked a lot of people to watch the movies and tell us where the boundaries between events were, using the method I described in Chapter 7: pushing a button to mark each time one ended and another began. This allowed her to classify objects based on whether there was an event boundary within 5 seconds of when the object went off-screen. Then she was ready to run her studies. She showed people the clips, and from time to time stopped and probed their memory. The test sounds simple: You see two objects, one of which was just on the screen 5 seconds ago, and you pick which one is correct. On some trials, the movie is paused just after an event boundary, so you have to reach back to the previous event to access the object. On other trials, the movie is paused in the middle of an event so that 5 seconds ago is still part of the current event. The results were dramatic: Accessing an object from the previous event—even though it was only 5 seconds ago—was much more difficult than accessing an object from the current event. For certain kinds of objects you *can* do it; but for others it's basically impossible.

Khena then repeated the experiment with participants in the fMRI scanner. As you'd expect, trying to decide which object was from the movie brought on a lot of brain changes—visual areas, which were probably involved in examining the visual features of the candidate objects; motor areas associated with making the response; and lots of others. But a few regions were working harder when our participants had to reach back to the previous event to recognize an object. Most prominent of these was the hippocampus, a structure in the temporal lobes on the bottom of the cortex.

The hippocampus has a storied history in cognitive neuroscience. (*Hippocampus* is Latin for "seahorse"; the structure got its name because of its shape.) You may recall my description of *place cells* in the hippocampus in Chapter 8. Those cells implement long-term memory maps of our spatial environment. The hippocampus is important for lots of other kinds of long-term memory. It was brought to prominence due to the patient known as H.M., a young man who in 1953 was suffering from violent seizures originating in his hippocampi. His neurosurgeon, William Scoville, proposed a surgery to remove the brain tissue that was causing the seizures. This treatment is invasive, but effective, and for some patients it's the best option available. This is still true today. But back in 1953 very few if any patients had undergone removal of their hippocampus on *both* sides. After H.M. underwent surgery, his seizures were effectively controlled—but at a grave price. He lost the ability to form new memories. His condition, called *anterograde amnesia*, is the one dramatized in the Christopher Nolan film *Memento*. Since H.M.'s surgery, we have learned that removal of the hippocampus consistently produces this effect, and that if both hemispheres are involved, the impairments are dramatic.[8]

Khena found that the hippocampus was selectively engaged when people had to retrieve object information across an event boundary. More specifically, we found this activity just for those objects that the behavioral results showed people could successfully recognize. Here's what we think this means: We think that for as long as an object was involved in the current event, people actively maintained it in cortical brain regions and could access some of its visual properties from those representations. But once a new event had begun, those properties were less likely to be actively maintained. When people *could* recover them, they did so by tapping into the hippocampus.

These studies, and others, show that a lot of memory updating happens at event boundaries. But probably some updating happens in the middle of events, too. Here is a metaphor I find helpful: Imagine yourself watching a movie—let's say it is a Western. As you watch the outlaws ride across the plain, think of your brain building a model of the movie situation out of Legos. The Lego model does not include parts corresponding to every single cactus and sagebrush on the screen; it is selective. The horses and riders are schematized—squared off by the nature of the blocks from which they are constructed. That's your model of the situation. When the outlaws come to the settlers' camp, that is an event boundary. Your brain knocks the model over, starting mostly from scratch, building up a set of sod huts and farm tools, and rebuilding the horses and riders. So a lot of the change in the model happens at this point. But in between the event boundaries, your brain may update features of the model as things change. If a dog runs out of the house, your brain probably adds a dog to the model. Now, suppose there is a cut and the dog changes from a spaniel to a retriever. If your brain has not gotten around to adding details about the dog to your model, you will probably not be able to detect the change.

Adding things to a model or updating them takes work. For visual information, adding a feature to a model usually requires that you fix your attention on it. Remember from Chapter 8 that your eyes are constantly flitting from object to object, landing for durations of about a quarter of a second on average. And remember that fixing your eyes on an object has two important effects: The objects receive more attention and so are more likely to make it through the bottleneck; and by bringing an object into your fovea you are able to get more information from it, because your fovea is more sensitive. These two effects enable you to add features of the object to your model—identity, size, shape, direction it is facing, and so forth.

How can we know whether someone has added a visual feature to their model? How can we determine whether this actually makes a difference in catching continuity errors? It turns out you can watch this process unfold as it happens—if you have the right equipment and a really sharp programmer. Both can be found at Andrew Hollingworth's laboratory at the University of Iowa.

Let me describe what they do, using one experiment as an example: You sit down in the lab in front of a computer with a precision digital camera pointed at your eye. The camera takes fast, high-resolution pictures of your eye as it jumps around the screen—images so good that the computer can measure exactly where you are looking 1,000 times a second. What you are looking at is a picture of an everyday scene—say, a kitchen. The computer watches where you look and waits until your eyes land on the toaster. It keeps waiting until you look away from the toaster. Then, the next time you move your eyes, the computer *switches* the toaster to a blender while your eyes are still moving. This is a really fancy programming trick: The computer has to keep track of where you are looking, figure out when you start to move your eyes, and then quickly change the screen before your eyes stop moving.

In this situation, people can detect about half of the switches. This is by no means perfect, but not bad. (Importantly, in these studies people know there are changes coming and are trying to detect them.) Performance holds up quite well even when the computer waits through several glances before making the switch. What if the switch happens *before* you fix your eyes on the toaster? You can't detect it at all. How much information about the object did Hollingworth's viewers incorporate into their model? Their models must have contained information about more than just the fact that it was a toaster, because they could tell whether the toaster was switched not to a blender but to a different toaster. They even could tell whether the toaster was rotated instead of switched. Rotations are harder to detect, but still well above chance performance. It makes sense that some changes are harder than others to catch. Your model of a situation is most likely to contain information that identifies the toaster as a toaster, and somewhat less likely to contain information about exactly what sort of toaster it is or which way it is facing.[9]

We also know a bit about what is happening in the brain when people try to detect continuity errors. There have been several experiments in which viewers tried to detect changes in simple scenes while brain activity was recorded with functional MRI. The experimenters compared brain activity when there was a switch across cuts—a continuity error—to when there was no switch. What to me is most interesting and consistent across these studies is which brain areas *don't* show a difference: early or middle stages in the visual processing stream. Instead, what you see is differences in the late stages of the visual streams, and in parts of the parietal and frontal cortex involved in all sorts of tasks that require attention and reasoning. In one study, researchers briefly disrupted activity in the right parietal lobe and found that this led people to miss more changes. If it's really the later stages of processing that are causally responsible for our ability to detect visual changes, this helps explain why we sometimes miss the switched scarf— or even the switched experimenter—but other times catch the turned toaster. We are not using our early visual system to detect the changes, but our event models.[10]

I think this relates directly to how the brain processes cuts, which I described in the last chapter. Remember the study that Joe Magliano and I ran using fMRI to look at the processing of cuts? In that study, cuts within a scene produced large increases throughout visual cortex, but at major scene breaks the areas involved in higher level visual processing showed *less* of this increase. One possibility is that within a scene, cuts provide few cues to potential mismatches in our event models. So when our visual system encounters a big visual discontinuity, it treats it like a blink or a saccade and bridges its representations from before and after the cut. This is physiologically demanding because the discontinuity introduces a lot of new visual information to be processed. At a major scene break, other parts of brain suppress some of this bridging because in those cases bridging would be counterproductive.

I have emphasized here how sketchy and schematic our models are. But I don't want to give the impression that these representations are inadequate or weak. On the contrary, these are the same representations that do all the wonderful things for comprehension that we have considered in the previous chapters. And they can do some pretty amazing things for memory. In Andrew Hollingworth's experiments, once viewers fixed their eyes on an object, they were pretty good at recognizing changes to the object even when they were tested at the end of the study rather than immediately.

But the best example comes from an amazing experiment published by Lionel Standing in 1973.[11] Standing showed college students the world's longest and most boring slide show: 10,000 snapshots, presented at a rate of one every 5 seconds. They watched the slides for about 3 hours a day for 5 days, and then came back for a test a couple days later. After all those pictures students could still differentiate between a picture they had seen and one they hadn't seen 83% of the time. How were they able to do it? Imagine being a participant in the experiment. Suppose you see a picture of a dock on a pine-rimmed lake, with swimming rafts offshore and fog rising from the water. Think of how many features there are in that snapshot that you *might* store in your model—the colors and shapes of the dock and rafts and trees, the location of the rafts relative to the dock and the shore, the transparency of the fog, the angle of the light…Even if you store only a fraction of those features, and even if only a fraction of *that* fraction make it into your long-term memory, you probably stored dozens of features of objects and their locations. Now, you get to the end of the experiment and the experimenter shows you two new pictures—say, the lake scene and a new picture of the inside of a schoolroom. For the lake scene, you match up some of those stored bits of your model. For the schoolroom, chances are that fewer features will match features from models in your memory from the sessions. You may have some false matches from similar pictures, especially if you happened to study a snapshot of something visually similar to a schoolroom, like an office, but often there will be more true matches than false matches. That is usually enough to give you confidence that you saw the lake and not the schoolroom.

So, one reason we may miss changes is that we can discriminate well among many previous events without storing a lot about each one. Another reason may be that we adopt a strategy of assuming of just going with what we see now unless we have some reason to consult our memories. This makes good sense—most of the time the world doesn't change out from under us.[12] I think these two ideas are different sides of the same coin: Our brains adapted to hold onto enough information to allow us to discriminate between different previous experiences and to guide our future behavior, but there's no reason to build a brain to detect continuity errors because they rarely happen in the real world.

All of this has major implications for film editing. It says, "Don't sweat it." You can make major continuity gaffes, and most of the time your audience won't catch them. Actually, film editors and directors know this. Despite all the work that goes into managing continuity, they often choose shots with errors rather than select an alternate take that is "clean" or reshoot the scene altogether. Expert filmmakers know that they can sacrifice continuity to the higher goals of the storytelling. Here is the film editor Walter Murch: "If you are considering a range of possible edits for a particular moment in the film, and you find that there is one cut that gives the right emotion *and* moves the story forward, *and* is rhythmically satisfying, *and* respects eye-trace and planarity, *but* it fails to preserve the continuity of three-dimensional space, then, by all means, that is the cut you should make."[13]

But still some filmmakers *do* sweat it. Why? One reason is craftsmanship. It's like a woodworker who makes perfect mortise and tenon joints for the back of a drawer. Nobody except another woodworker would ever look at those joints, but doing it right is a point of pride. I think there is another reason that filmmakers are obsessive about continuity: Even small numbers add up over lots and lots of viewers. Suppose I were the script supervisor on *The King's Speech*. After a day of filming the death of King George V, director Tom Hooper is watching the dailies. He isn't quite happy with one sequence, in which the archbishop of Canterbury (played by Derek Jacobi) is performing last rites. The next day we go back to redo a few shots. The take comes off perfectly—but that evening we realize that the archbishop was wearing a cross that is different from the day before. What to do? Certainly fewer than half of viewers will notice it, probably many fewer. Say it's 1 in a 100. Not a big deal, right? Well, as of May 2011, about 53 million people had seen the film. So, about 5 million would have noticed and might have found it distracting.[14]

Or consider James Cameron's *Titanic*. Continuity buffs have found more than 250 continuity errors in this film. Again, let's suppose each viewer catches only 1 in 100 of these. By the end of the film, you would have been left scratching your head more than three times on average. (Did you see *Titanic*? Do you remember being bugged by any of these?)[15]

Either way you count, these little errors add up. And if script supervisors did not work so hard to try to prevent them, there would be vastly many more. My bet is that on a complex commercial film, going cheap on preventing continuity errors would wind up diminishing viewers' experience. I do not mean to minimize how blind we are to continuity errors, but even our dim vision is enough to make tracking these errors worthwhile.

Dan Levin suggests the body of science has one last implication for filmmakers: "Be aware that your intuitions about which properties will be visible to an audience are often incorrect." The scientific results "invite filmmakers to be a little more empirical. It may be that there are a lot of things you can do to a sequence that you would think people would be aware of that they might not be aware of." Some of these things may affect the tone of the movie and the viewer's emotional response but not register in awareness. Trying things out, running little experiments on yourself and your friends, may be a valuable way to get control over your film's effect.

What about implications for audiences? Do we need to keep up with the latest science to follow a movie? Of course not. "If you just want to enjoy film, you don't have to read a book. But if you *really* want to enjoy it, being aware of how perceptual experiences are generated may give a richer experience—and may cause you to enjoy a wider range of films."[16]

10 ■

Virtual Futures

When the ads for Mars vacations came on the TV, Doug Quaid couldn't turn away. He thought about Mars at work, dreamed about it at night, badgered his wife about going there. She reminded him that they couldn't afford it—and anyway, Saturn is much nicer. But he could not get Mars out of his head. So after work at the construction site, he went to visit Rekall, Incorporated. Salesman Bob McClane described their memory implant services:

Bob: When you go Rekall, you get nothing but first class memories. Private cabin on the shuttle, deluxe suite at the Hilton, plus all the major sites: Mount Pyramid, the Grand Canal, and of course, Venusville.

Doug: But how real does it seem?

Bob: As real as any memory in your head.

Doug: Come on, don't bullshit me.

Bob: No, I'm telling you, Doug, your brain will not know the difference—and that's guaranteed, or your money back.

Doug was sold. Within a few minutes, he was being sedated and slid into a large circular machine to have his artificial memories inserted directly into his brain. But something went wrong, and the next thing he knew he was on the run from a gang of men with big guns. His wife revealed that she was an enemy agent and tried to kill him herself; he discovered he was being tracked by a bug in his head; and he learned that he had a whole life that had been taken from him by artificial memory manipulation. He threw on a disguise and headed to Mars to get some answers.

The film is Paul Verhoeven's 1990 *Total Recall*, with Arnold Schwarzenegger as Douglas Quaid. The theme is one that has come up repeatedly in the movies of the last few decades: directly manipulating memory using hypothetical future neuroscience techniques. In *Eternal Sunshine of the Spotless Mind* (2004), Jim Carrey as Joel Barish is interested in obliviating a memory rather than creating one; the outfit he visits is called Lacuna Corporation. In an ad that was created as part of a website for the fictional company, they promise to sort him out:

> Remember the Alamo. Remember the Sabbath day, and keep it holy. But why remember a destructive love affair? Here at Lacuna, we have perfected a safe, effective technique for the focused erasure of troubling memories. Our patented nonsurgical procedure will rid you of painful memories and allow you a new and lasting peace of mind you never imagined possible. Don't forget: with Lacuna, you can forget.

Joel and his once-lover Clementine Kruczynski (Kate Winslett) chase each other through cycles of memory erasure and rediscovery with the aid of the not-quite-trustworthy staff of Lacuna. Once they start messing with their memories, though (and this is true in *Total Recall* as well), it becomes quite difficult to sort out fact from fiction, real from virtual. Every experience is questioned.

And because our memory for our lives is so tied up with who we think we are, it also becomes a challenge to sort out who is in charge. In *Total Recall*, Quaid is addressed by video images recorded by his previous self, a bad guy called Hauser. In the last message, just before he is due to have his Quaid memories erased and Hauser's memories restored, Hauser tells him, "I would like to wish you happiness and long life, old buddy, but unfortunately this is not going to happen. You see, that's *my* body you've got there, and I want it back."

In *The Matrix* (1999), Keanu Reaves as Neo discovers that his entire conscious experience has been artificially created by direct stimulation of his nervous system. In the world of *The Matrix*, humans are plugged into a giant computer system with direct brain connections at birth and spend their entire lives suspended in liquids in huge racks of pods, living virtual lives inside their brains. Neo is freed by the mysterious Morpheus and his small band of rebels. His training with the rebels is done mostly by direct download using the interface cable in the back of his neck. In one oft-cited scene, Neo lies on a gurney in the rebels' ship, plugged into the training computer, with his eyes closed but twitching and his neck and arms jerking slightly. Then he quiets, opens his eyes, turns to Morpheus, and says "I know kung fu."

Another movie from 1999, David Cronenberg's *eXistenZ*, emphasizes the invasive physicality of wiring directly to an alternate reality. Characters jack in using "bioports" in their lower backs using plugs that bear more than a passing resemblance to sex toys. Like *The Matrix*, *eXistenZ* plays up how immersing one's self in an alternate reality risks decoupling from the reality we're used to.

Christopher Nolan's *Inception* (2010) imagines a technology that allows people to sneak into others' dreams by wiring their heads together. This device is inspired by research on lucid dreaming, which is a kind of training designed to teach people how to hold on to information about their dreams in their waking life and use their waking intentions to guide what happens in the dream.[1] In a succession of offices, safehouses, and bombed-out-looking warehouses, Cobb (Leonardo DiCaprio) and his team strap electrical leads to their scalps, close their eyes, and go to work implanting memories, ideas, or dispositions by making suggestions in others' dreams. Cobb is employed by industrial conglomerates to implant a suggestion in a rival CEO. The big job is just a subtle change of direction, but one that will affect billions of dollars of business.[2]

One thing I find fascinating about these films is how fast the future ages. In the midst of a vision of what might come to be, obsolete technologies stick out like sore thumbs. In *Total Recall*, Mars has been colonized and scientists can directly program memories, but video images are shown on cathode ray tubes; and when Quaid emerges from the subway, he walks under a huge billboard for Fuji film. (Remember film? Plastic strips coated with chemicals for making pictures?)

In both *Total Recall* and *Eternal Sunshine of the Spotless Mind*, memory manipulation is done with devices that look suspiciously like PET (positron emission tomography) scanners. PET is an imaging technique that is used widely in medicine and with some frequency in research. PET requires injecting or inhaling radioactive tracers, so it will probably be replaced with less invasive imaging technologies eventually, and when that happens, I suspect those movies will look more and more dated. (In *The Matrix* and *Inception*, the neural interface looks more like tubes or cables that plug directly into the subject.) But there is an important difference between the approach taken by Michel Gondry in *Eternal Sunshine of the Spotless Mind* and the approaches of the other films. Whereas the rest are set in a hypothetical future, *Eternal Sunshine* is set in a version of the present (as of 2004) that has been tweaked. It is the difference between science fiction and fantasy. I suspect that as a result, it will age better.

Rekall, Inc., Lacuna Corp., Neo's training, and Cobb's illicit activities all suggest something important about the possibilities for direct-download movies: They could be used for a lot more than entertainment. Doug's adventure in *Total Recall* starts out as a vacation, but it turns out the memory implant is a way to program a secret agent who doesn't know he is one. (The agent-against-his-will theme was borrowed from *The Manchurian Candidate*, but in that movie the implant technology was hypnosis rather than neural stimulation.) In the future, will we be downloading experiences to teach ourselves martial arts, cure our depression, or implement a business strategy? The technologies that these movies envision are pretty unrealistic (and so is hypnosis for this purpose). But in this chapter I'll explore some techniques that are a little closer to being ready for prime time.

First, let's consider one more plot. Men and women in lab coats surround an operating table. Their faces are hidden by surgical masks and hats. The table is completely covered by sterile sheets, except for a rectangle, about 6 by 4 inches, through which pulsing brain tissue can be seen. One of the people in lab coats, a man, lifts a thin probe, leans in, and touches it to the exposed living brain. From beneath the sheet comes a voice: "I can see the most wonderful lights." A little later, "Did you pour cold water on my hand?" Then, "I can smell burnt toast."[3]

Another science fiction film? No, this is real. And it's not even the latest thing—not by a long shot. I just described a brain surgery conducted in 1934 to treat a patient with a severe seizure disorder. The surgeon was Wilder Penfield, who became famous for his use of electrical stimulation during brain surgery. Penfield studied as an undergraduate at Princeton, and then traveled to Oxford on a Rhodes Scholarship where he studied physiology with Sir Charles Sherrington. Sherrington had been awarded the Nobel Prize for his work using electrical stimulation to study the brains of dogs and other nonhuman animals. Sherrington had found that by applying gentle electrical currents to parts of a dog's brain, he could cause the animal to execute simple movements, to sniff as if scenting something, to cock its ears. As Penfield completed his training in medicine and surgery, he wondered whether this technique could be applied during brain surgery to better home in on damaged tissue and to avoid healthy tissue that was important for, say, speaking or moving. In 1934, Penfield was appointed the founding director of the new Montreal Neurological Institute, and he had a chance to put his ideas into action.

One of the strange and fortunate things about the brain is that it has no sensory neurons, so touching the brain or stimulating it with electrical current does not itself produce any discomfort. Penfield and his surgical team were able to apply local anesthetic to the scalp, cut through to expose the brain, and probe its surface while the patient was awake. Sherrington's stimulation studies with dogs had been informative, but a dog cannot tell you much about what it is experiencing. People can. Here is Penfield's description of one surgery:

> M.M., a young woman of twenty-six, had minor attacks that began with a sense of familiarity followed by a sense of fear and then by "a little dream" of some previous experience. When the right hemisphere was exposed at operation, I explored the cerebral cortex with an electrode, placing numbered squares of paper on the surface of the brain to show the position each time a positive response was obtained. At point 2 she felt a tingling in the left thumb; at point 3, tingling in the left

side of the tongue; at 7 there was movement of the tongue. It was clear then that 3 had been placed on the primary somatosensory cortex and 7 on the primary motor cortex.[4]

Penfield's photograph of M.M.'s exposed brain, with paper tags, is shown here in Figure 10.1.You can see that tags 3 and 7 are on opposite sides of a sulcus (fissure). This is the central sulcus, which we discussed in Chapter 1, with the somatosensory cortex on one side and the motor cortex on the other. In other patients who have lesions in other parts of the brain, Penfield stimulated the primary visual cortex, and the patients told him they saw flashes of light. Stimulating the

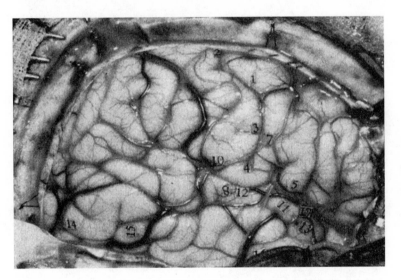

FIGURE 10.1 Photograph taken during M.M.'s brain surgery. The paper tags were placed to mark locations where the surgeon stimulated. The right side of the brain is exposed; the front of the head is toward the right, and the back of the head to the left. The central sulcus runs right between tags 2, 3, and 4 and tags 1 and 7; the somatosensory cortex is on the posterior bank (left), and the motor cortex is on the anterior bank (right).

Penfield, W. (1975). *The mystery of the mind: A critical study of consciousness and the human brain.* Princeton, NJ: Princeton University Press, pp. 22–26.

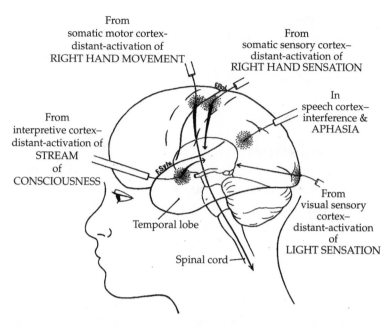

From
somatic motor cortex-
distant-activation of
RIGHT HAND MOVEMENT

From
somatic sensory cortex–
distant-activation of
RIGHT HAND SENSATION

In
speech cortex–
interference &
APHASIA

From
interpretive cortex–
distant-activation of
STREAM
of
CONSCIOUSNESS

From
visual sensory
cortex–
distant-activation
of
LIGHT SENSATION

Temporal lobe

Spinal cord

FIGURE 10.2 Penfield's depiction of the effects of brain stimulation during surgery.

Penfield, W. (1975). *The mystery of the mind: A critical study of consciousness and the human brain.* Princeton, NJ: Princeton University Press, pp. 22–26.

primary auditory cortex produced impressions of sound. These findings are summarized in Figure 10.2.

What about stimulating outside the primary sensory and motor areas? Here is Penfield's description of what this did to M.M.:

> Stimulating at tag 11: "I heard something, I do not know what it was."
>
> Repeating stimulation at this site without warning: "Yes, Sir, I think I heard a mother calling her little boy somewhere. It seemed to be something that happened years ago." When asked to explain, she said, "It was somebody in the neighborhood where I live." Then

she added that she herself "was somewhere close enough to hear."

Stimulating at tag 12: "Yes. I heard voices down along the river somewhere—a man's voice and a woman's voice calling....I think I saw the river."

Stimulating at tag 15: "Just a tiny flash of a feeling of familiarity and a feeling that I knew everything that was going to happen in the near future."

Stimulating at tag 17c using a depth electrode to stimulate within the sulcus: "Oh! I had the same very, very familiar memory, in an office somewhere. I could see the desks. I was there and someone was calling to me, a man leaning on a desk with a pencil in his hand."

A clever control: I warned her I was going to stimulate, but I did not do so, "Nothing."

Stimulating at tag 18a: "I had a little memory—a scene in a play—they were talking and I could see it—I was just seeing it in my memory."[5]

The technique Penfield and his colleagues developed proved enormously valuable for improving the safety and efficacy of brain surgery. These methods are now standard procedure in neurosurgery units around the world. Over decades, Penfield and his colleagues were able to establish that the evoked visual responses in primary sensory and motor areas, and in parts of the brain controlling speech, are predictable and replicable. Creating experience by directly stimulating the brain is by no means science fiction; it is an everyday part of medical practice.

But it has limits. The sensory and motor experiences that we can evoke by stimulation are crude at best. Touch sensation—the feeling of being touched on, say, the left hand, or the right leg—is probably where the highest fidelity responses can be obtained. In the visual system, we can reliably evoke flashing lights and if we are lucky we can control roughly where in the visual field they appear, but we certainly cannot reliably create particular shapes or colors. Stimulating the auditory cortex will cause the patient to hear *something*, but we cannot predict much about *what* they will hear; the situation is similar for olfaction.

And of course, there is the obvious practical limitation: You have to have your skull cut open to try it out. This reminds me of an old riff from the comedian George Carlin: "Did you ever have a hatchet go right through your face? You know, I'm talking about a good shot. Isn't it strange? It's the funniest feeling because just after the hatchet goes in, before you feel any pain, you feel this blast of cool air on the middle of your brain. I love that, it feels so good, but you know, that's the only way I can attain it so I try not to get too hung up on it."[6] A deal-breaker, huh? Well, yes and no. I doubt anyone will be showing up for elective brain surgery as entertainment, but it turns out that there are new tools that enable neuroscientists to stimulate the brain in ways that are relatively safe, noninvasive, and with little lasting consequence. These methods may make it possible to take some of Penfield's techniques out of the operating room.

Here is one option: The business end of the machine looks like an infinity symbol, a figure eight encased in white plastic. The device is called a *transcranial magnetic stimulator*, and it is one of the more dramatic tools in the neuroscientist's toolkit. Transcranial magnetic stimulation (TMS) uses magnetic fields to stimulate small bits of brain—in healthy people, without any surgery, and, in most cases, with minimal aftereffects.

The TMS stimulator is an electromagnet, specially designed to produce a tightly focused magnetic field that can be rapidly switched on and off. This switching rapidly induces an electric current, oriented crosswise to the magnetic field. Magnetic fields are relatively unaffected by skin, bone, blood, and brain. So, if we hold the coil next to your head, the focus of the magnetic field, and thus the induced current, will be inside your brain. That electric current changes the membranes of neurons in the current's vicinity and will cause many of them to fire. Hence the device's name: *transcranial*, because it goes right through the skull; *magnetic*, because it works by manipulating a magnetic field; and *stimulation*, because the result is to stimulate neurons to fire.

Let's be very clear about what TMS can and cannot do. The unique features of TMS are that it can alter the workings of a pretty small piece of brain, do so very quickly (in a few hundredths of a second), and just as quickly shut off the effect. However, compared to stimulating with a small electrode, TMS is a pretty blunt instrument. A TMS pulse affects a small patch of brain under the magnetic coil—but a small patch of brain is still millions of neurons. It cannot cause any particular neuron or group of neurons in that volume to fire. And the firing induced by the TMS pulse is quite different from normal neural activity. During normal neural activity, only a modest subset of the neurons in a brain region is firing at any given time. Which neurons fire, and when, is determined by an exquisite coupling within and across brain regions. Within a region, different types of neurons excite and inhibit their neighbors. Across regions, groups of neurons provide feedback signals and timing coordination. Think of a big newspaper building with huge numbers of reporters, editors, and production specialists talking to their nearby neighbors and communicating with others by phone and email. When a TMS pulse comes in, it is like ringing everyone's phone at the same time. Ongoing activity is interrupted, and a large pool of neurons all fire at once. Thus, the result of a TMS pulse is a transient disruption of processing in a patch of tissue. Neuroscientists often think of TMS as working like a quick instantaneous brain lesion that we can turn on and off.

Is this safe? Quite. Dosed out as one or a few pulses at a time, TMS has been shown to have virtually no long-term consequences for brain function. The main drawback is that, depending on where the targeted area is located, some current may be induced in the scalp as well as in the brain. You can't feel current in the brain, but current in the scalp can cause muscles to twitch and can stimulate pain receptors in the skin, producing a pinching or pricking sensation.[7] I find it to be no big deal, as do most people who try it.

The effects we can produce with TMS are similar to those that Penfield discovered with his electrodes applied directly to the brain. It will not create a detailed shape or a particular sound, but it could still do some things that might be pretty entertaining. Imagine you are watching a car chase. The Mustang's brakes are out, and the car is headed for a cliff. As the car swerves, we zap the part of your brain responsible for your sense of balance and you feel for a moment as though your body is turning suddenly. At the last instant the hero dives out of the car and hits the ground. We zap the part of your brain responsible for body sensation and you feel a touch as the protagonist makes contact. The car hurtles over the edge and crashes into the canyon. We zap your auditory cortex, and the sound of the crash is augmented by sound signals generated inside your head. The camera zooms in as the car bursts into flame, the inferno filling the screen. At the same time, we zap your visual cortex and the bright image combines with even brighter flashes all over your visual field.

As should be pretty clear from this description, TMS is not going to give us *Total Recall*. But it can do some things that might be pretty entertaining. Sound like fun? I hereby coin a term for this entertainment medium of the future: *Magnovision*.

Is Magnovision really practical? Not just yet, but I think it's quite likely that some kind of electromagnetic brain stimulation for entertainment will become practical in the not-too-distant future. There are some safety concerns and logistical issues that will need to be resolved before this kind of brain stimulation could become available for entertainment. First is safety. Although single-pulse TMS in the lab is quite safe, it would need to be combined with careful monitoring to be safe in an entertainment setting.

The closest analogy may be the defibrillator machines used to restart a heart after cardiac arrest. Defibrillators can save a life, but because they rely on massive shocks to restart the heart, improper use can be deadly. Just a few years ago, defibrillators were deployed almost exclusively in hospitals and ambulances, where they could be operated only by trained professionals. The problem was that after a heart attack, every second is precious, and people could lose their lives waiting for a trained professional. So engineers and physicians developed sensors and programs to allow the machines to assess the patient's condition, adjust its parameters appropriately, and monitor the consequences of the shock. You have probably seen the defibrillator machines that now hang on the wall in lots of malls, universities, and office buildings. In an emergency, anyone can pull one of these things down and have a good shot at saving someone's life. The safety monitoring required for TMS is quite a bit simpler, and the risks are smaller, so I can easily imagine a smarter TMS machine that could calibrate its pulses based on monitoring your brain and shut itself down if anything looked risky.

The logistics may prove a bigger challenge. First, for Magnovision, the precise spatial location of the magnet relative to your brain matters. So, in order to join the Magnovision audience, you will need either a comfortable headrest so that you can hold perfectly still through the movie, or a system that can move with your head to keep the magnetic field focused. Popcorn may be tricky. Second, TMS depends on strong magnets, which interfere with cell phones, credit cards, and each other. It may be hard to sit people close together and administer TMS; maybe you will need to check your gadgets and cards outside and be seated alone in a shielded booth. So Magnovision may take us back to the mode of the nickelodeon. The last challenge is perhaps the trickiest. Each of us has a head and a brain that is unique in size and shape. For TMS experiments now, participants usually undergo an MRI before the session to measure their head and brain. The MRI data are used to target the stimulator. This is expensive and time-consuming. It is not necessarily a deal-breaker, though. You need to do it only once, so you could imagine going down to the MRI center at the mall to get fitted for your stimulator settings. Thereafter, whenever you would go to a Magnovision theater, the attendants would load up your data into the machine. Another likely possibility is that we will develop cheaper and faster ways of focusing the stimulator.

Everything I have said so far applies to single magnetic pulses or short trains of a couple of pulses. In clinical and research applications, the same devices are used in another mode called *repeated-train TMS*. Repeated-train TMS involves sending a continuous stream of pulses to a brain area for up to 10s of minutes. During stimulation, neurons are excited and fire more frequently; the exact effects depend on how strong the current is and the frequency at which it oscillates. After the stimulation is turned off, activity in the area is suppressed or facilitated for a period that lasts at least 15 minutes.[8] Depending on where the stimulation is applied, it can affect perception and memory, emotional state, and other aspects of functioning. It also can produce changes in the connections of the stimulated neurons that last for days, weeks, or months. These synaptic changes have been exploited for clinical purposes. The most successful example of repeated-train TMS in use is in the treatment of depression. For a long time we have known that particular parts of the brain are misregulated in depression. These include the parts of the temporal lobe, on the bottom of the cerebrum near the middle, including the hippocampus and surrounding tissue. Repeated-train

TMS to these areas has proved an effective treatment for difficult cases of depression. The exact mechanism is not known, but it probably involves resetting these areas.[9] One side effect is a modest memory impairment for events that happened just before and after the treatment. This is a reasonable trade-off in cases of severe depression, but not for a night at the movies. Moreover, who wants to experience an entertainment that wipes itself from memory? Another risk of repeated-train stimulation is the induction of brain seizures. These are rare in cognitive protocols but more common in some of the clinical uses. Repeated-train TMS is a great clinical tool, but these risks probably mean it will never be widely deployed for recreational purposes.

Let's turn back to Keanu Reeves and "I know kung fu." Will TMS allow us to bypass traditional education and just implant skills directly into our brains? No. First, if we could tweak our brains however we wanted, we don't know what set of tweaks would make someone a kung fu master. Second, even if we did know, TMS is too crude an instrument to do it. It can't stimulate individual cells, just large areas, and the stimulation is too different from real neural activity to work right.

Much more modestly, there are intriguing data coming out right now suggesting that brain stimulation *does* have the capacity to enhance traditional learning. One line of research has examined motor learning of the sort that we undergo when we learn to play a piece on the piano or to type on a computer keyboard. In these studies, researchers teach people to perform a motor sequence, usually by presenting a sequence of visual cues and instructing the learners to press a key corresponding to each cue. If you have ever used piano-teaching software, it's kind of like that. Repeated-train TMS over the motor cortex can improve this kind of learning.[10]

Other studies have used very mild electrical stimulation rather than magnetic stimulation. This technique has even bigger spatial spread than TMS, and it can't easily be used to produce visual or auditory effects. But it can modulate ongoing patterns of activity, including patterns induced by learning. One set of studies has used both TMS and electrical stimulation in patients with early-stage Alzheimer's disease. As you probably know, Alzheimer's is a progressive disease affecting the brain, which generally starts showing effects on people in their 60s and 70s. In the early and middle stages, it is marked by major declines in memory, understanding, and problem-solving. The brain's frontal lobes are one of the areas that are especially affected during this stage. Parts of the frontal lobes, particularly the dorsolateral prefrontal cortex (*dorso* for "upper," *lateral* "for side"), are important for many kinds of memory, reasoning, and problem-solving. Stimulating these areas regularly for a few weeks produced substantial improvements in memory and problem-solving, and these gains held for up to 4½ months.[11]

Another set of studies looked at the learning of mathematics. In these studies, the researchers wanted to see whether stimulating particular parts of the brain can speed the learning of numerical digits or arithmetic. The problem with both of these is that you can't teach them to adults— they already know! So, in these studies, the researchers created "new math" and taught it to people in the lab. In the first study, the scientists taught people a new set of symbols representing numerical digits. They used a training task designed to approximate what it is like to learn your numbers for the first time. Each of the participants practiced for six 2-hour sessions. During the training sessions some of them were receiving mild electric stimulation to their right parietal cortex. This area is known to be important for numerical cognition; lesions in it produce a syndrome called *dyscalculia*, which is a specific impairment of numerical thinking. At the end of the training, the researchers used several tests to see how well participants had learned the numerical value of the symbols. Those who had received stimulation to the right parietal cortex had learned the new digits better than those who received sham stimulation or stimulation to the left hemisphere. In the second study, the scientists taught people a new version of arithmetic and some of the learners received stimulation of their dorsolateral prefrontal cortex, a region in the front of the brain that is important for juggling information during problem-solving. In a final test of the new arithmetic, the students who had received the stimulation performed better. As we learn more about how these stimulation effects work, we may be able to target them and thereby increase the efficacy.[12]

The idea of tweaking your brain purely for entertainment is fun, no doubt. And techniques such as electrical stimulation and TMS appeal to me because these are the tools my colleagues and I use in our research. But *all* movies are brain tweaks—they just stimulate our brains the old-fashioned way, by putting signals in through the eyes and ears. Even how we do that is changing.

Take the visual signal. Back in Chapter 6 I described some of the dramatic changes that the recording and display of visual images is undergoing. One change is the transition from analog film recording to digital recording, which is more or less complete. This has been accompanied by an increase in resolution and in control over color and light. Today's high-resolution digital movie cameras can resolve finer information than all but the highest-resolution specialized film cameras.[13] Digital cameras also can shoot at a higher frame rate—more than 120 frames per second.

Another change is the range of devices that movies are being shown on. For many years, people could watch movies at home as well as in a theater, but the home viewing experience was a poor step-cousin. Televisions had much lower resolution, poor contrast, and inferior sound. The TV screen also had a different, taller shape than a theater screen, so that most films had to have their sides lopped off to fit. (The technique is called *pan and scan*, because the cropping rectangle is adjusted from frame to frame to try to keep key information such as actors' faces in the frame.) These days, plasma and LCD screens are large and vivid, and they are often hooked up to sound systems that rival anything in the neighborhood multiplex. But at the same time, audiences are increasingly experiencing movies on small-screen portable devices such as smartphones and tablets.

As I write, probably the most excitement in theaters and televisions is about so-called 3-D viewing. Why "so-called"? Indulge me in a little bit of a rant here. "3-D" movies/TV refers to what a scientist would call *stereoscopic* projection. *Stereoscopic* means "two-eyed": Different images are presented to the two eyes. Stereoscopy (stereo for short) is an important cue to depth. Because your two eyes are in slightly different locations, your two retinas capture slightly different images of the world. Objects that are far away wind up in about the same place on the left and right retinas. But objects that are close to the eyes fall on quite different places on the two retinas. By comparing visual features across the two eyes, your brain acquires information about the distance of objects. This comparison happens mainly in area MT, the same area that we talked about in Chapter 6, where we learned that it is also the brain's major center for motion processing.

But stereo is by no means the only depth cue we use. Here are just some of the depth cues we use all the time:

- *Occlusion:* When the outline of one object cuts out the outline of another, you see it as being in front.
- *Linear perspective:* When straight lines converge, you see them as parallel lines receding in distance. (Think of a pair of railroad tracks.)

- *Foreshortening:* This is related to linear perspective. When you look at an object with two equal-sized parts, one being closer to you than the other, the closer part will produce a larger visual image.
- *Atmospheric perspective:* Things that are far away look desaturated and fuzzy because of the atmosphere.
- *Motion parallax:* When you move your head, the image of a nearby object shifts a long distance on your retina, but the image of a faraway object shifts only slightly.

Stereo doesn't work for things that are too close to the eyes because we can't align the corresponding points in the image. It's not much use for things that are very far away either because a large difference in depth is required to produce a detectable disparity. For close-up and faraway things, we depend on these other cues. You can quickly verify that these other cues are more than sufficient to produce good depth perception by simply covering up one eye. Does the world suddenly look flat? Of course not. In fact, a sizeable minority of the population actually has little or no stereoscopic vision. This happens if you have a visual problem such as amblyopia (lazy eye) as a child and it is not corrected in time. As the visual system develops, it is unable to establish the correspondences between the eyes. People without stereo vision still see the world in 3-D. They may have a little more trouble tracking a baseball pitch or a tennis serve, but can drive and sew and golf and appreciate sculpture. If we remove cues that show you the screen is flat—particularly the edges—you can experience a really strong sense of depth while viewing with only one eye.[14] So, to a perceptual psychologist it is pretty silly to call stereoscopically presented movies "3-D"—*all* movies are 3-D.

OK, that's the end of the rant. Stereoscopic presentation is actually pretty cool. It *is* a great cue to depth. Even if you remove all other depth cues, it can produce a vivid perception of depth by itself. By exaggerating the disparities between the images, one can construct a hyper-real depth impression in which objects seem to "pop out." So it is no surprise that technologists and filmmakers are interested in the possibilities of stereoscopic presentation for entertainment.

Stereoscopic image viewing has actually been around for a *long* time. The first popular wave of stereoscopic viewing was in the Victorian era, around 1838. A photographer would take two images from slightly different locations, print them, and display them using a special handheld viewer. By the late 19th century, these were a popular home entertainment—and a very similar viewer, the Viewmaster, is still available as a children's toy.

Bruce Bridgeman, a cognitive psychologist at the University of California at Santa Cruz, had a pretty amazing experience with stereoscopic movies. Bruce was born with almost no stereoscopic vision due to having been wall-eyed (exotropic) as a child. Here's how he describes it: "My eyes were pointed in two different directions. Normally, the two eyes receive slightly different images, so corresponding locations in the two eyes have small disparities. The brain can learn to use these disparities as a cue to distance. I never had that correspondence." As a result, Bruce's brain didn't develop sensitivity to the relations between the eyes' two images. Bruce describes his visual experience this way: "Just imagine watching a regular movie or regular TV. You get plenty of depth cues from occlusion, parallax, foreshortening and the rest, but you don't get stereoscopic disparity. You don't have a sense of depth of things jumping out." And this: "When we'd go out and people would look up and start discussing some bird in the tree, I would still be looking for the bird when they were finished. For everybody else, the bird jumped out. But to me, it was just part of the background." Then, he went to see Martin Scorsese's *Hugo* in stereo. For Bruce (and this has been documented in other cases as well), seeing the exaggerated depth cues retrained his brain to respond to stereoscopic depth. Suddenly, he had a whole new visual experience: "Things were separated from each other in ways they hadn't been before. I drove my wife crazy. Some of the most interesting things were to look at trees. I ride my bicycle to work each day and part of the ride has a forest on one side. Each tree is a sculpture of its own. It's as though the forest were a solid thing rather than a picture."[15]

Bruce pointed out to me that without knowing anything about the brain you can figure out that it must be using a special pathway to process stereoscopic depth cues. You can get almost the same disparity information that you get from stereo vision by just moving your head back and forth. If you close your left eye, look, and then move your head a few inches to the left, you'll see the same pair of images as if you had looked with both eyes. But Bruce confirmed that for him this produced nothing like the sense of popping out that stereo vision gives. I suspect you'll feel the same way. One of the players in this specialized processing is likely to be area MT, the motion specialist. Perhaps—and this is just a hunch—what produces the special experience of depth from stereo is the convergence in MT of information about movement with information about depth.

How do stereoscopic movies work? The key ingredient is presenting two different images to the two eyes. Inventors have come up with lots of ways to do this. The simplest is called *anaglyphic* presentation. The images for the right eye and the left eye are superimposed on the screen. The viewer wears different filters on each eye so that only one of the two images makes it through to each eye. The old red-green stereoscopic movies and pictures you may have seen are anaglyphic images. By wearing a red or green lens of each eye, you filter out one of the two images in the picture. The problem with this method is that you give up a lot of color signal to gain depth. Another kind of anaglyphic presentation uses polarized light. The two images are superimposed, projected in polarized light, and viewed through polarized lenses such that only one of the two images gets through to each eye. The glasses for this kind of presentation have plastic polarized lenses, which let through only one of the two polarized images. This system handles color better, but it still darkens the image considerably because each lens filters out half of the light reflected from the screen.

One of the first stereoscopic movie technologies to be commercially deployed was also one of the most technologically impressive. In 1922, the inventor Laurens Hammond patented a system to present alternating frames and synchronize them with mechanical shutters that were mounted on stands in front of each seat in the theater. He called the system "Teleview," and it debuted at the Selwyn Theatre on Broadway in the same year. It appears that only one movie was ever shot for the Teleview system, a science fiction film called *The Man From M.A.R.S.* The Teleview system caused a minor stir in the *New York Times*, with the director D. W. Griffith supporting stereoscopic projection but with movie patrons expressing alarm. Audience members reported that the effects were striking but that eyestrain and the awkward posture required for the viewers were a drawback. The one thing everyone agreed on was that *The Man From M.A.R.S.* was a tedious bore. The Teleview premiere closed after about a month, and shutter systems were not again deployed for commercial viewing for about another 90 years. Laurens Hammond made out okay, though—he went on to invent the Hammond electric organ.[16]

Probably the best-looking systems deployed in theaters use glasses with LCD shutters in each lens that can open and shut very quickly. Images for each eye are presented in alternation, and the shutters in the glasses are synchronized to the alternation on the screen using radio-frequency signals from the projector. This method produces great-looking images, but it is sensitive and expensive. Polarized lenses are cheap enough to throw away, but LCD shutter glasses have fancy electronics and a radio for synchronization on board, so they are quite expensive. This system also cuts the effective frame rate of the projector in half (and leaves the image for each eye dark for half of the time), so you need a very fast, bright projector for it to look good.

As I write this, TV manufacturers are making a big push to deploy these technologies. There is one more stereoscopic presentation method that is worth mentioning because it is showing up in TVs too. This system uses a set of lenses or barriers built into the screen, alternating in thin stripes, so that each eye sees only the odd or only the even stripes. One way to do this is with *lenticular lenses*. I remember these mostly from Cracker Jack boxes when I was a kid. Do you remember the little pictures with the ridged surfaces that moved when you moved your head? Those were lenticular lenses. Same thing on the billboards whose images change as you drive by. Here's how they work. You take two (or sometimes more) pictures, chop each one up into tall thin stripes, and alternate them on the cardboard or the screen. Then, you slap a sheet of plastic over the pasted-together images. The plastic sheet has a bunch of lenses that alternate in line with the stripes in the image. From any particular viewing angle, the lenses allow you to see only one set of stripes. For stereoscopic TV, the image is created with an LCD display, and the lenses are set up so that if you view them from the right angle, each eye sees one of the two sets of stripes. The great thing about this system is that it doesn't require any fancy glasses. The big limitation is that the image looks right only when you are sitting in just the right place. (Another problem is that you give up half of the horizontal resolution of the screen, and half of the brightness the screen can give off.)

All of these systems can produce a vivid sense of depth—but there are costs. You generally give up some combination of resolution, frame rate, and brightness to display in stereo. Stereo may also produce a little more eyestrain and motion sickness than regular viewing.[17]

It's not just the sights that are changing at the movies, but the sounds too. Movies, of course, were originally silent. Hugo Münsterberg, contemplating the future of movies from the vantage of 1916, speculated on the possibility of adding sound. He was not enthusiastic:

> Those who, like Edison, had a technical, scientific, and social interest but not a genuine esthetic point of view in the development of the moving pictures naturally asked themselves whether this optical imitation of the drama might not be improved by an acoustical imitation too.... Even if the voices were heard with ideal perfection and exactly in time with the movements on the screen, the effect on an esthetically conscientious audience would have been disappointing. A photoplay cannot gain but only lose if its visual purity is destroyed.[18]

Of course, a few years later, "talkies" would take over, and the movie industry has rarely looked back. (Münsterberg would no doubt have been gratified by the success of *The Artist*, a silent film, in the 2012 Oscars.)

Movies were originally accompanied by live music, or in a pinch by a phonograph. Successful synchronized movie sound was accomplished by adding a strip to the side of the film that recorded the sound as a pattern of light and dark. Because the soundtrack was printed on the same film strip as the images, the two could easily be kept in synchrony. That basic scheme endured through to the digital transition of the 1990s and 2000s. Over the decades, reproduction and amplification improved dramatically, and the audio was divided into two channels for stereo reproduction. When the world went digital, theaters went to more channels of sound reproduction. One popular standard that your home theater may use has five audio channels plus a subwoofer.

What is coming for movie sound reproduction? I think that advances in recording and speaker technology will probably continue to morph the audio experience in the theater. Take recording. Back in the day, sound for a film was recorded with a single needle onto wax. Then we got a microphone, or two microphones for stereo recording, and then the ability to mix and edit sounds after recording. Now, it is possible to put dozens or even hundreds of microphones on a set and record many different sound sources individually. With digital filtering, we can isolate individual sound sources and store their output separately. At the same time, speakers have become dramatically better and cheaper. It is not unreasonable to imagine that a new theater would have hundreds of small speakers arranged around the space. So, instead of distributing a soundtrack with five channels, film companies could wind up distributing a soundtrack in which each actor, each car, each instrument in the orchestra is represented separately, with information about its location in space at each moment. The audio system in the theater would then spread these signals out to the speakers based on a model of the speaker locations and the room acoustics. Currently, if a character walks across the screen from left to right, their voice might be mixed from the left front speaker to the center speaker to the right. In the system I am contemplating, the same dialogue might move across dozens of speakers. This sort of system would also allow for some new effects: Imagine sitting in the middle of a chorus, with one voice coming from each of the speakers around you. Or imagine in the middle of a suspense film a voice whispering from just behind your seat. All of this is pretty much doable with today's technology.[19]

But why stick to sight and sound? Over the years, film-makers have experimented with adding other sensory modalities to the film experience. One that keeps coming back is olfaction—the sense of smell. This makes sense to me. There is a popular belief that odors are strong memory cues, and that belief turns out to be true. So, adding smell to film has the promise of not just enriching the experience directly, but also by calling up related memories. The 1960 film *Scent of Mystery*, starring Elizabeth Taylor, was released in "Smell-O-Vision," a system that piped scents in through the theater's air conditioning system. It was not a hit; the *New York Times* wrote, "If there is anything of lasting value to be learned from Michael Todd's *Scent of Mystery* it is that motion pictures and synthetic smells do not mix." After a brief run, Smell-O-Vision wafted away. Smell has been brought back from time to time as a gimmick or as a joke, as in John Waters's 1981 *Polyester*. Waters distributed scratch and sniff cards to viewers, calling the system "Odorama."

There are two tricky things about making olfactory stimuli work in a theater setting. The first is delivery—it's hard to get odors where you want, when you want. Current technologies include forced air, heated wax, and ink-jet printing of odorants. Their ability to control the dispersal of an odor over time and space has gotten a lot better; it is not unreasonable to envision computer-controlled odorant systems in theaters that would produce realistic scents time-locked to what is happening on screen. That still leaves us with a second tricky thing about smell. Our other senses provide a lot of quantitative information as well as qualitative information. You can sense not just what color a light is but also how bright it is, not just whether a sound is a trumpet or a violin but also whether it is loud or soft. Our sense of smell, on the other hand, is optimized to detect *what* we are smelling without making fine discriminations about how much of the smell there is. If you are young and not stuffed up, you can probably detect a very low concentration of odorant and identify it if it's a smell you know. For example, say the building on screen is on fire and you smell smoke. Just a whiff might get your heart racing. But if we double the concentration of an odorant, it may not have a big effect on your experience. Double up the concentration of cotton candy or lemon, and it may not be qualitatively different. This is not necessarily a bad thing for smell in the movies—on the upside, it means you don't have to fuss too much about the concentration of scent in the air to give a realistic impression. On the downside, though, it means you really need to clear a scent out quickly and completely to avoid mixed olfactory messages. So, is Smell-O-Vision set for a comeback? Well, a few years ago, a Japanese company tried again to make a hit with scent, deploying a system of under-the-seat air pipes in theaters. It doesn't seem to have caught on.[20]

If smelling a burning building doesn't get you shaking in your seat, how about actually shaking the seat? Movie producers and exhibit designers have used motorized seats to intensify theater experiences for decades. I have a vivid recollection of the old "Mission to Mars" ride at Disney World, which had seats that shook during takeoff and then dropped suddenly to simulate the release of gravity. That ride was no doubt influenced by the early film experiments. The best known of these is probably William Castle's *The Tingler*, released in 1959. It was deployed to theaters along with Castle's "Perceptro" system and a truckload of hype. Perceptro consisted of buzzers inserted into the theater seats, wired to a switch in the projectionist's booth that was pressed at key moments during the action.

One inheritor of Perceptro in the 2010s is a system called "Motion Code," made by the Canadian company D-Box. Theater seats are outfitted with motors to tilt and shift, and with vibrators to add shake. Movies encoded with this system have specific motion cues synchronized to the on-screen action. Systems like this actually stimulate several sensory modalities: Through our skin and muscles we sense pressure from the motors and vibration from the vibrators. Through our inner ears we sense acceleration. Pressure, vibration, and acceleration are all processed differently in the central nervous system. So motors in the seats really do triple duty. Another company, CJ Group of South Korea, is deploying a theater system that combines seat motors with wind machines, fog, and scents. As of this writing I'm hundreds of miles from the nearest theater equipped with these seats, but when they show up in my city you can be sure I'll give them a try.[21]

There is one more big change shaking up movies even as we speak: interaction. Movies may be merging with video games.

On the movie side, cinema is becoming more interactive. Debates about movies on fan sites now start long before the movie is released. (Peter Jackson's *Lord of the Rings* series was discussed ferociously, for years, by devotees of the Tolkien books from which it was adapted—before the movie was even edited and screened.) Interactive goodies—the director's commentary track, games, alternative endings, extra material that was edited out—have become a ubiquitous part of DVD releases. Online promotions for movies include lots of interactive features, some reaching the complexity and scope of commercial video games. And of course many action movies are produced from the start with tie-ins to games. Production may include extra footage shot specifically for the game.

On the game side, video games are becoming more movie-like. Many games are designed to take players through a story via a connected set of events. The players may have control over exactly which scenes are played, their order, and of course how they turn out, but the game is structured according to a larger narrative whose parameters are set by the game's designers. At the same time, the gap between animation and live action continues to close, and game designers are increasingly mixing the two in their creations.

This is a *big deal*. Working out its implications would take another book. You may have noticed that in this book I have mostly tried to duck the topic of video games because it is just too large in scope. But let me very briefly lay out what I think are the biggest issues presented by the fusing of movies and games. First, interactivity increases immersion in a set of events. My hunch is that movie-like, interactive video games will pick up customers from the base of traditional moviegoers because they will offer a more immersive narrative experience. Second, at the same time that interactive movies give a more immersive experience, they lessen the sense of shared experience provided by noninteractive stories. If you and I watch a blockbuster or read a novel or go to a baseball game, we can talk about the *same* events, line by line or frame by frame. This shared experience is important; audiences like it. Gamers certainly have shared components of experience and can talk about their experiences in the game, but unless they were playing together, they did not have the same experience in the game. Third, research on source memory that I described in Chapter 4 tells us that interactivity changes how we differentiate vicarious experiences from real ones. My hunch is that, for this reason, interactivity will promote source confusion—we will be more likely to confuse information we learned from an interactive movie with real life than information we learned from a noninteractive one. Finally—and this is the one I think is most exciting—I think that interactive movies may provide stronger opportunities to learn things from cinema. Take social learning. As we've discussed, narrative arts provide great opportunities to learn about our social world. Watching a character make a bad choice and suffer the consequences teaches you something about how to behave. Making the bad choice yourself is probably loads better. In a game, you can make bad choices and suffer only vicariously as your character reaps what you have sown. The same thing goes for nonsocial learning—interactive movies may prove great vehicles for teaching us how to cook, fish, navigate in the wilderness, operate a tractor; there are lots of activities where you can see the potential. These possibilities have opened up a whole new field called "serious games," which aims to use interactive media for training and learning.

So where does all this leave us? Will stereo presentation succeed this time round? Industry insiders are starting to write that it may have peaked. Will Smell-O-Vision make a big comeback? Will motorized seats? Too soon to say. Eventually, I think we will have recreational and educational brain stimulation too. And we definitely are seeing more interactivity in the theater, perhaps to the point where games and movies are seamlessly merged. Will any of this fundamentally shift how we experience movies?

Some of these changes will be big, no doubt. When cinema came along and took its place alongside the play and the novel as a major form of narrative art, it was a big change. Bigger screens with higher contrast and higher resolution increase our sense of immersion, just like shaking seats and stereoscopic depth. Even brain stimulation to produce the sensation of sight and sound is on that continuum, should it come about. But at the end of the day, I think all of these technological developments are of a piece with continuous improvements in video and sound reproduction technology. The underlying grip of movies is that they program our brains to have experiences. They create events in our heads. For tens of thousands of years, maybe more, we have been stimulating each others' brains by telling stories and acting them out. As soon as we figured out how to write, we started writing stories. As soon as we developed systems to record our voices and movements, we recorded ourselves portraying events that others could watch for entertainment. Even interactive stories, I believe, are on this continuum. Technologies for telling stories are going to keep morphing and expanding, but my bet is that in another hundred years we will still recognize them as descendants of the movies we watch now. They'll still be devices we use to program each other by constructing representations of events in each others' heads—sometimes events too remote, too abstract, too dangerous or transgressive or gross to want to live out in real life. *That's* the attraction of film.

EPILOGUE
Stinger

At the end of *Ferris Beuller's Day Off,* after all of the credits have run, Matthew Broderick appears in a bathrobe and shoos the remaining audience out of the theater: "You're still here? It's over. Go home. Go!" In a book, that little scene would be an epilogue; in a movie it's sometimes called a "stinger." So does this movie book get an epilogue or a stinger? Call it what you will; here are a couple parting thoughts.

If you have a love affair with film, I hope that reading these pages has deepened your relationship. If you happen to be involved in making films, let me make a pitch: Psychology and neuroscience can be of real practical use in helping you make choices as a film artist. Science can't replace artistry—it can't tell you what choices to make—but it can help you to understand what will happen to your audience depending on how you choose. That can't hurt, right?

If you happen to be a psychologist or a neuroscientist, there's a pitch here for you too: Filmmakers know a terrific amount about perception, comprehension, and memory. Just to make a simple action sequence or dialogue scene that is intelligible and interesting requires exquisite control over the viewer's attention, emotion, and inferences. We can learn a lot about the mind and brain by leveraging the generations of wisdom accumulated in filmmaking practice.

Whatever the nature of your love affair with movies, I hope that reading this book has you falling (more) in love with the scientific study of minds and brains. Writing it has deepened my wonder at how natural selection has shaped our minds and brains into devices of complexity, power, and beauty. Throughout, I have been struck by the point that I used to title Chapter 1: Your brain wasn't built for movies. It wasn't built for computers or newspapers or airplanes or cities, either. When we reach out to understand how our minds and brains function in the modern world, we are well served to keep this in mind.

OK, that's really it. You're still here? It's over. Go home. Go!

NOTES

PROLOGUE

1. http://blog.moviefone.com/2011/10/26/the-worst-movie-mistakes-in-history/.

CHAPTER 1

1. James (1890), p. 522. James attributes the term "ideo-motor action" to a paper by William Carpenter in 1852. Somewhere along the way, researchers lost the hyphen. James's description goes on like this: "Whilst talking I become conscious of a pin on the floor, or of some dust on my sleeve. Without interrupting the conversation I brush away the dust or pick up the pin. I make no express resolve, but the mere perception of the object and the fleeting notion of the act seem of themselves to bring the latter about."

2. These studies are reviewed in Chartrand, Maddux, & Lakin (2005). The ducking study is from Bavelas, Black,

Chovil, Lemery, & Mullett (1988). The rubbing/shaking study is from Chartrand & Bargh (1999).

3. Brass, Bekkering, Wohlschläger, & Prinz (2000).

4. Maslovat, Chua, & Hodges (2013).

5. These studies are reviewed in the chapter by Chartrand et al. (2005).

6. Rizzolatti, Fogassi, & Gallese (2001).

7. The *success rule*, or *operant conditioning*, has a long and distinguished history in experimental psychology and neuroscience. Another form of learning that has been studied even longer is *classical conditioning*. In operant conditioning, an animal learns to associate a stimulus with a successful response; in classical conditioning, the animal learns to associate a stimulus with another stimulus. This is what Pavlov did in his famous experiments in which dogs were conditioned to associate the sound of a bell with the delivery of meat powder.

8. Kamitani & Tong (2005); Tootell, Devaney, Young, Postelnicu, Rajimehr, & Ungerleider (2008).

9. Reddy & Kanwisher (2006); Quiroga, Reddy, Kreiman, Koch, & Fried (2005); Amedi, Malach, Hendler, Peled, & Zohary (2001).

10. Preuss, Stepniewska, & Kaas (1996); Fried, Katz, McCarthy, Sass, Williamson, Spencer, et al. (1991); Penfield & Rasmussen (1950).

11. Schwenkreis, El Tom, Ragert, Pleger, Tegenthoff, & Dinse (2007); Elbert, Pantev, Wienbruch, Rockstroh, & Taub (1995); Bangert & Schlaug (2006).

12. Meltzoff & Moore (1983) describe the infant social imitation study.

13. Náñez (1988).

14.   Rizzolatti, Fadiga, Gallese, & Fogassi (1996).

15.   Iacoboni & Dapretto (2006); Rizzolatti & Craighero (2004).

16.   Chapman & McGhie (1964).

17.   Shallice, Burgess, Schon, & Baxter (1989).

18.   Lhermitte, Pillon, & Serdaru (1986); Archibald, Mateer, & Kerns (2001).

CHAPTER 2

1.   Thanks to Robyn Husa for pointing out the aptness of this passage.

2.   The notion of a model in psychology has a long history but was articulated most fully by Philip Johnson-Laird (1983). The role of models in reading comprehension has been studied by psychologists including Gordon Bower, Walter Kintsch, Art Graesser, G. A. Radvansky, & Rolf Zwaan. A review of much of this work can be found in Zwaan & Radvansky (1998).

3.   Proulx (1999).

4.   For those who would like to know *much* more about this topic, G. A. Radvansky and I have written a book (Radvansky & Zacks, in 2014) in which we give a detailed theoretical account of the psychology of event model construction and use, and review lots of psychological and neurophysiological data.

5.   Humphries, Liebenthal, & Binder (2010).

6.   This property is called *isomorphism*, which means "same shape."

7.   Two of the pioneering studies were done by Andreas Bartels and Uri Hasson. Bartels's study used a method similar to the one we used. He and his colleagues showed viewers commercial films that were coded for different

features and asked what was happening in their brains when particular types of content appeared on the screen. Hasson's study turned this approach on its head. His group again showed people a commercial film (*The Good, the Bad & the Ugly*), but instead of starting with the film content they looked for elements of brain activity that were most consistent across viewers. Once they found an area that "ticked together" across individual viewers, they found the times that area was most active and asked what was going on in the film. See Bartels & Zeki (2004); Hasson Nir, Levy, Fuhrmann, & Malach (2004).

8. Zacks, Speer, & Reynolds (2009); Zacks, Speer, Swallow, & Maley (2010).

9. Epstein (2008).

10. Both of these results converge nicely with what was observed by Hasson and colleagues (2004).

11. Adapted from Barker & Wright (1951), pp. 57–60.

12. Murphy (2013).

13. The two studies described here are Buccino, Binkofski, Fink, Fadiga, Fogassi, Gallese, et al. (2001); and Hauk, Johnsrude, & Pulvermuller (2004). Another important and relevant study is Tettamanti, Buccino, Saccuman, Gallese, Danna, Scifo, et al. (2005).

14. One of the early studies of simulation during motor imagery comes from my laboratory: Michelon, Vettel, & Zacks (2006). The question of whether and where visual imagery elicits retinotopic activity is contested. A very good recent review is Ganis & Schendan (2011). In the domain of motor imagery, see Ehrsson, Geyer, & Naito (2003).

15. In other experiments, including the first one on this paper, readers did have to establish *some* relationship between the picture and the sentence. In that experiment readers

were asked not just to name the eagle, but to say whether the picture showed something mentioned in the story. The results were the same.

16. Interview conducted January 23, 2013. I've edited slightly for clarity. These ideas are developed more fully in Guber (2011).

17. James (1881), p. 39.

18. Montgomery (1947).

19. There are definitely exceptions. Google "movie better than the book" and you will find that lots of people have lists of movie adaptations they like better than the original books.

20. Keane (1998).

21. Brady (1981), p. 163.

CHAPTER 3

1. Maupin (2008).

2. Münsterberg wrote this at an unhappy time in his life. An ardent promoter of German-American friendship, and one used to being received warmly by the American public, he wrote frequently in the newspapers in support of Germany during the run-up to World War I. He took a lot of heat for this, and felt himself sorely misunderstood. He dropped dead from a stroke while lecturing on December 16, 1916, shortly after the publication of *The Photoplay*. See H. Münsterberg (1916); M. A. A. Münsterberg (1922).

3. Dimberg, Thunberg, & Elmehed (2000).

4. Hsee, Hatfield, Carlson, & Chemtob (1990).

5.   See Darwin (1998). This edition includes a thoughtful introductory essay, upon which I have drawn heavily here.

6.   Darwin (1988), p. 248.

7.   Darwin (1988), pp. 55–57.

8.   Darwin (1988), p. 288.

9.   There is a lot more to it than good and bad, of course. The core emotions probably include at least these: anger, disgust, fear, happiness, sadness, surprise, and contempt. Fine shadings of appraisal can give us embarrassment, shame, pride, love, desire, sympathy, and more. But the good/bad dimension is a fine place to start because it is universal, arises early in development, and shows up quickly in response to emotion-inducing stimuli. See Keltner, Oatley, & Jenkins (2013), Ch. 8.

10. Barrett, Mesquita, Ochsner, & Gross (2007).

11. James (1890), pp. 449–50.

12. James (1890), pp. 464–65. (James goes on with another paragraph of quotes—he clearly got a kick out of these actors' introspections about their emotional experiences.)

13. Strack Martin, & Stepper (1988); Larsen Kasimatis, & Frey (1992).

14. Lee, Josephs, Dolan, & Critchley (2006).

15. Barrett et al., 2007; Wicker, Keysers, Plailly, Royet, Gallese, & Rizzolatti (2003).

16. Roy, Shohamy, & Wager (2012).

17. LeDoux (2000); Phelps (2006).

18. James (1890), Ch. 25; Damasio (1994); Barrett et al. (2007).

19. The view that we understand others' mental states by simulating them is called *simulation theory*. It can be

contrasted with the view that we reason about others' mental states by using theories of how other people work, much the same way we have theories of how things like bicycle pumps or thermostats work; that view is called *theory theory*. A brief introduction to these ideas can be found in Cruz & Gordon (2006). The proposal that simulation is the mechanism underlying emotional experience from fiction—particularly written fiction—was first developed in psychology by Keith Oatley (1999). An overview of the brain systems involved in mindreading can be found in Waytz & Mitchell (2011).

20. Truffaut (1978), pp. 110–11.

21. Truffaut (1978), p. 299.

22. Retrieved February 27, 2012, from http://www.imdb.com/title/tt0086425/reviews.

23. G. M. Smith (2003). While Smith works out in detail the establishment and maintenance of mood states by film, the same idea is at the heart of an excellent book by Ed Tan (1996, p. 250). Here's how he puts it: "In general, narration may be seen as the systematic evocation of emotion in an audience, according to a preconceived plan. Narration by means of film is one way of doing this."

24. The film theorist Carl Plantinga raises many of these issues (see Plantinga, 2013, as well as other works). Plantinga parses out different kinds of emotional movie experiences a little differently than I do. Plantinga distinguishes between *global* emotions, which are long-lasting, and *local* ones, which are briefer and more intense. He distinguishes between *direct* responses to the unfolding narrative (e.g., curiosity, suspense), *sympathetic* responses to the characters' situations (e.g., compassion, pity), and *meta-emotions*, which are directed at your own responses as a viewer (e.g., pride, guilt). Finally, he distinguishes between responses

to the *fiction* of the movie's story and responses to the *arti-fact* that is the movie itself.

25. Alcock (2001), p. 117.

26. Thanks to Kevin Maffitt for suggesting this.

CHAPTER 4

1. This intriguing study was presented at the Annual Meeting of the Psychonomic Society in 2006. As far as I know, it was never written up in a peer reviewed publication, unfortunately. See d'Ydewalle & Sevenants (2006).

2. These papers provide a good introduction to the phenomena of the reminiscence bump and develop the theoretical accounts: Conway (2005); Rubin, Wetzler, & Nebes (1986); Janssen, Chessa, & Murre (2005). In a *New Yorker* essay, neurobiologist Robert Sapolsky (1998) made some thoughtful speculations about why our preferences for music, art, and food seem to coalesce around the same time as the bump—and he even collected some data.

3. Copeland, Radvansky, & Goodwin (2009).

4. The cultural script explanation makes a counterintuitive prediction: If people use such scripts to think about their lives, they ought to show a reminiscence bump not just when looking back on their lives but also when looking forward as children. Arnette Bohn and Dorte Bernsten (2010) tested exactly this proposal. They asked kids in third through eighth grades to imagine how their life might turn out, and then looked at the shape of these imagined lives. Sure enough, there was a bump.

5. Kalisky & Uzzell (1996).

6. Two pieces of this story are controversial. First, Reagan's advocates claimed he never made this confusion, that it was a misunderstanding by two separate Israeli

government leaders. Second, some of Reagan's biographers have suggested he was suffering the early stages of Alzheimer's disease by this point in his presidency. Joan Didion's (1997) piece in the *New York Review of Books* and the following exchange of letters lays out the issues.

7.   Johnson (2006).

8.   Butler, Zaromb, Lyle, & Roediger (2009); Umanath, Butler, & Marsh (2012).

9.   Poague (2004), pp. 57–58.

10.   Poague (2004), pp. 59–60.

11.   Hovland, Lumsdaine, & Sheffield (1949); Shepard (n.d.).

12.   My characterization of the behavioral and neurophysiological properties of source memory is based mostly on Johnson, Raye, Mitchell, & Ankudowich (2012).

13.   Thanks to Lindsay Margolis for suggesting this example.

14.   Endel Tulving (2002) provides an overview of this aspect of memory.

15.   "The New Pictures" (1942).

16.   Interview conducted February 25, 2013.

17.   Marsh & Fazio (2006).

18.   Gerrig & Rapp (2004); Prentice, Gerrig, & Bailis (1997).

19.   Jacoby (1999).

20.   Johnson (2006).

CHAPTER 5

1.   Eron, Huesmann, Lefkowitz, & Walder (1972).

2.   Huesmann (1986).

3.   Anderson, Berkowitz, Donnerstein, Huesmann, Johnson, Linz, et al. (2003).

4. Anderson et al. (2003).

5. Douglas O. Linder at the University of Missouri in Kansas City has collected the Hinckley letters entered as evidence at the trial on a web page, with materials from other famous trials (Linder, n.d.).

6. This verdict was hugely controversial. A good case can be made that although Hinckley was insane he should still have been convicted, because he was able to plan out his actions and understand their consequences. See Taylor (1982).

7. Gogtay, Giedd, Lusk, Hayashi, Greenstein, Vaituzis, et al. (2004).

8. Singer, Seymour, O'Doherty, Kaube, Dolan, & Frith (2004).

9. Beah (2008), p. 13.

10. Beah (2008), p. 19.

11. Beah (2008), p. 125.

12. Sapolsky (1996); Bremner (1999).

13. Beah (2008), p. 13.

14. Thomas (1982).

15. Anderson et al. (2003).

16. Hasan, Bègue, Scharkow, & Bushman (2013).

17. Ramos, Ferguson, Frailing, & Romero-Ramirez (2013).

18. The meta-analyses as of 2003 are reviewed (a meta-meta-analysis!) in Anderson et al. (2003). To my knowledge the largest meta-analysis is Bushman & Huesmann (2006).

19. Ferguson & Kilburn (2009).

20. Interview conducted, March 5, 2013.

21. Interview conducted, March 7, 2013.

22. Bushman & Anderson (2001).

23. Bushman & Anderson (2001).

24. Freedman (1984).

25. Bushman & Anderson (2001).

26. Dove Foundation (2008).

27. The media surveys are reviewed in American Academy of Pediatrics (2009). Jack Valenti's testimony can be read in full at U.S. Congress (1990).

28. Signorielli (2003), p. 54.

29. Liptak (2011).

30. I retrieved the MPAA rating retrieved from filmratings.com and the Common Sense Media ratings from commonsensemedia.org on June 13, 2011.

CHAPTER 6

1. Roget (1825). This is a bit hard to visualize. Michael Bach has created a very nice interactive demonstration: http://michaelbach.de/ot/mot_Roget/.

2. Muybridge was an interesting character. Before his famous motion studies, he made a tidy living from dramatic landscape photography in the Yosemite Valley and surrounding Sierra Nevada—decades before Ansel Adams. He also had an explosive personality. He was tried for shooting his wife after discovering her adulterous affair, and as near as can be reconstructed was acquitted simply because at that time and place his fellow citizens did not object to his behavior.

3. A terrific website on the history of the origins of film, on which I've relied heavily, can be found at http://www.cinemaprehistory.net. Eadweard Muybridge is depicted vividly in Solnit (2003).

4. Sperling (1960).

5. For visual persistence to make sense as an explanation of how movies work, it has to mean persisting activity in the earliest parts of the visual system, the parts that are functionally coupled to the retina. There are many forms of memory throughout the visual system, some of which we will see become quite abstract. Visual persistence in the early stage can be distinguished from memory effects later in the system by looking at what happens when you move your eyes: If moving your eyes doesn't disrupt the persistence effect, then it is operating at a higher level than the retina. For reviews of these issues and overviews of experiments fixing the temporal duration of visual persistence and distinguishing this form of persistence from others, see Breitmeyer (1980); and Breitmeyer, Kropfl, & Julesz (1982).

6. The example of two-point motion without a change in position dates back to the research of Exner in the 1880s, summarized in Smith & Snowden (1994). We can even perceive motion when absolutely nothing is moving. This happens in the "waterfall illusion." Here is how it works: First, you stare at something like a waterfall or a moving train for about 15 seconds. Then, you look away to some that isn't moving—a tree or a wall. The still object will appear to be moving in the opposite direction. For both the two-light effect and the waterfall illusion, you have the sensation of motion without any sense that the objects have changed position. For a demonstration, see http://www.georgemather.com/MotionDemos/MAEQT. html. For a review of the idea of visual persistence in film and its troubles, see Anderson & Anderson (1993).

7. Newsome, Britten, & Movshon (1989).

8. L.M.'s case is summarized in Heywood & Zihl's (1999) nicely readable chapter. The initial case report

and follow-up were presented in these chapters: Zihl, von Cramon, & Mai (1983); Zihl, von Cramon, Mai, & Schmid (1991).

9.   Humphreys & Riddoch (1987), pp. 25–26.

10. Humphreys & Riddoch (1987), p. 29.

11. Humphreys & Riddoch (1987), p. 33.

12. Vision scientists don't measure size in thumbs, but in *degrees*. We know that 360 degrees is the full arc around you. Your visual field fills about 180 degrees horizontally. Your thumb at arms length covers about 2 degrees (1.1%) of your visual field. Visual speed is measured in degrees per second. So the person walking on the other side of the street would be moving at about ½ a degree per second, and the car driving right in front of you would be moving at about 24 degrees per second. I obtained the sensitivity estimates from McKee & Watamaniuk (1994). Data on the responses of MT cells to stimuli moving different distances with different lags can be found in Churchland & Lisberger (2001); Churchland, Huang, & Lisberger (2007). Thanks to Kevin Maffitt for pointing me to these sources.

13. Vary (2011).

14. The data using the moving-screen apparatus are reported in Kuroki, Nishi, Kobayashi, Oyaizu, & Yoshimura (2007); and Kuroki (2012). Watson and his colleagues have been working on this problem for quite a while. Quite a while ago they developed an elegant formal model, and also collected data on the relationship between motion speed and the frame rate needed to give a smooth perceptual experience. See Watson, Ahumada, & Farrell (1986); and Watson (2013). (Watson's estimate is from a personal communication, March 21, 2013.)

15. LCD and DLP (digital light path) projectors can sometimes flicker if the voltage to the illuminating lamp

fluctuates. But unlike film projectors and CRT (cathode ray tube) monitors, this is not an intrinsic part of the projection mechanism.

Chapter 7

1. Murch (2001).

2. The films of Georges Méliès stand up surprisingly well today. Many of them can be viewed online on YouTube.

3. Levaco (1974).

4. This version is from http://youtu.be/zUZCPPGeJ1c. Kuleshov may have made several versions of this demonstration, and as far as I can tell the original footage has been lost. See Levaco (1974).

5. This quotation is from Truffaut (1978), p. 185. I have edited the transliteration of the Russian name "Mozzhukhin" for consistency with the one used by Levaco (1974).

6. Goodale & Humphrey (1998).

7. Rayner & Castelhano (2007); Karson (1983); Murch (2001).

8. RadioLab did a great story on the Nakano study, in which they interviewed Walter Murch: http://www.radiolab.org/blogs/radiolab-blog/2009/oct/05/blink/. Nakano, Yamamoto, Kitajo, Takahashi, & Kitazawa (2009); Murch (2001).

9. Smith and Henderson did find one hint that saccades can hide cuts. When they looked specifically at cuts placed just after a character looked at something new (gaze match cuts), they found a lot of concurrent saccades. The funny thing, though, is that these cuts were actually quite easy for viewers to detect. Smith & Henderson (2008).

10. Hochberg & Brooks (2006).

11. Hood, Willen, & Driver (1998); Driver, Davis, Ricciardelli, Kidd, Maxwell, & Baron-Cohen (1999).

12. O'Regan, Rensink, & Clark (1999). You can view examples of the effect at http://nivea.psycho.univ-paris5.fr/Mud splash/Nature_Supp_Inf/Nature_Supp_Inf.html.

13. Shimamura, Cohn-Sheehy, & Shimamura (in press).

14. Münsterberg (1916).

15. Tim Smith (2012) has developed an account of these techniques that bridges the practical knowledge of filmmakers with the psychology. The article and commentaries make for great reading.

16. Long-range apparent motion is also called "beta" motion, and has been studied for a long time. The Gestalt psychologist Max Wertheimer noted that it is quite different from the experience of real motion. Short-range apparent motion, on the other hand, is basically indistinguishable from real motion, both in terms of physiology and phenomenology. Wertheimer also discovered a special kind of long-range apparent motion illusion, which he called "phi" motion, in which you have the impression of something moving but not of a change in the objects' positions. Weird, huh? For a demonstration, see http://www1.psych.purdue.edu/Magniphi/MagniPhi.html. Steinman, Pizlo, & Pizlo (2000); Mikami (1991).

17. Thanks to Zach Schmitz for showing me this example.

18. Thanks to James Cutting for setting me straight on this.

19. Schwan & Ildirar (2010); see also Ildirar & Schwan (in press).

20. These figures come from Barry Salt's database of hand-coded films, at www.cinemetrics.lv. I downloaded the data in April 2011 and calculated the shot length means for each decade. The site also includes a larger database of data contributed by others; those data are noisier but give similar results.

21. Rideout, Foehr, & Roberts (2010), p. 79.

22. Here are a few of the studies showing effects of video game play on attention and imagery: Bavelier, Green, Han, Renshaw, Merzenich, & Gentile (2011); Feng, Spence, & Pratt (2007); Hubert-Wallander, Green, & Bavelier (2011); Wu & Spence (2013).

    However, some researchers, including Kristjánsson (2013), have questioned whether video game play is causally responsible for improvements in visual attention.

CHAPTER 8

1. The figures I used for this estimate are as follows: frame rate: 24 frames per second (48 is also common); resolution: 2048 × 1556 pixel (the "2k" digital cinema standard, which is now being superseded by the higher-resolution "4k" standard); bits per pixel: 24; diameter of a piece of popcorn: 1 cm.

2. http://www.wired.com/gadgetlab/2010/06/iphone-4-retina-2/.

3. An important and too often neglected component of the paper is that a lot hangs on what is considered an "item." Miller showed that often the same set of physical stimuli can be processed as if they are one or many items. For example, when we read, the individual letters aren't usually the items, but the words. We'll return to this later.

4. Cowan (2001).

5. Shay (1993).

6. Two excellent introductions to attentional neglect and related phenomena are De Renzi (1982); and Robertson (2004).

7. In some theories, you can think of all the ropes pulling at the same time and the spotlight's final direction reflecting

the combination of all these forces. In other accounts, you can think of the visual salience ropes as restricting the spotlight to some parts of space, and the task-driven monkeys pulling to move the rope around within that restricted space. Jeremy Wolfe, the author of one of the dominant current accounts, has written a thoughtful and readable overview (2003) of the key issues. For a fuller description of the current version of his model, see Wolfe (2007).

8. Corbetta & Shulman (2002); Kelley, Serences, Giesbrecht, & Yantis (2008); Posner & Petersen (1990).

9. Rayner & Castelhano (2007).

10. Hasson, Vallines, & Heeger (2011, March 9). Personal communication. For a related analysis using these stimuli, see Hasson, Landesman, Knappmeyer, Vallines, Rubin, & Heeger (2008). Also, Tim D. Smith conducted a fascinating eye movement analysis of a scene in *There Will Be Blood*, described on David Bordwell's blog (Smith, 2011).

11. Simons & Chabris (1999).

12. The term *inattentional blindness* was coined by Arien Mack and Irvin Rock, who used a simpler paradigm that is in some ways even more dramatic than the basketball paradigm. In their experiments, viewers looked at the middle of a screen and were asked to respond quickly when a crosshair appeared, indicating whether the cross's vertical or horizontal arm was longer. The crosshair was quickly replaced by a splotch of visual noise to stop residual processing in the retina. Here, the crosshair functions like the basketball pass counting in the Simons and Chabris experiment—it focuses attention on a particular set of features. After a few trials of this task, the experimenters presented a small red square just offset from the crosshair's center. The square was large enough to be easily

visible, was presented quite near the center of the viewer's visual field, and was visually distinctive from the background and the crosshair. Yet about 25% of the time the viewers failed to notice the square. Mack & Rock (1998).

13. The first seven principles come from Palmer (1999). To these I have added an eighth based on work by Mary Peterson and her colleagues; for a review, see Peterson (2003).

14. Levin (2010). Interestingly, frequent viewers of *Friends* did a little better. This is because *Friends* was filmed, like most serial comedies, using a set that had a missing fourth wall where the audience sat. This means the range of camera angles you see on the show is much reduced, making the task a lot easier. *ER* was filmed on a set that allowed the cameras to shoot from most angles, which is more like real life.

15. http://en.wikipedia.org/w/index.php?title=The_X-Files& oldid=417753932.

16. http://x-files.wikia.com/wiki/J._Edgar_Hoover_FBI_ Building, retrieved March 8, 2011.

17. O'Keefe & Nadel (1978); Taube (2007); Moser, Kropff, & Moser (2008); Doeller, Barry, & Burgess (2010); Ekstrom, Kahana, Caplan, Fields, Isham, Newman, et al. (2003); Epstein (2008); Jacobs, Weidemann, Miller, Solway, Burke, Wei, et al. (2013).

18. http://www.imdb.com/title/tt0068646/usercomments? filter=prolific, retrieved March 10, 2011.

19. Kael, 1991, pp. 17, 188, and 488–489.

20. Labov & Waletzky (2003).

21. Larsson (2009), p. 42.

22. Baker (1998), p. 1.

23. Newtson (1976); Speer, Swallow, & Zacks (2003).

24. Lichtenstein & Brewer (1980).

25. Zacks, Tversky, & Iyer (2001). For another measure of hierarchical segmentation, see Hard, Tversky, & Lang (2006).

26. Kurby & Zacks (2008); Zacks, Speer, Swallow, Braver, & Reynolds (2007).

27. We and others have done this, and indeed you do observe massive activity when people push buttons at the event boundaries. See Hanson, Negishi, & Hanson (2001); Zacks, Braver, Sheridan, Donaldson, Snyder, Ollinger, et al. (2001).

28. The fMRI signal lags the neural activity that causes it by a few seconds. Here I'm describing a best estimate of the time course of the increase in neural firing.

29. Magliano & Zacks (2011).

30. Surprisingly, we observed little change in brain activity at action discontinuities themselves. There were increases in parts of the lateral occipital cortex and decreases in the superior parietal cortex and in the upper part of the posterior temporal lobe and the premotor cortex in the left hemisphere. Are they just harder to localize in time, or is forming a new event representation so efficient that it doesn't register much in the scanner?

31. These guesses are based on discussions of cuts in Hochberg & Brooks (1978); Smith & Henderson (2008); Bordwell (2002); Anderson (1996); Murch (2001).

32. James (1890), p. 246.

33. James (1890), p. 488.

34. Baird & Baldwin (2001); Hespos, Saylor, & Grossman (2009); Hespos, Grossman, & Saylor (2010); Wynn (1996).

35.   This interview excerpt comes from Marcel (1983). Many thanks to Tony Marcel for calling my attention to this case.

36.   Hirtle & Jonides (1985); Moar & Bower (1983); Tversky (1981).

CHAPTER 9

1.   Interview conducted, April 4, 2012.

2.   The original research studies described here are from the following papers: Levin & Simons (1997); Levin, Simons, Angelone, & Chabris (2002); Chris Chabris and Dan Simons discuss this work together with their research on inattentional blindness (which we talked about in Chapter 3) in a great book called *The Invisible Gorilla* (2010). This research has received a lot of attention in the media and has generated a number of spin-offs, some more sensible than others. My favorite is a series of commercials (the "awareness test" series) encouraging drivers to look more strategically, from the London transportation department.

3.   Simons, Franconeri, & Reimer (2000).

4.   Levin, Momen, Drivdahl, & Simons (2000).

5.   I do *not* want to give the impression that we don't hold on to anything in visual memory. A lot of continuity errors are missed, especially when we're focused on enjoying a film, but a lot of continuity errors can be detected when we are looking for them. Vision researchers have shown that a certain amount of detail about specific objects is accessible after a brief disruption, and a certain amount is even accessible hours or days later. For a review of the evidence about what sorts of visual information we *do* hold on to across changes and delays, see Hollingworth (2006).

6.   Thanks to Zach Schmitz for this example.

7. These studies are described in Swallow, Zacks, & Abrams (2009); and Swallow, Barch, Head, Maley, Holder, & Zacks (2011).

8. Corkin (2002).

9. These experiments are reviewed in Hollingworth (2006). This particular study comes from Hollingworth & Henderson (2002).

10. A couple of caveats are in order with respect to the neurophysiological studies on continuity errors. First, these experiments all involved fairly simple images—a pair of faces in which one may switch persons at a cut, or an array of bars in which one may switch which way it is leaning. Second, different experimental preparations have produced somewhat different activation patterns. See Beck, Rees, Frith, & Lavie (2001); Beck, Muggleton, Walsh, & Lavie (2006); Pessoa & Ungerleider (2004).

11. Standing (1973).

12. Thanks to Khena Swallow for suggesting this.

13. Murch (2001), p. 19.

14. The continuity error in *The King's Speech* comes from www.imdb.com. The sales statistics for the movie come from www.the-numbers.com.

15. Retrieved May 25, 2014, from www.moviemistakes.com.

16. Interview conducted, April 4, 2012.

Chapter 10

1. LaBerge (2000).

2. A group at MIT recently published a really neat paper in which they implanted a fear memory in mice using brain stimulation—and they described themselves as inspired

by *Inception* and *Total Recall*. Ramirez, Liu, Lin, Suh, Pignatelli, Redondo, et al. (2013); T. Beck (2013).

3. This account comes from *Heritage Minutes*, a series on great Canadians produced by the Canadian government. Retrieved June 24, 2011, at http://www.histori.ca/min utes/minute.do?id=10211.

4. Excerpted from Penfield (1975), pp. 22–24. I have edited the text slightly to use modern terms, and because Penfield refers to additional figures that are not reproduced here.

5. Penfield (1975), pp. 24–26. Again, I have edited slightly. Penfield takes pains to point out that the parts of the brain that are responsible for these effects need not—in fact, probably are not—the parts that are directly stimulated. Electrical stimulation directly affects the tissue that is stimulated, causing massive uncoordinated firing of neurons. Penfield suggested that these chaotic disturbances were probably sufficient to produce simple sound or light sensations, but not elaborated experiences of events. However, stimulation also affects the neurons to which the directly stimulated neurons are connected. The activity in these "downstream" regions is more subtle and probably is what is responsible for the conscious experiences.

6. Carlin, Hamza, Kurtz, Carlin, & Santos (1984).

7. Wagner, Valero-Cabre, & Pascual-Leone (2007).

8. Gerschlager, Siebner, & Rothwell (2001).

9. The stimulation of the temporal lobes to treat depression long predates TMS. In electroconvulsive therapy (ECT), a strong electric current is passed through the brain to induce a seizure affecting the medial temporal lobes. This is an effective treatment, but the seizure carries some

risks and the experience is quite unpleasant. TMS allows physicians to disrupt function more focally, limiting risks and side effects.

10. Reis, Robertson, Krakauer, Rothwell, Marshall, Gerloff, et al. (2008).

11. Boggio, Valasek, Campanhã, Giglio, Baptista, Lapenta, et al. (2011).

12. The digit learning study is reported in Cohen Kadosh, Soskic, Iuculano, Kanai, and Walsh (2010). The arithmetic study is reported in Snowball, Tachtsidis, Popescu, Thompson, Delazer, Zamarian, et al. (2013). A recent issue of the journal *NeuroImage* was devoted to the topic of enhancing cognition with magnetic and electrical stimulation. This opening article by Clark and Parasuraman (2014) gives a nice overview of the topic.

13. IMAX is the most popular ultra-high-resolution film standard, used for projection with an extremely wide field of view. IMAX has debuted a digital standard, but so far it is not quite up to the resolution of the film setup.

14. Vishwanath & Hibbard (2013).

15. The quotes from Bruce Bridgeman come from a telephone interview I conducted (May 7, 2013; edited for clarity), a manuscript Bruce sent me describing his experience (April 23, 2013), and an article written about him (Peck, 2012). Thanks to Patricia Ho for finding this story.

16. Rownd (2010).

17. Yang, Schlieski, Selmins, Cooper, Doherty, Corriveau, et al. (2012).

18. Münsterberg (1916).

19. Glanz (1999).

20. Kaye (2004).

21. Newcomb (2012) and Tecca (2012) describe the CJ Group system (thanks to Noam Kupfer for these). The websites for the CJ Group and D-Box are www.cj4dx.com and www.d-box.com, respectively.

References

Alcock, J. (2001). *Animal behavior: An evolutionary approach* (7th ed.). Sunderland, MA: Sinauer Associates.

Amedi, A., Malach, R., Hendler, T., Peled, S., & Zohary, E. (2001). Visuo-haptic object-related activation in the ventral visual pathway. *Natural Neuroscience, 4,* 324–30.

American Academy of Pediatrics. (2009). Media violence. *Pediatrics, 124,* 1495–503.

Anderson, C. A., Berkowitz, L., Donnerstein, E., Huesmann, L. R., Johnson, J. D., Linz, D., et al. (2003). The influence of media violence on youth. *Psychological Science in the Public Interest, 4,* 81–110.

Anderson, J. (1996). *The reality of illusion: An ecological approach to cognitive film theory.* Carbondale: Southern Illinois University Press.

Anderson, J., & Anderson, B. (1993). The myth of persistence of vision revisited. *Journal of Film and Video, 45,* 3–12.

Archibald, S., Mateer, C., & Kerns, K. (2001). Utilization behavior: Clinical manifestations and neurological mechanisms. *Neuropsychology Review, 11,* 117–30.

Associated Press. (2006, April 13). Smell-o-vision comes to the big screen. *Sydney Morning Herald.*

Baird, J. A., & Baldwin, D. A. (2001). Making sense of human behavior: Action parsing and intentional inference. In B. F. Malle, L. J. Moses, & D. A. Baldwin (Eds.), *Intentions and intentionality: Foundations of social cognition* (pp. 193–206). Cambridge, MA: MIT Press.

Baker, N. (1988). *The mezzanine.* New York: Weidenfeld & Nicholson.

Bangert, M., & Schlaug, G. (2006). Specialization of the specialized in features of external human brain morphology. *European Journal of Neuroscience, 24,* 1832–34.

Barker, R. G., & Wright, H. F. (1951). *One boy's day: A specimen record of behavior.* New York: Harper & Brothers.

Baron-Cohen, S., Ring, H. A., Wheelwright, S., Bullmore, E. T., Brammer, M. J., Simmons, A., & Williams, S. C. R. (1999). Social intelligence in the normal and autistic brain: An fMRI study. *European Journal of Neuroscience, 11*(6), 1891–98.

Barrett, L. F., Mesquita, B., Ochsner, K. N., & Gross, J. J. (2007). The experience of emotion. *Annual Review of Psychology, 58,* 373–403.

Bartels, A., & Zeki, S. (2004). Functional brain mapping during free viewing of natural scenes. *Human Brain Mapping, 21,* 75–85.

Bavelas, J. B., Black, A., Chovil, N., Lemery, C. R., & Mullett, J. (1988). Form and function in motor mimicry: Topographic evidence that the primary function is communicative. *Human Communication Research, 14,* 275–99.

Bavelier, D., Green, C. S., Han, D. H., Renshaw, P. F., Merzenich, M. M., & Gentile, D. A. (2011). Brains on video games. *Nature Reviews Neuroscience, 12,* 763–68.

Beah, I. (2008). *A long way gone: Memoirs of a boy soldier.* New York: Farrar, Straus and Giroux.

Beck, D. M., Muggleton, N., Walsh, V., & Lavie, N. (2006). Right parietal cortex plays a critical role in change blindness. *Cerebral Cortex, 16,* 712–17.

Beck, D. M., Rees, G., Frith, C. D., & Lavie, N. (2001). Neural correlates of change detection and change blindness. *Nature Neuroscience, 4,* 645–50.

Beck, T. (2013). *Inception-style memory experiment performed on mice was inspired by the movie "Total Recall."* Retrieved September 24, 2013, from http://www.fastcolabs.com/3015419/inception-style-memory-experiment-performed-on-mice-was-inspired-by-the-movie-total-recall.

Boggio, P. S., Valasek, C. A., Campanhã, C., Giglio, A. C. A., Baptista, N. I., Lapenta, O. M., et al. (2011). Non-invasive brain stimulation to assess and modulate neuroplasticity in Alzheimer's disease. *Neuropsychological Rehabilitation, 21,* 703–16.

Bohn, A., & Berntsen, D. (2010). The reminiscence bump reconsidered. *Psychological Science, 22,* 197–202.

Bordwell, D. (2002). Intensified continuity: Visual style in contemporary American film. *Film Quarterly, 55,* 16–28.

Brady, J. J. (1981). *The craft of the screenwriter: Interviews with six celebrated screenwriters.* New York: Simon and Schuster.

Brass, M., Bekkering, H., Wohlschläger, A., & Prinz, W. (2000). Compatibility between observed and executed finger movements: Comparing symbolic, spatial, and imitative cues. *Brain and Cognition, 44,* 124–43.

Breitmeyer, B. G. (1980). Unmasking visual masking: A look at the "why" behind the veil of the "how." *Psychological Review, 87,* 52–69.

Breitmeyer, B. G., Kropfl, W., & Julesz, B. (1982). The existence and role of retinotopic and spatiotopic forms of visual persistence. *Acta Psychologica, 52,* 175–96.

Bremner, J. D. (1999). Does stress damage the brain? *Biological Psychiatry, 45,* 797–805.

Buccino, G., Binkofski, F., Fink, G. R., Fadiga, L., Fogassi, L., Gallese, V., et al. (2001). Action observation activates premotor and parietal areas in a somatotopic manner: An fMRI study. *European Journal of Neuroscience, 13,* 400–404.

Bushman, B. J., & Anderson, C. A. (2001). Media violence and the American public: Scientific facts versus media misinformation. *American Psychologist, 56,* 477–89.

Bushman, B. J., & Huesmann, H. L. (2006). Short-term and long-term effects of violent media on aggression in children and adults. *Archives of Pediatrics & Adolescent Medicine, 160,* 348–52.

Butler, A. C., Zaromb, F. M., Lyle, K. B., & Roediger, I. (2009). Using popular films to enhance classroom learning: The good, the bad, and the interesting. *Psychological Science, 20,* 1161–68.

Carlin, B., Hamza, J., Kurtz, B., Carlin, G. (Producers), & Santos, S. J. (Director). (1984). George Carlin: *Carlin on campus* [Motion picture]. United States: Cable Stuff Productions.

Chabris, C., & Simons, D. (2010). *The invisible gorilla: and other ways our intuitions deceive us.* New York: Crown Archetype.

Chapman, J., & McGhie, A. (1964). Echopraxia in schizophrenia. *The British Journal of Psychiatry, 110,* 365–74.

Chartrand, T. L., & Bargh, J. A. (1999). The chameleon effect: The perception–behavior link and social interaction. *Journal of Personality and Social Psychology, 76,* 893–910.

Chartrand, T. L., Maddux, W. W., & Lakin, J. L. (2005). Beyond the perception-behavior link: The ubiquitous utility and motivational moderators of nonconscious mimicry. In R. R. Hassin, J. S. Uleman, & J. A. Bargh (Eds.), *The new unconscious* (pp. 334–61). New York: Oxford University Press.

Churchland, A. K., Huang, X., & Lisberger, S. G. (2007). Responses of neurons in the medial superior temporal visual area to apparent motion stimuli in macaque monkeys. *Journal of Neurophysiology, 97,* 272–82.

Churchland, M. M., & Lisberger, S. G. (2001). Shifts in the population response in the middle temporal visual area parallel perceptual and motor illusions produced by apparent motion. *The Journal of Neuroscience, 21,* 9387–402.

Clark, V. P., & Parasuraman, R. (2014). Neuroenhancement: Enhancing brain and mind in health and in disease. *NeuroImage, 85, Part 3,* 889–94.

Cohen Kadosh, R., Soskic, S., Iuculano, T., Kanai, R., & Walsh, V. (2010). Modulating neuronal activity produces specific and long-lasting changes in numerical competence. *Current Biology, 20,* 2016–20.

Conway, M. A. (2005). Memory and the self. *Journal of Memory and Language, 53,* 594–628.

Copeland, D., Radvansky, G., & Goodwin, K. (2009). A novel study: Forgetting curves and the reminiscence bump. *Memory, 17,* 323–36.

Corbetta, M., & Shulman, G. L. (2002). Control of goal-directed and stimulus-driven attention in the brain. *Nature Reviews Neuroscience, 3,* 215–29.

Corkin, S. (2002). What's new with the amnesic patient H.M.? *Nature Reviews Neuroscience, 3,* 153–60.

Cowan, N. (2001). The magical number 4 in short-term memory: A reconsideration of mental storage capacity. *Behavioral and Brain Sciences, 24,* 87–114.

Cruz, J., & Gordon, R. M. (2006). Simulation theory. In L. Nadel (Ed.), *Encyclopedia of cognitive science.* Chichester: John Wiley & Sons.

Damasio, A. R. (1994). *Descartes' error: Emotion, reason, and the human brain.* New York: Putnam.

Darwin, C. (1998). *The expression of the emotions in man and animals* (3rd ed.). New York: HarperCollins.

De Renzi, E. (1982). *Disorders of space exploration and cognition.* Chichester, UK: John Wiley and Sons.

Didion, J. (1997, December 18). The lion king. *The New York Review of Books.*

Dimberg, U., Thunberg, M., & Elmehed, K. (2000). Unconscious facial reactions to emotional facial expressions. *Psychological Science, 11,* 86–89.

Doeller, C. F., Barry, C., & Burgess, N. (2010). Evidence for grid cells in a human memory network. *Nature, 463,* 657–61.

Dove Foundation. (2008). *The Dove Foundation's 2006-07 studio report card.* Retrieved April 17, 2014, from http://www.dove.org/the-dove-foundations-2006-07-studio-report-card/

Driver, J., Davis, G., Ricciardelli, P., Kidd, P., Maxwell, E., & Baron-Cohen, S. (1999). Gaze perception triggers reflexive visuospatial orienting. *Visual Cognition, 6*(5), 509–540.

D'Ydewalle, G., & Sevenants, A. (2006). Semantic, aesthetic, and cognitive effects of flashbacks in film. *Abstracts of the Psychonomic Society* (Vol. 11, p. 9). Houston, TX: Psychonomic Society.

Ehrsson, H. H., Geyer, S., & Naito, E. (2003). Imagery of voluntary movement of fingers, toes, and tongue activates corresponding body-part-specific motor representations. *Journal of Neurophysiology, 90,* 3304–316.

Ekstrom, A. D., Kahana, M. J., Caplan, J. B., Fields, T. A., Isham, E. A., Newman, E. L., et al. (2003). Cellular networks underlying human spatial navigation. *Nature, 425,* 184–87.

Elbert, T., Pantev, C., Wienbruch, C., Rockstroh, B., & Taub, E. (1995). Increased cortical representation of the fingers of the left hand in string players. *Science, 270,* 305–307.

Epstein, R. (2008). Parahippocampal and retrosplenial contributions to human spatial navigation. *Trends in Cognitive Sciences, 12,* 388–96.

Eron, L. D., Huesmann, L. R., Lefkowitz, M. M., & Walder, L. O. (1972). Does television violence cause aggression? *American Psychologist, 27,* 253–63.

Feng, J., Spence, I., & Pratt, J. (2007). Playing an action video game reduces gender differences in spatial cognition. *Psychological Science, 18,* 850–55.

Ferguson, C. J. (2009). Media violence effects: Confirmed truth or just another X-file? *Journal of Forensic Psychology Practice, 9,* 103–26.

Ferguson, C. J., & Kilburn, J. (2009). The public health risks of media violence: A meta-analytic review. *The Journal of Pediatrics, 154,* 759–63.

Freedman, J. L. (1984). Effect of television violence on aggressiveness. *Psychological Bulletin, 96,* 227–46.

Fried, I., Katz, A., McCarthy, G., Sass, K. J., Williamson, P., Spencer, S. S., et al. (1991). Functional organization of human supplementary motor cortex studied by electrical stimulation. *Journal of Neuroscience, 11,* 3656–66.

Ganis, G., & Schendan, H. E. (2011). Visual imagery. *Wiley Interdisciplinary Reviews: Cognitive Science, 2,* 239–52.

Gerrig, R. J., & Rapp, D. N. (2004). Psychological processes underlying literary impact. *Poetics Today, 25,* 265–81.

Gerschlager, W., Siebner, H. R., & Rothwell, J. C. (2001). Decreased corticospinal excitability after subthreshold 1 Hz rTMS over lateral premotor cortex. *Neurology, 57,* 449–55.

Glanz, J. (1999, November 16). Recorded music gets dose of reality. *The New York Times.*

Gogtay, N., Giedd, J. N., Lusk, L., Hayashi, K. M., Greenstein, D., Vaituzis, A. C., et al. (2004). Dynamic mapping of human cortical development during childhood through early adulthood. *Proceedings of the National Academy of Sciences of the United States of America, 101,* 8174–79.

Goodale, M. A., & Humphrey, G. (1998). The objects of action and perception. *Cognition, 67,* 181–207.

Guber, P. (2011). *Tell to win: Connect, persuade, and triumph with the hidden power of story.* New York: Crown Business.

Hanson, S. J., Negishi, M., & Hanson, C. (2001). Connectionist neuroimaging. In S. Wermter, J. Austin, & D. Willshaw (Eds.), *Emergent neural computational architectures based on neuroscience: Towards neuroscience-inspired computing* (pp. 560–77). Berlin: Springer.

Hard, B. M., Tversky, B., & Lang, D. (2006). Making sense of abstract events: Building event schemas. *Memory & Cognition, 34,* 1221–35.

Hasan, Y., Bègue, L., Scharkow, M., & Bushman, B. J. (2013). The more you play, the more aggressive you become: A long-term experimental study of cumulative violent video game effects on hostile expectations and aggressive behavior. *Journal of Experimental Social Psychology, 49,* 224–27.

Hasson, U., Landesman, O., Knappmeyer, B., Vallines, I., Rubin, N., & Heeger, D. (2008). Neurocinematics: The neuroscience of film. *Projections, 2,* 1–26.

Hasson, U., Nir, Y., Levy, I., Fuhrmann, G., & Malach, R. (2004). Intersubject synchronization of cortical activity during natural vision. *Science, 303,* 1634–640.

Hasson, U., Vallines, I., & Heeger, D. J., (2011, March 9). Personal communication.

Hauk, O., Johnsrude, I., & Pulvermuller, F. (2004). Somatotopic representation of action words in human motor and premotor cortex. *Neuron, 41,* 301–307.

Hespos, S. J., Grossman, S. R., & Saylor, M. M. (2010). Infants' ability to parse continuous actions: Further evidence. *Neural Networks, 23,* 1026–32.

Hespos, S., Saylor, M., & Grossman, S. (2009). Infants' ability to parse continuous actions. *Developmental Psychology, 45,* 575–85.

Heywood, C. A., & Zihl, J. (1999). Motion blindness. In G. W. Humphreys (Ed.), *Case studies in the neuropsychology of vision* (pp. 1–16). Hove, UK: Psychology Press.

Hirtle, S. C., & Jonides, J. (1985). Evidence of hierarchies in cognitive maps. *Memory & Cognition, 13,* 208–17.

Hochberg, J., & Brooks, V. (1978). The perception of motion pictures. In E. C. Carterette & M. P. Friedman (Eds.), *Handbook of perception* (Vol. 10, pp. 259–304). New York: Academic Press.

Hochberg, J., & Brooks, V. (2006). Film cutting and visual momentum. In M. A. Peterson, B. Gillam, & H. A. Sedgwick (Eds.), *In the mind's eye: Julian Hochberg on the perception of pictures, films, and the world* (pp. 206–28). New York: Oxford University Press.

Hollingworth, A. (2006). Visual memory for natural scenes: Evidence from change detection and visual search. *Visual Cognition, 14,* 781–807.

Hollingworth, A., & Henderson, J. M. (2002). Accurate visual memory for previously attended objects in natural scenes. *Journal of Experimental Psychology: Human Perception and Performance, 28,* 113–36.

Hood, B. M., Willen, J. D., & Driver, J. (1998). Adult's eyes trigger shifts of visual attention in human infants. *Psychological Science, 9,* 131–34.

Hovland, C. I., Lumsdaine, A. A., & Sheffield, F. D. (1949). *Experiments on mass communication: Vol. 3. Studies in social psychology in World War II.* Princeton, NJ: Princeton University Press.

Hsee, C. K., Hatfield, E., Carlson, J. G., & Chemtob, C. (1990). The effect of power on susceptibility to emotional contagion. *Cognition and Emotion, 4,* 327–40.

Hubert-Wallander, B., Green, C. S., & Bavelier, D. (2011). Stretching the limits of visual attention: The case of action video games. *Wiley Interdisciplinary Reviews: Cognitive Science, 2,* 222–30.

Huesmann, L. R. (1986). Psychological processes promoting the relation between exposure to media violence and aggressive behavior by the viewer. *Journal of Social Issues, 42,* 125–39.

Humphreys, G. W., & Riddoch, M. J. (1987). *To see but not to see: A case study of visual agnosia.* Hove, UK: Psychology Press.

Humphries, C., Liebenthal, E., & Binder, J. R. (2010). Tonotopic organization of human auditory cortex. *NeuroImage, 50,* 1202–11.

Iacoboni, M., & Dapretto, M. (2006). The mirror neuron system and the consequences of its dysfunction. *Nature Reviews Neuroscience, 7,* 942–51.

Ildirar, S., & Schwan, S. (in press). First-time viewers' comprehension of films: Bridging shot transitions. *British Journal of Psychology.*

Jacobs, J., Weidemann, C. T., Miller, J. F., Solway, A., Burke, J. F., Wei, X.-X., et al. (2013). Direct recordings of grid-like neuronal activity in human spatial navigation. *Nature Neuroscience, 16,* 1188–90.

Jacoby, L. L. (1999). Deceiving the elderly: Effects of accessibility bias in cued-recall performance. *Cognitive Neuropsychology, 16,* 417–36.

James, H. (1881). *Washington Square; The pension Beaurepas; A bundle of letters.* B. Tauchnitz.

James, W. (1890). *The principles of psychology* (Vol. 1). New York: Henry Holt.

Janssen, S., Chessa, A., & Murre, J. (2005). The reminiscence bump in autobiographical memory: Effects of age, gender, education, and culture. *Memory, 13,* 658.

Johnson, M. K. (2006). Memory and reality. *American Psychologist,* *61,* 760–71.

Johnson, M. K., Raye, C. L., Mitchell, K. J., & Ankudowich, E. (2012). The cognitive neuroscience of true and false memories. In R. F. Belli (Ed.), *True and false recovered memories: Toward a reconciliation of the debate* (pp. 15–52). *Vol. 58: Nebraska Symposium on Motivation.* New York: Springer.

Johnson-Laird, P. N. (1983). *Mental models: Towards a cognitive science of language, inference, and consciousness.* Cambridge, MA: Harvard University Press.

Kael, P. (1991). *5001 nights at the movies.* New York: Henry Holt.

Kamitani, Y., & Tong, F. (2005). Decoding the visual and subjective contents of the human brain. *Nature Neuroscience, 8,* 679–85.

Karson, C. N. (1983). Spontaneous eye-blink rates and dopaminergic systems. *Brain, 106,* 643–53.

Kaye, J. (2004). Making scents: Aromatic output for HCI. *Interactions, 11,* 48–61.

Keane, C. (1998). *How to write a selling screenplay: A step-by-step approach to developing your story and writing your screenplay by one of today's most successful screenwriters and teachers.* Random House Digital.

Kelley, T. A., Serences, J. T., Giesbrecht, B., & Yantis, S. (2008). Cortical mechanisms for shifting and holding visuospatial attention. *Cerebral Cortex, 18,* 114–25.

Keltner, D., Oatley, K., & Jenkins, J. M. (2013). *Understanding emotions* (3rd ed.). Chichester, UK: Wiley-Blackwell.

Kristjánsson, Á. (2013). The case for causal influences of action videogame play upon vision and attention. *Attention, Perception, & Psychophysics, 75,* 667–72.

Kurby, C. A., & Zacks, J. M. (2008). Segmentation in the perception and memory of events. *Trends in Cognitive Sciences, 12,* 72–79.

Kuroki, Y. (2012). Improvement of 3D visual image quality by using high frame rate. *Journal of the Society for Information Display, 20,* 566–74.

Kuroki, Y., Nishi, T., Kobayashi, S., Oyaizu, H., & Yoshimura, S. (2007). A psychophysical study of improvements in motion-image quality by using high frame rates. *Journal of the Society for Information Display, 15,* 61–68.

LaBerge, S. (2000). Lucid dreaming: Evidence and methodology. *Behavioral and Brain Sciences, 23,* 962–64.

Labov, W., & Waletzky, J. (2003). Narrative analysis: Oral versions of personal experience. In C. B. Paulston & G. R. Tucker (Eds.), *Sociolinguistics: The essential readings* (pp. 74–104). Malden, MA: Blackwell.

Larsen, R. J., Kasimatis, M., & Frey, K. (1992). Facilitating the furrowed brow: An unobtrusive test of the facial feedback hypothesis applied to unpleasant affect. *Cognition & Emotion, 6,* 321–38.

Larsson, S. (2009). *The girl who played with fire: Book 2 of the millennium trilogy.* New York: Knopf.

LeDoux, J. E. (2000). Emotion circuits in the brain. *Annual Review of Neuroscience, 23,* 155–84.

Lee, T.-W., Josephs, O., Dolan, R. J., & Critchley, H. D. (2006). Imitating expressions: Emotion-specific neural substrates in facial mimicry. *Social Cognitive and Affective Neuroscience, 1,* 122–35.

Levaco, R. (1974). *Kuleshov on film: Writings by Lev Kuleshov.* Berkeley: University of California Press.

Levin, D. T. (2010). Spatial representations of the sets of familiar and unfamiliar television programs. *Media Psychology, 13,* 54–76.

Levin, D. T., Momen, N., Drivdahl, S. B., & Simons, D. J. (2000). Change blindness blindness: The metacognitive error of overestimating change-detection ability. *Visual Cognition, 7,* 397–412.

Levin, D. T., & Simons, D. J. (1997). Failure to detect changes to attended objects in motion pictures. *Psychonomic Bulletin & Review, 4,* 501–506.

Levin, D. T., Simons, D. J., Angelone, B. L., & Chabris, C. F. (2002). Memory for centrally attended changing objects in an incidental real-world change detection paradigm. *British Journal of Psychology, 93,* 289–302.

Lhermitte, F., Pillon, B., & Serdaru, M. (1986). Human autonomy and the frontal lobes. Part I: Imitation and utilization behavior: A neuropsychological study of 75 patients. *Annals of Neurology, 19,* 326–34.

Lichtenstein, E. D., & Brewer, W. F. (1980). Memory for goal-directed events. *Cognitive Psychology, 12,* 412–45.

Linder, D. O. (n.d.). The Hinckley trial: Hinckley's communications with Jodie Foster. Retrieved March 6, 2012, from http://law2.umkc.edu/faculty/projects/ftrials/hinckley/jfostercommun.HTM.

Liptak, A. (2011, June 27). Justices reject ban on violent video games for children. *The New York Times.*

Mack, A., & Rock, I. (1998). *Inattentional blindness.* Cambridge, MA: MIT Press.

Magliano, J. P., & Zacks, J. M. (2011). The impact of continuity editing in narrative film on event segmentation. *Cognitive Science, 35,* 1489–517.

Marcel, A. J. (1983). Conscious and unconscious perception: An approach to the relations between phenomenal experience and perceptual processes. *Cognitive Psychology, 15,* 238–300.

Marsh, E. J., & Fazio, L. K. (2006). Learning errors from fiction: Difficulties in reducing reliance on fictional stories. *Memory & Cognition, 34*(5), 1140.

Maslovat, D., Chua, R., & Hodges, N. J. (2013). When unintended movements "leak" out: A startling acoustic stimulus can elicit a prepared response during motor imagery and action observation. *Neuropsychologia, 51,* 838–44.

Maupin, A. (2008). *Michael Tolliver lives.* New York: HarperCollins.

McKee, S. P., & Watamaniuk, S. N. (1994). The psychophysics of motion perception. In A. T. Smith & R. J. Snowden (Eds.), *Visual detection of motion* (pp. 85–114). London: Academic Press.

Meltzoff, A. N., & Moore, M. K. (1983). Newborn infants imitate adult facial gestures. *Child Development, 54,* 702–709.

Michelon, P., Vettel, J. M., & Zacks, J. M. (2006). Lateral somatotopic organization during imagined and prepared movements. *Journal of Neurophysiology, 95,* 811–22.

Mikami, A. (1991). Direction selective neurons respond to short-range and long-range apparent motion stimuli in macaque visual area MT. *International Journal of Neuroscience*, *61*, 101–12.

Moar, I., & Bower, G. H. (1983). Inconsistency in spatial knowledge. *Memory & Cognition*, *11*, 107–13.

Montgomery, R. (Director). (1947). *Lady in the lake* [Motion picture]. United States: Metro-Goldwyn-Mayer.

Moser, E. I., Kropff, E., & Moser, M.-B. (2008). Place cells, grid cells, and the brain's spatial representation system. *Annual Review of Neuroscience*, *31*, 69–89.

Münsterberg, H. (1916). *The photoplay: A psychological study.* New York: D. Appleton.

Münsterberg, M. A. A. (1922). *Hugo Münsterberg: His life and work.* New York: D. Appleton.

Murch, W. (2001). *In the blink of an eye: A perspective on film editing.* Los Angeles: Silman-James Press.

Murphy, K. (2013, February 2). Catching up with the animator John Kahrs. *The New York Times.*

Nakano, T., Yamamoto, Y., Kitajo, K., Takahashi, T., & Kitazawa, S. (2009). Synchronization of spontaneous eyeblinks while viewing video stories. *Proceedings of the Royal Society B: Biological Sciences*, *276*, 3635–44.

Náñez, J. (1988). Perception of impending collision in 3- to 6-week-old human infants. *Infant Behavior and Development*, *11*, 447–63.

Newcomb, T. (2012, July 10). 4D movies: Experience for the entire body coming to U.S. theaters? Retrieved April 29, 2014, from http://entertainment.time.com/2012/07/10/smell-your-mo vie-are-4d-films-coming-to-theater-near-you.

Newsome, W., Britten, K., & Movshon, J. (1989). Neuronal correlates of a perceptual decision. *Nature*, *341*, 52–54.

Newtson, D. (1976). Foundations of attribution: The perception of ongoing behavior. In J. H. Harvey, W. J. Ickes, & R. F. Kidd (Eds.), *New directions in attribution research* (pp. 223–48). Hillsdale, NJ: Lawrence Erlbaum Associates.

Niedenthal, P. M. (2007). Embodying emotion. *Science*, *316*, 1002–1005.

Oatley, K. (1999). Why fiction may be twice as true as fact: Fiction as cognitive and emotional simulation. *Review of General Psychology, 3*, 101–17.

O'Keefe, J., & Nadel, L. (1978). *The hippocampus as a cognitive map.* Oxford: Oxford University Press.

O'Regan, J. K., Rensink, R. A., & Clark, J. J. (1999). Change-blindness as a result of "mudsplashes." *Nature, 398*, 34.

Palmer, S. E. (1999). *Vision science: photons to phenomenology.* Cambridge, MA: MIT Press.

Peck, M. (2012, July 19). How a movie changed one man's vision forever. Retrieved April 29, 2014, from http://www.bbc.com/future/story/20120719-awoken-from-a-2d-world/1.

Penfield, W. (1975). *The mystery of the mind: A critical study of consciousness and the human brain.* Princeton, NJ: Princeton University Press.

Penfield, W., & Rasmussen, T. (1950). *The cerebral cortex of man.* New York: Macmillan.

Pessoa, L. & Ungerleider, L. G. (2004). Neural correlates of change detection and change blindness in a working memory task. *Cerebral Cortex, 14*, 511–20.

Peterson, M. A. (2003). On figures, grounds, and varieties of surface completion. In R. Kimchi, M. Behrmann, & C. Olson (Eds.), *Perceptual organization in vision: Behavioral and neural perspectives* (pp. 87–116). Mahwah, NJ: Lawrence Erlbaum Associates.

Phelps, E. A. (2006). Emotion and cognition: Insights from studies of the human amygdala. *Annual Review of Psychology, 57*, 27–53.

Plantinga, C. (2013). The affective power of movies. In A. P. Shimamura (Ed.), *Psychocinematics: Exploring cognition at the movies.* (pp. 94–111). New York: Oxford University Press.

Poague, L. (Ed.). (2004). *Frank Capra: Interviews.* Jackson: University Press of Mississippi.

Posner, M., & Petersen, S. (1990). The attention system of the human brain. *Annual Review of Neuroscience, 13*, 25–42.

Prentice, D. A., Gerrig, R. J., & Bailis, D. S. (1997). What readers bring to the processing of fictional texts. *Psychonomic Bulletin & Review, 4*, 416–20.

Preuss, T. M., Stepniewska, I. & Kaas, J. H. (1996). Movement representation in the dorsal and ventral premotor areas of owl monkeys: A microstimulation study. *The Journal of Comparative Neurology, 371,* 649–76.

Proulx, A. (1999). *The shipping news.* New York: Simon and Schuster.

Quiroga, R. Q., Reddy, L., Kreiman, G., Koch, C., & Fried, I. (2005). Invariant visual representation by single neurons in the human brain. *Nature, 435,* 1102–107.

Radvansky, G. A., & Zacks, J. M. (2014). *Event cognition.* New York: Oxford University Press.

Ramirez, S., Liu, X., Lin, P.-A., Suh, J., Pignatelli, M., Redondo, R. L., et al. (2013). Creating a false memory in the hippocampus. *Science, 341,* 387–91.

Ramos, R. A., Ferguson, C. J., Frailing, K. & Romero-Ramirez, M. (2013). Comfortably numb or just yet another movie? Media violence exposure does not reduce viewer empathy for victims of real violence among primarily Hispanic viewers. *Psychology of Popular Media Culture, 2,* 2–10.

Rayner, K., & Castelhano, M. (2007). Eye movements. *Scholarpedia, 2,* 3649.

Reddy, L., & Kanwisher, N. (2006). Coding of visual objects in the ventral stream. *Current Opinion in Neurobiology, 16,* 408–14.

Reis, J., Robertson, E. M., Krakauer, J. W., Rothwell, J., Marshall, L., Gerloff, C., et al. (2008). Consensus: Can transcranial direct current stimulation and transcranial magnetic stimulation enhance motor learning and memory formation? *Brain Stimulation, 1,* 363–69.

Rideout, V. J., Foehr, U. G., & Roberts, D. F. (2010). *Generation M2: Media in the lives of 8- to 18-year-olds* (p. 79). Menlo Park, CA: Henry J. Kaiser Family Foundation.

Rizzolatti, G., & Craighero, L. (2004). The mirror-neuron system. *Annual Review of Neuroscience, 27,* 169–92.

Rizzolatti, G., Fadiga, L., Gallese, V., & Fogassi, L. (1996). Premotor cortex and the recognition of motor actions. *Cognitive Brain Research, 3,* 131–41.

Rizzolatti, G., Fogassi, L., & Gallese, V. (2001). Neurophysiological mechanisms underlying the understanding and imitation of action. *Nature Reviews Neuroscience, 2*, 661–61–70.

Robertson, L. C. (2004). *Space, objects, minds and brains.* New York: Psychology Press.

Roget, P. M. (1825). Explanation of an optical deception in the appearance of the spokes of a wheel seen through vertical apertures. *Philosophical Transactions of the Royal Society of London, 115*, 131–40.

Rownd, H. W. F. (2010). Early 3D: A case study: The teleview and *The Man from M.A.R.S. Bright Lights Film Journal, 68.*

Roy, M., Shohamy, D. & Wager, T. D. (2012). Ventromedial prefrontal-subcortical systems and the generation of affective meaning. *Trends in Cognitive Sciences, 16*, 147–56.

Rubin, D. C., Wetzler, S. E., & Nebes, R. D. (1986). Autobiographical memory across the lifespan. In D. C. Rubin (Ed.), *Autobiographical memory.* (pp. 202–21). New York: Cambridge University Press.

Sapolsky, R. M. (1996). Why stress is bad for your brain. *Science, 273*, 749–50.

Sapolsky, R. M. (1998, March 30). Open season. *The New Yorker,* 57–58.

Schwan, S., & Ildirar, S. (2010). Watching film for the first time. *Psychological Science, 21*, 970–76.

Schwenkreis, P., El Tom, S., Ragert, P., Pleger, B., Tegenthoff, M., & Dinse, H. R. (2007). Assessment of sensorimotor cortical representation asymmetries and motor skills in violin players. *European Journal of Neuroscience, 26*, 3291–302.

Shallice, T., Burgess, P. W., Schon, F., & Baxter, D. M. (1989). The origins of utilization behaviour. *Brain, 112*, 1587–98.

Shay, D. (1993). *The making of Jurassic Park.* New York: Ballantine Books.

Shepard, Roger N. (n.d.). Carl Iver Hovland, June 12, 1912. *The National* Academies Press: *Biographical Memoirs.* Retrieved May 17, 2011, from http://www.nap.edu/readingroom.php?book= biomems&page=chovland.html.

Shimamura, A. P., Cohn-Sheehy, B. I., & Shimamura, T. A. (2014). Perceiving movement across film edits: a psychocinematic analysis. *Psychology of Aesthetics, Creativity, and the Arts, 8*(1), 77–80.

Signorielli, N. (2003). Prime-time violence 1993–2001: Has the picture really changed? *Journal of Broadcasting & Electronic Media, 47,* 36–58.

Simons, D. J., & Chabris, C. F. (1999). Gorillas in our midst: Sustained inattentional blindness for dynamic events. *Perception, 28,* 1059–74.

Simons, D. J., Franconeri, S. L., & Reimer, R. L. (2000). Change blindness in the absence of a visual disruption. *Perception, 29,* 1143–54.

Singer, T., Seymour, B., O'Doherty, J., Kaube, H., Dolan, R. J., & Frith, C. D. (2004). Empathy for pain involves the affective but not sensory components of pain. *Science, 303,* 1157–62.

Smith, A. T., & Snowden, R. J. (1994). Motion detection: An overview. In A. T. Smith & R. J. Snowden, *Visual Detection of Motion* (pp. 1–15). London: Academic Press.

Smith, G. M. (2003). *Film structure and the emotion system.* Cambridge, UK: Cambridge University Press.

Smith, T. D. (2011, February 14). Observations on film art: Watching you watch *There Will Be Blood.* Retrieved March 14, 2011, from http://www.davidbordwell.net/blog/?p=12417.

Smith, T. J. (2012). The attentional theory of cinematic continuity. *Projections, 6,* 1–27.

Smith, T. J., & Henderson, J. M. (2008). Edit blindness: The relationship between attention and global change in dynamic scenes. *Journal of Eye Movement Research, 2,* 1–17.

Snowball, A., Tachtsidis, I., Popescu, T., Thompson, J., Delazer, M., Zamarian, L., et al. (2013). Long-term enhancement of brain function and cognition using cognitive training and brain stimulation. *Current Biology, 23,* 987–92.

Solnit, R. (2003). *River of shadows: Eadweard Muybridge and the technological wild west.* New York: Viking.

Speer, N. K., Swallow, K. M., & Zacks, J. M. (2003). Activation of human motion processing areas during event perception. *Cognitive, Affective & Behavioral Neuroscience, 3,* 335–45.

Sperling, G. (1960). The information available in brief visual presentations. *Psychological Monographs: General and Applied, 74,* 1–29.

Standing, L. (1973). Learning 10,000 pictures. *Quarterly Journal of Experimental Psychology, 25,* 207–22.

Steinman, R. M., Pizlo, Z., & Pizlo, F. J. (2000). Phi is not beta, and why Wertheimer's discovery launched the Gestalt revolution. *Vision Research, 40,* 2257–64.

Strack, F., Martin, L. L., & Stepper, S. (1988). Inhibiting and facilitating conditions of the human smile: A nonobtrusive test of the facial feedback hypothesis. *Journal of Personality and Social Psychology, 54,* 768–77.

Swallow, K. M., Barch, D. M., Head, D., Maley, C. J., Holder, D., & Zacks, J. M. (2011). Changes in events alter how people remember recent information. *Journal of Cognitive Neuroscience, 23,* 1052–64.

Swallow, K. M., Zacks, J. M., & Abrams, R. A. (2009). Event boundaries in perception affect memory encoding and updating. *Journal of Experimental Psychology: General, 138,* 236–57.

Tan, E. (1996). *Emotion and the structure of narrative film.* Hillsdale, NJ: Lawrence Erlbaum Associates.

Taube, J. S. (2007). The head direction signal: Origins and sensory-motor integration. *Annual Review of Neuroscience, 30,* 181–207.

Taylor, S. (1982, September 1). Too much justice: The John Hinckley Jr. case. *Harper's,* 53–66.

Tecca. (2012, July 11). Coming soon: 200 theaters that let you smell and feel the movies. Retrieved April 29, 2014, from http://news.yahoo.com/blogs/technology-blog/coming-soon-200-theaters-let-smell-feel-movies-041057432.html

Tettamanti, M., Buccino, G., Saccuman, M. C., Gallese, V., Danna, M., Scifo, P., et al. (2005). Listening to action-related sentences activates fronto-parietal motor circuits. *Journal of Cognitive Neuroscience, 17,* 273–81.

The new pictures. (1942, May 11). *Time.*

Thomas, M. H. (1982). Physiological arousal, exposure to a relatively lengthy aggressive film, and aggressive behavior. *Journal of Research in Personality, 16,* 72–81.

Tootell, R. B. H., Devaney, K. J., Young, J. C., Postelnicu, G., Rajimehr, R., & Ungerleider, L. G. (2008). fMRI mapping of a morphed continuum of 3D shapes within inferior temporal cortex. *Proceedings of the National Academy of Sciences, 105,* 3605–609.

Truffaut, F. (1978). *Hitchcock: François Truffaut.* St. Albans, UK: Granada.

Tulving, E. (2002). Episodic memory: From mind to brain. *Annual Review of Psychology, 53,* 1–25.

Tversky, B. (1981). Distortions in memory for maps. *Cognitive Psychology, 13,* 407–33.

Umanath, S., Butler, A. C., & Marsh, E. J. (2012). Positive and negative effects of monitoring popular films for historical inaccuracies. *Applied Cognitive Psychology, 26,* 556–67.

U.S. Congress. (1990). *Implementation of the Television Program Improvement Act of 1990.* Retrieved April 11, 2012, from http://archive.org/details/implementationoftvoounit.

Vary, A. B. (2011, April 12). "The Hobbit" shooting at 48 frames per second. So what's the big deal? *Entertainment Weekly.*

Vishwanath, D., & Hibbard, P. B. (2013). Seeing in 3-D with just one eye stereopsis without binocular vision. *Psychological Science, 24,* 1673–85.

Wagner, T., Valero-Cabre, A., & Pascual-Leone, A. (2007). Noninvasive human brain stimulation. *Annual Review of Biomedical Engineering, 9,* 527–65.

Watson, A. B. (2013). High frame rates and human vision: A view through the window of visibility. *SMPTE Motion Imaging Journal, 122,* 18–32.

Watson, A. B., Ahumada, A. J., Jr., & Farrell, J. E. (1986). Window of visibility: A psychophysical theory of fidelity in time-sampled visual motion displays. *Journal of the Optical Society of America A, 3,* 300.

Waytz, A., & Mitchell, J. P. (2011). Two mechanisms for simulating other minds. *Current Directions in Psychological Science, 20,* 197–200.

Wicker, B., Keysers, C., Plailly, J., Royet, J.-P., Gallese, V., & Rizzolatti, G. (2003). Both of us disgusted in my insula: The common neural basis of seeing and feeling disgust. *Neuron, 40,* 655–64.

Wolfe, J. (2007). Guided Search 4.0: Current progress with a model of visual search. In W. Gray (Ed.), *Integrated models of cognitive systems* (pp. 99–119). New York: Oxford.

Wolfe, J. M. (2003). Moving towards solutions to some enduring controversies in visual search. *Trends in Cognitive Sciences, 7,* 70–76.

Wu, S., & Spence, I. (2013). Playing shooter and driving videogames improves top-down guidance in visual search. *Attention, Perception, & Psychophysics, 75,* 673–86.

Wynn, K. (1996). Infants' individuation and enumeration of actions. *Psychological Science, 7,* 164–69.

Yang, S., Schlieski, T., Selmins, B., Cooper, S. C., Doherty, R. A., Corriveau, P. J:, et al. (2012). Stereoscopic viewing and reported perceived immersion and symptoms. *Optometry and Vision Science, 89,* 1068–80.

Zacks, J. M., Braver, T. S., Sheridan, M. A., Donaldson, D. I., Snyder, A. Z., Ollinger, J. M., et al. (2001). Human brain activity time-locked to perceptual event boundaries. *Nature Neuroscience, 4,* 651–55.

Zacks, J. M., Speer, N. K., & Reynolds, J. R. (2009). Segmentation in reading and film comprehension. *Journal of Experimental Psychology: General, 138,* 307–27.

Zacks, J. M., Speer, N. K., Swallow, K. M., Braver, T. S., & Reynolds, J. R. (2007). Event perception: A mind/brain perspective. *Psychological Bulletin, 133,* 273–93.

Zacks, J. M., Speer, N. K., Swallow, K. M., & Maley, C. J. (2010). The brain's cutting-room floor: Segmentation of narrative cinema. *Frontiers in Human Neuroscience, 4,* 1–15.

Zacks, J. M., Tversky, B., & Iyer, G. (2001). Perceiving, remembering, and communicating structure in events. *Journal of Experimental Psychology: General, 130,* 29–58.

Zihl, J., von Cramon, D., & Mai, N. (1983). Selective disturbance of
movement vision after bilateral brain damage. *Brain, 106* (Pt 2),
313–40.

Zihl, J., von Cramon, D., Mai, N., & Schmid, C. (1991). Disturbance of movement vision after bilateral posterior brain damage. Further evidence and follow up observations. *Brain, 114*
(Pt 5), 2235–52.

Zwaan, R. A., & Radvansky, G. A. (1998). Situation models in language comprehension and memory. *Psychological Bulletin, 123,*
162–85.

Zwaan, R. A., Stanfield, R. A., & Yaxley, R. H. (2002). Language
comprehenders mentally represent the shape of objects. *Psychological Science, 13,* 168–71.

INDEX ■

Page numbers followed by the italicized letter f indicate material found in figures.

auditory cortex (*Cont.*)
  primary, 254
  TMS and, 258
autism, 18
autobiographical memory, 92
autonomic nervous system, 120
awareness test, 300n2

babies
  chunking and, 226
  looming by, 16
  mirror rule and, 15–16
Bacall, Lauren, 116–17
Bailis, Daniel, 108
Baker, Nicholson, 86, 213
Barish, Joel (fictional character),
    235–36, 248
Barker, Roger, 38–39
Bartels, Andreas, 283n7
Batman, 86
The Battle of Britain, 99–100, 99f, 102
Battleship Potemkin, 166
Beah, Ishmael, 120, 121
belief
  with continuity errors, 233
  in memory, 103–4
  suspension of disbelief, 108
Ben Hur, 93
Bernsten, Dorte, 288n4
beta motion. *See* long-range apparent
    motion
Bickle, Travis (fictional character), 117
Bigelow, Kathryn, 95
Big Night, 63
The Big Sleep, 53
The Black Swan, 106
Blade Runner, 56
  violence in, 129
blindness
  change blindness, 232–33
  change blindness blindness, 233
  color-blindness, 13, 153
  inattentional blindness, 205, 297n12,
    300n2
  motion blindness, 151–54
blinking, of eyes, 174–76
Blomkamp, Neill, 93
Blomquist, Mikhail (fictional
    character), 52
Bloom, Leopold, 213

Bloom, Leopold (fictional character),
    86
bodily experience, emotion and, 75
Bogart, Humphrey, 52–53, 216–17
  observational learning from, 117
Bohn, Arnette, 288n4
Bond, James (fictional character), 179
books
  event models and, 42, 48
  mental models for, 48–49
  movie adaptations from, 54–57
  movies and, 27–30
bottlenecks, 198–99, 205–6
  chunking and, 227
  continuity errors and, 234
  temporal chunking and, 216–17
Bowman, Tom (fictional character),
    224
The Brady Bunch (TV program), 223–24
brain. *See also specific structures or areas*
  chunking and, 219
  continuity edits and, 222–23
  continuity errors and, 241–42
  cuts and, 169–72, 193–94
  echopraxia and, 20
  emotions and, 71–76
  event models and, 42–43
  eyes and, 172–73
  jump cuts and, 184–85
  memory and, 89–90, 103–4, 251–55,
    253f, 254f
  mirror neurons in, 16–18
  motion perception and, 146–56
  movies and, 3–23
  MT in, 171
  plasticity and, 14–15
  spatial representation and, 202–3,
    209–11
  spotlights and, 200–201
  TMS and, 256–63
  utilization behavior and, 20
  visual bridging and, 242
Brewer, Bill, 215–16
Bridgeman, Bruce, 266–67
brightness
  with digital projectors, 161
  flicker and, 158
  motion perception and, 158–59
  V1 and, 12
  visual areas of brain and, 12

eyes (*Cont.*)
  digital cameras and, 240–41
  dorsal visual stream and, 172
  event boundaries and, 238–39
  fovea of, 156, 172, 203–4
  gaze of, 176–77, 177*f*, 182, 204–5, 204*f*
  retina of, 146, 147
  saccades of, 172, 174–76, 203–4,
    294n9
  spotlights and, 203–4
  vision and, 172

facial expressions
  emotion and, 70–73, 72*f*, 76
  fMRI for, 71–73
  James, W., and, 70–71
  mirror rule and, 6–7, 15–16, 62–63
factual information, in fiction, 107–8
fades, 188, 223–24
Fazio, Lisa, 107
fear, 73, 75
feeling
  with continuity errors, 233
  of emotions, 73
Ferguson, Chris, 124
Ferris Bueller's Day Off, 177, 177*f*, 279
fiction
  factual information in, 107–8
  memory and, 104–22
  movie adaptations of, 104–22
  responses to, 288n24
  transportation and, 108
Fight Club, 56
fight-or-flight response, 120–21
figure-ground segmentation, 206–9,
    207*t*
"file drawer" problem, 123–24
film cameras, 160
film projectors
  apertures in, 159
  frame rate and, 159–60
  invention of, 145
  shutter in, 159, 160
Fincher, David, 87
First Amendment, 130
5001 Nights at the Movies (Kael), 212–13
flashbacks, 86
Flett, Daisy Goodwill (fictional
    character), 90–91
flicker

brightness and, 158
  digital recording and, 161
  frame rate and, 158–62
fMRI. *See* functional MRI
food, movies as, 133–35
force-feedback, in video games, 22
foreshortening, 265
Foster, Jodie, 117
fovea, 156, 172
  spotlights and, 203–4
frame rate, 197
  film projectors and, 159–60
  flicker and, 158–62
  of movies, 155–62
  MT and, 155–57
  playback speed and, 159
Freedman, Jonathan, 126–28
Friends (TV program), 298n14
functional MRI (fMRI), 35–38, 41,
    42–43, 237, 299n28
  of chunking, 217–18
  of continuity errors, 241
  of cuts, 242
  of emotion, 75–76
  of event boundaries, 218, 237
  of facial expressions, 71–73
  motor cortex and, 43

Galton, Francis, 88
Game Change, 102–3
Gandhi, 85
Garland, Judy, 77
gaze
  eyeline match and, 182
  of eyes, 176–77, 177*f*, 182, 204–5, 204*f*
  spotlights and, 204–5, 204*f*
Gerrig, Richard, 108
The Girl Who Played With Fire, 213–14
Girl with the Dragon Tattoo, 52
gist of scene, continuity errors and,
    235
Glenberg, Art, 44, 46–47, 48–49
global emotions, 287n24
Glory, 95
The Godfather, 212
Goldman, William, 55
Gondry, Michel, 186–87, 235–36,
    250–51
Goodwin, Kerry, 90–91
Gould, Stephen Jay, 66

sex
"Hayes Code" and, 131
PG-13 rating and, 132
Shallice, Time, 20
The Sheltering Sky, 189
Sheridan, Jim, 204
Sherrington, Charles, 252
Shields, Carol, 90–91
Shimamura, Art, 181
The Shipping News, 28
short-range apparent motion, 183, 295n16
shot/reverse shot, 182
shots, 163
long, 189
over-the-shoulder, 3, 194
point-of-view, 53
shot/reverse, 182
tracking, 168–69, 168*f*
shutter, in film projectors, 159, 160
shutters, LCD shutter glasses, for 3-D,
268–69
Sidney, Sylvia, 78
Simon, Paul (Senator), 130
Simons, Dan, 205, 229–33, 230*f*, 300n2
simulation
event models and, 32
theory, 286n19
Sin City, 201–2
sitcoms, laugh track in, 7
skin, neural maps and, 31
Skyfall, 179
slapstick, 60
sleeper effect, 101
Sleepy Hollow, 144*f*
Sloper, Catherine (fictional character),
51–52
smell
emotion and, 74
in movies, 272–73
Smell-O-Vision, 272
Smith, Greg, 81, 287n23
Smith, Tim, 175, 295n15
smoking
observational learning and, 116–17
utilization behavior and, 20
violence and, 124–25
social interactions
maturation story and, 90
mirror rule and, 15–16
success rule in, 10–11

Sokurov, Alexander, 190
somatic marker hypothesis, 75
somatosensory cortex, 31, 253, 253*f*
memory and, 104
right-handedness and, 37
text and, 43
sound, in movies, 270–71
"spandrels," 66
spatial representation
brain and, 202–3, 209–11
brightness contour and, 148–49
chunking and, 206–12
figure-ground segmentation and,
206–9, 207*t*
head and, 31
hippocampus and, 210–11
parahippocampal place area and,
36–37
part segmentation and, 206–7
spotlights and, 199–206
special effects
cuts as, 165
in movies, 26, 68, 160–61, 165
specialization, in visual areas of
brain, 12
Speer, Nicole, 38
Sperling, George, 146–47
Spider-Man, 197, 205–6
spotlights, 199–206
eyes and, 203–4
Standing, Lionel, 242–43
Star Wars, Episode IV, 220
statistically significant effect, 128
The Stepford Wives, 55
stereoscopic projection (3-D), 195,
264–70
anaglyphic presentation in, 267–68
LCD shutter glasses for, 268–69
MT and, 267
Stewart, James, 167
stimuli, 282n7
for emotions, 73
success rule and, 10, 32
supernormal, 82
stingers, 279–80
The Stone Diaries (Shields), 90–91
stories
chronological order of, 86–88
confabulations, 93–94
cuts for, 168–69

Twain, Mark, 110
2001, 224

U-571, 95–96
Ulysses (Joyce), 40, 85–86, 213
uncertainty principle, of Heisenberg, 217
understanding, event models and, 35
utilization behavior, 20

V1. *See* primary visual cortex
V2. *See* secondary visual cortex
Vader, Darth (fictional character), 220
Valenti, Jack, 130–31
ventral frontal cortex, 73–74
ventral visual stream, 171–72
ventromedial prefrontal cortex, 74
    mind reading and, 77
Verhoeven, Paul, 248
Victor/Victoria, 67, 81–82
Victory, 42, 202
video games
    desensitization from, 121–22
    movies and, 22–23, 274–76
violence
    children and, 113–16, 124
    commercial enterprises and, 126–27
    desensitization to, 119–23
    empathy and, 122
    enjoyment of, 126
    First Amendment and, 130
    libertarians and, 130
    meta-analysis on, 123–24
    in movies, 114–35
    null results on, 123–24, 127–28
    observational learning of, 116–17
    regulation of, 130–31
    self-regulation of, 131–32
    smoking and, 124–25
    on TV, 113–16, 129, 131
virtual reality, video games and, 22
vision
    as active process, 171–73
    continuity edits and, 173–80
    cuts and, 173–80
    eyes and, 172
    jump cuts and, 184–85
    prediction in, 172–73
visual areas of brain, 149*f*, 169–72
    brightness and, 12

color and, 12–13
cuts and, 169–72
event boundaries and, 222, 237–39
hierarchical arrangement of, 12, 148
memory and, 103
orientation and, 12
specialization in, 148
visual bridging, 188, 194, 221–24
    brain and, 242
visual cortex. *See also* primary visual cortex
    color and, 35
    cuts and, 242
    event boundaries and, 222
    neglect and, 201
    neural maps in, 30–31
    stroke and, 201
    TMS and, 258
    V2, 149–50, 185
visual persistence, 292n5
    continuity errors and, 233–34
    motion perception and, 142–43, 147
visual questions
    cuts and, 176–77, 177*f*, 180, 181–82
    eyeline match as, 181–82
visual salience, 201–2
    inattentional blindness and, 205
von Trier, Lars, 187–88

Wall Street, 76
war movies
    desensitization from, 121
    The Hurt Locker, 95
    Three Kings, 95, 109
    U-571, 95–96
Washington, Denzel, 126
Washington Square, 50–52
waterfall illusion, 292n6
Waters, John, 272
Watson, Andrew B., 158
Weiss, Kaspar (fictional character), 15
Welles, Orson, 86, 189
westerns, 117
Why We Fight (U.S. Army), 98
Wii, 22–23
willing suspension of disbelief, 108
Winslet, Kate, 235–36, 248
wipes, 188, 223–24
The Wizard of Oz, 77